FOURTH EDITION

State Board Review Questions to Accompany

The Professional Cosmetologist

John W. Dalton

West Publishing Company
St. Paul   New York   Los Angeles   San Francisco

WEST'S COMMITMENT TO THE ENVIRONMENT

In 1906, West Publishing Company began recycling materials left over from the production of books. This began a tradition of efficient and responsible use of resources. Today, up to 95% of our legal books and 70% of our college texts are printed on recycled, acid-free stock. West also recycles nearly 22 million pounds of scrap paper annually—the equivalent of 181,717 trees. Since the 1960s, West has devised ways to capture and recycle waste inks, solvents, oils, and vapors created in the printing process. We also recycle plastics of all kinds, wood, glass, corrugated cardboard, and batteries, and have eliminated the use of styrofoam book packaging. We at West are proud of the longevity and the scope of our commitment to our environment.

Production, Prepress, Printing and Binding by West Publishing Company.

COPYRIGHT © 1992 by WEST PUBLISHING CO.
610 Opperman Drive
P.O. Box 64526
St. Paul, MN 55164–0526

ISBN 0–314–00786–5

Table of Contents

Post-Tests

Practical Tests

Answer Key

INTRODUCTION

This test book has been written to follow testing guidelines established by Educational Testing Service (ETS), The National Interstate Council of State Boards of Cosmetology, individual State Boards of Cosmetology, and State Departments of Education for technical-vocational training. A comprehensive set of questions covers each chapter. The practical questions, toward the end of the book, will assist you in studying for the practical examination. The practical questions are clearly referenced by a drawing. Knowledge of these questions will assist you in preparing for your licensing test.

The revision of this test book is part of the "Dalton Concept" of providing current, professional learning materials for cosmetology students. For the benefit of the student, the next few paragraphs explain why written tests are a necessary part of any cosmetology program.

WHY SHOULD YOU TAKE TESTS?

Student testing is important because it permits your instructor to determine whether or not you, the student, have learned certain facts, principles, and procedures. For each task (service) you want to be able to do, there are some things you must "know" in order to do them safely and correctly. For example, it would be very difficult to give a cold wave if you didn't know how to wrap, process, and neutralize it. Maybe you don't even know what a cold wave rod looks like. Another thing to consider is the safety of the person to whom you would like to give the cold wave. Your instructor must know whether you can use professional cold waves safely – without burning the person with the chemicals found in cold waving solutions – before allowing you to do this task.

WHAT ARE PRE-TESTS AND POST-TESTS?

Tests in this book have title headings such as "Pre-Test" or "Post-Test." These tests can be used in different ways. For instance, if you are a transfer student from another school and want to show your instructor what you already know, take the Pre-Test for the subjects you learned at the other school. If your score is below a range of 75–85% on a test, you may have to review, or re-learn that material. The next time you take the test(s), you would take the Post-Test(s). They are basically the same questions (with some new questions too), but in a different order . If you are a regular student, you would attend class and complete reading and workbook assignments; then, take the Pre-Test(s). If your score is below 85% (or whatever percentage is required by your instructor), you should review the material in the textbook; then, take the Post-Test(s). Using the tests from (THE PROFESSIONAL COSMETOLOGIST) State Board Review Book, your instructor has at least two different tests to use, which is preferable to taking the same test twice.

WHY ARE MULTIPLE CHOICE TESTS USED?

Multiple choice test questions are used because they seem to be the fairest type of question for the student. Multiple choice questions usually begin with a phrase that should give you a "clue" to what part of a certain subject your mind should be "tuned in to." This phrase is followed by four choices (called distractors) lettered "A., B., C., and D.," which change the phrase into a complete sentence. So, given the "clue" of the phrase, you should be able to "recognize" the correct answer. If you have listened in class, and studied, the question should be quite easy to answer. It should be added that multiple choice tests are scored more accurately than other types of tests.

BE CAREFUL

Carefully read the phrase of the question to be sure you know "what is being asked." Before answering any question, read through all the choices, then pick the best one.

TAKE IT EASY

Understandably, there will be apprehensions, anxieties, or tensions the day before you go for your test. Developing a system makes test taking easier. The following system should be helpful--try it!

DO's

1. Thumb through THE PROFESSIONAL COSMETOLOGIST glossaries.

2. Review these test questions and your workbook.

3. Have classmates ask you questions.

4. Get some form of vigorous exercise, but even walking helps.

5. Eat regular meals.

6. Review briefly just before bedtime.

7. Go to bed early.

8. Eat your regular breakfast.

9. Allow time in the morning for delays, i.e., car trouble, bus late, etc.

DON'Ts

1. Wait 'til the last minute to study.

2. Study continuously all day.

3. Stay inside all day.

4. Get involved in a quarrel with your boss, boyfriend, girlfriend, or parents.

5. Skip meals.

6. Decide to have a party.

7. Stay out late.

8. Skip your regular breakfast.

9. Get lost traveling to the place where the test is going to be held.

GOOD LUCK!

26 Questions

___ 1. The name given to the preservation of personal or public health is

A. hygiene
B. cosmetology
C. chemistry
D. biology

___ 2. The science that prevents individual disease, and promotes good health is

A. individual development
B. good grooming
C. personal hygiene
D. public sanitation

___ 3. Personal hygiene is defined as the daily routine followed to preserve and promote the well being of the

A. town
B. individual
C. society
D. community

___ 4. The easiest way to keep the body clean is to use

A. perfume sprays
B. body powder
C. deodorant sprays
D. soap and water

___ 5. All full-time employees in a beauty salon must be paid

A. a state or federal minimum commission
B. the state or federal minimum wage
C. for at least one hour of work
D. the company's hourly salary

___ 6. Hairstyles are judged in a contest for

A. originality
B. adaptability
C. trend
D. all of the above

___ 7. Participation as a platform artist will help build

A. recognition
B. a large clientele
C. a good income
D. all of the above

___ 8. A good manager–operator should have

A. 2 to 3 years work experience
B. some bookkeeping experience
C. skill in all basic salon services
D. some experience in supply purchasing

___ 9. A salon owner's experience should include

A. five years of experience in a salon
B. one year of management in a salon
C. two years of platform work
D. one year as a field technician

___ 10. Individuals that have known skin or respiratory allergies should

A. discuss the problem with a good friend to determine what to do
B. consult their doctor
C. not be concerned about the problem
D. all of the above

___ 11. Cosmetology instructors are required to

A. complete a number of college courses
B. work part-time in a beauty salon
C. participate annually in a hairstyling competition
D. all of the above

___ 12. Personal hygiene includes

A. bathing or showering daily
B. oral and dental care
C. a well-balanced diet
D. all of the above

___ 13. A newly licensed, full-time cosmetologist is usually paid

A. on a commission basis
B. on a part-time, hourly basis
C. an hourly minimum wage
D. weekly

14. Nonverbal communication refers to
   A. listening to what is said
   B. communicating with body movements
   C. communicating with your hands
   D. keeping steady eye contact during conversation

15. A student who has a positive attitude
   A. is reliable
   B. gets along with other people
   C. learns when convenient
   D. A and B

16. The educational requirement for entry into a registered beauty school in some states is
   A. an eighth-grade education
   B. a twelfth-grade education
   C. a four-year college education
   D. variable from city to city

17. Upon completion of beauty school, attendance at local workshop seminars is needed to keep
   A. pace with ever-changing hairstyles
   B. up with new products being used
   C. in touch with old school mates
   D. A and B

18. A research technician
   A. tests newly developed products
   B. works at a cosmetic manufacturing company
   C. must be at least twenty-five years old
   D. A and B

19. One of the main things needed for good health is
   A. little or no exercise
   B. vigorous physical exercise
   C. poor posture
   D. little or no relaxation

20. The extra money paid to you for the sale of conditioners and shampoos is your
   A. profit
   B. retail commission
   C. bonus
   D. spiff

21. To work efficiently and with a minimum amount of physical back strain, the cosmetologist should
   A. relax on a shampoo bowl
   B. maintain good erect posture
   C. take frequent coffee breaks
   D. work three-day weeks

22. Tonsorial is a term to describe a person that does what type of work?
   A. the nails
   B. the feet
   C. hair coloring
   D. barbering

23. Regular physical examination by a doctor may lead to a discovery of
   A. physical exercise
   B. prophylaxis
   C. public hygiene
   D. disease

24. A cosmetologist who is in good health helps prevent the spread of
   A. soda
   B. disease
   C. cavities
   D. osmosis

25. One of the main things needed for good health is
   A. very little exercise
   B. personal dehydration
   C. a well-balanced diet
   D. freedom from hangnails

26. Most state laws require that any technician practicing on a living person must have
   A. a cosmetology license
   B. five years of experience in a salon
   C. a junior instructor's license
   D. a senior instructor's license

Poss.	Wrong	%	Right
26	0	100%	26
26	1	96%	25
26	2	92%	24
26	3	88%	23
26	4	85%	22

26	5	81%	21
26	6	77%	20
26	7	73%	19
26	8	69%	18
26	9	65%	17
26	10	62%	16
26	11	58%	15

2 ETHICS IN COSMETOLOGY PRE-TEST 1

16 Questions

___ 1. Ethics is a system that measures human behavior that is

A. voluntary
B. involuntary
C. imposed by local police
D. imposed by the federal government

___ 2. The governing body in most states that is supposed to discipline members that violate professional ethics is the

A. bureau of ethics
B. state legislature
C. state association
D. state board

___ 3. A professional attitude is

A. natural
B. given when you are licensed
C. acquired in enrollment
D. learned

___ 4. Responsibility means your own reliability and

A. integrity
B. honesty
C. discipline
D. punctuality

___ 5. It is your responsibility to

A. give as much service as needed by the client
B. learn new methods of hairstyling
C. give services based on quality and price
D. all of the above

___ 6. Your professional responsibility to your co-workers should include NOT

A. recruiting employees from other salons
B. saying that another's work is inferior
C. learning new techniques
D. attending educational classes

___ 7. A professional code of ethics

A. is always enforced by the state board
B. is not necessary for cosmetology
C. is always covered by rules and regulations
D. goes beyond laws and regulations

___ 8. Proper behavior toward other people, such as clients, employer, and co-workers, is known as professional

A. attitude
B. ethics
C. sincerity
D. diligence

___ 9. It is very unethical to

A. condition hair
B. gossip
C. give cold waves
D. shape hair

___ 10. The cosmetologist who is dependable will earn

A. the honor and praise of others
B. the respect and loyalty of others
C. the advice and counsel of others
D. fame and fortune

3

11. Professional ethics are expressed in

A. rules
B. regulations
C. codes
D. traditions

12. Ethical codes are set for the beauty industry especially to earn the respect and confidence of

A. other members
B. barbers
C. the public
D. the state board

13. Competence means mastering information and

A. art
B. skill
C. science
D. craft

14. The responsible cosmetologist will

A. overcharge according to what the traffic will bear
B. falsely advertise products and services
C. talk about one client to another
D. provide only needed services

15. You are conducting yourself in an ethical way toward your employer if you

A. promote a good reputation for the salon
B. provide only quality service
C. keep private information given to you in confidence
D. all of the above

16. An employer has to assume responsibility for

A. services given by employees
B. giving advance training classes
C. setting fair and equal prices
D. all of the above

Poss.	Wrong	%	Right
16	0	100%	16
16	1	94%	15
16	2	88%	14
16	3	81%	13
16	4	75%	12

3 SANITATION AND STERILIZATION PRE-TEST 1

31 Questions

1. To equal the strength of 70% ethyl alcohol, you would have to use

A. 20% isopropyl alcohol
B. 39% isopropyl alcohol
C. 85% isopropyl alcohol
D. 99% isopropyl alcohol

2. If cosmetology implements are aseptic, then they are

A. free from bacteria
B. unsanitary
C. soiled
D. covered

3. A person immune to a disease, but who can infect others, is known as a(n)

A. clinical
B. medical
C. agent
D. carrier

4. Things that may be considered a health hazard are

A. forced air furnaces
B. impurities in the air
C. clean body and clothes
D. hygienic salon practices

_____ 5. The germicidal light used in some dry sanitizers is known as

   A. fluorescent light
   B. ultra-violet light
   C. infrared light
   D. incandescent light

_____ 6. Uncleanliness can produce germs that cause

   A. good health
   B. local canities
   C. disease
   D. malnutrition

_____ 7. Another name for public hygiene is

   A. grooming
   B. hair care
   C. sanitation
   D. community

_____ 8. Disease is caused mainly from the lack of

   A. cleanliness
   B. deodorizers
   C. cold water
   D. hairspray

_____ 9. The electrical device that removes stale air from the salon is called a(n)

   A. humidifier
   B. ceiling fan
   C. exhaust fan
   D. dehumidifier

_____ 10. Practices in the beauty salon that help preserve the health of the public are called

   A. fumigation/deodorization
   B. salon grooming
   C. cleaning/washing
   D. sanitation/sterilization

_____ 11. To be effective, a solution of quaternary ammonium compound solution requires

   A. mixing with alcohol
   B. lengthy contact time
   C. mixing with peroxide
   D. short contact time

_____ 12. An article that would melt if exposed to heat may be sanitized using

   A. a soapy water solution
   B. a hydrogen peroxide solution
   C. a disinfectant solution
   D. infrared rays

_____ 13. A dry sanitizer is only effective when it contains

   A. formaldehyde fumes
   B. 10% alcohol
   C. hydrogen peroxide
   D. disinfectant solutions

_____ 14. If the eye has been chemically burned, what should be done?

   A. flush eye with cool water
   B. flush eye with boric acid
   C. apply alcohol
   D. apply quats

_____ 15. When removing implements from a wet sanitizer you should wear

   A. an operator apron
   B. a hair net
   C. rubber gloves
   D. a neutralizing bib

_____ 16. An example of the chemical method of sanitization is

   A. boiling
   B. quats
   C. infrared rays
   D. steaming

_____ 17. To be effective for sanitation, the strength of the quats to be used should be at least

   A. 1:100
   B. 1:200
   C. 1:1000
   D. 1:2000

_____ 18. What do electronic air precipitators remove from the air?

   A. viruses
   B. bacteria
   C. disinfectants
   D. A, B, and C

5

___ 19. Formaldehyde discs are used in a

    A. towel sanitizer
    B. opened container
    C. dry sanitizer
    D. wet sanitizer

___ 20. Generally, bacteria are classified into how many types?

    A. three
    B. five
    C. seven
    D. nine

___ 21. Quaternary ammonium compound is used mainly in the school or salon as a(n)

    A. soapy solution
    B. astringent
    C. disinfectant
    D. wave set

___ 22. Hair cutting implements are sanitized with

    A. 70% alcohol
    B. 40% alcohol
    C. 30% formalin solution
    D. 30% alcohol

___ 23. Disinfectants and germicides affect the growth of bacteria by

    A. destroying growth
    B. decreasing growth
    C. increasing growth
    D. halting growth

___ 24. A carrier is a person who has a disease that is

    A. acute
    B. occupational
    C. common
    D. contagious

___ 25. Nonpathogenic bacteria is defined by the cosmetologist as being

    A. beneficial
    B. harmless
    C. disease producing
    D. A and B

___ 26. Which virus causes the AIDS disease?

    A. rhinovirus
    B. HIV virus
    C. influenza virus
    D. cold virus

___ 27. How is the AIDS disease transmitted from one person to another?

    A. blood
    B. semen
    C. vaginal secretions
    D. all of the above

___ 28. What route of transmission does the AIDS disease follow?

    A. sexual contact
    B. injection
    C. touching
    D. A and B only

___ 29. What other route(s) of transmission does the disease follow?

    A. injection
    B. blood transfusion
    C. maternal
    D. all of the above

___ 30. Blow combs should be sanitized by immersion in a solution that is

    A. 10% formalin
    B. soapy
    C. 5% formalin
    D. none of the above

___ 31. Which sanitation method is most often used in the salon?

    A. moist heat
    B. chemicals
    C. autoclave
    D. boiling water

Poss.	Wrong	%	Right
31	5	84%	26
31	6	81%	25
31	7	77%	24
31	8	74%	23
31	9	71%	22
31	10	68%	21
31	11	65%	20

Poss.	Wrong	%	Right
31	0	100%	31
31	1	97%	30
31	2	94%	29
31	3	90%	28
31	4	87%	27

3 SANITATION AND STERILIZATION PRE-TEST 2

32 Questions

___ 1. Metal electrodes should be sanitized with

A. 2% quats
B. 20% peroxide
C. 70% alcohol
D. 80% ammonium

___ 2. When not in use, a sanitized comb should be kept in a(n)

A. wet sanitizer
B. dry sanitizer
C. ordinary drawer
D. uniform pocket

___ 3. A clean, laundered towel should be used

A. for every third person
B. for each person
C. when the one in use looks soiled
D. when the one in use becomes stained

___ 4. Sterilization is a process in which

A. foul odors are destroyed
B. both types of bacteria are destroyed
C. only beneficial bacteria are destroyed
D. bacteria remain alive

___ 5. Moist heat sanitizing is done by

A. cooking in an oven
B. fumes in cup
C. boiling
D. frying in a pan

___ 6. Soiled towels should be stored in a covered

A. linen basket
B. closed container
C. plastic container
D. laundry basket

___ 7. Wet sanitizers should contain a solution that is

A. 1/2% formalin
B. 1/2% alcohol
C. 1/2% hydrogen peroxide
D. a disinfectant

___ 8. Sharp metallic implements, such as a scissors, should be sanitized with

A. 40% alcohol
B. 50% alcohol
C. 60% alcohol
D. 70% alcohol

___ 9. An article that would melt if exposed to heat may be sanitized using

A. a disinfectant solution
B. a hydrogen peroxide solution
C. infrared rays
D. a soapy water solution

___ 10. With flammable salon chemicals, what should be your most important consideration?

A. light
B. heat
C. moisture
D. air

___ 11. To be effective, a quaternary ammonium compound solution requires

A. mixing with alcohol
B. lengthy contact time
C. short contact time
D. mixing with peroxide

___ 12. A 70 percent alcohol solution would be used to sanitize which of the following items?

A. wet sanitizer
B. scissors and razor
C. dry sanitizer
D. styling chair

___ 13. An ammonium solution or Lysol is used mainly to sanitize a

A. pressing comb
B. cosmetologist's shoe
C. manicuring chair
D. shampoo bowl

___ 14. Which of the items below is used to store sanitized combs and brushes?

A. wet sanitizer
B. ultraviolet sanitizer
C. cleanser
D. alcohol

___ 15. After combs and brushes are removed from a formalin solution, they should be placed in a(n)

A. opened drawer
B. roller tray
C. ultraviolet sanitizer
D. all of the above

___ 16. By law, which of the following must each beauty salon have available?

A. a fire blanket
B. a hot water dispenser
C. an emergency eye wash station
D. a fire extinguisher

___ 17. After implements are removed from the ultraviolet sanitizer, they should be placed in a(n)

A. dry sanitizer
B. opened sanitizer
C. wet sanitizer
D. cold sanitizer

___ 18. Blow combs should be sanitized by a solution that is

A. soapy
B. 10% formalin
C. 5% formalin
D. none of the above

___ 19. What do electronic air precipitators remove from the air?

A. viruses
B. bacteria
C. chemicals
D. A, B, and C

___ 20. Generally, bacteria are classified into how many types?

A. three
B. five
C. seven
D. nine

___ 21. Nonpathogenic bacteria is defined by the cosmetologist as being

A. beneficial
B. harmless
C. disease producing
D. A and B

___ 22. If a salon has a fire extinguisher, how often must it be serviced and inspected?

A. monthly
B. bi-monthly
C. semi-annually
D. annually

___ 23. A carrier is a person who has a disease that is

A. acute
B. contagious
C. occupational
D. common

___ 24. Disinfectants and germicides affect the growth of bacteria by

A. increasing growth
B. decreasing growth
C. halting growth
D. destroying growth

___ 25. How is the AIDS disease transmitted from one person to another?

A. blood
B. semen
C. vaginal secretions
D. all of the above

26. What route of transmission does the AIDS disease follow?

    A. injection
    B. blood transfusion
    C. maternal
    D. all of the above

27. How is the AIDS virus destroyed outside the body?

    A. exposure to air and heat
    B. cold water
    C. rubbing with a towel
    D. wiping with a sponge

28. Which of the following would be the best choice for destroying the AIDS virus on a metal implement?

    A. water
    B. 70% alcohol
    C. shampoo
    D. hand soap

29. What common chemical would kill the AIDS virus on an implement?

    A. household bleach
    B. water
    C. 1% hydrogen peroxide
    D. 20% alcohol

30. What strength hydrogen peroxide would destroy the AIDS virus on an implement?

    A. 1%
    B. 2%
    C. 3%
    D. all of the above

31. When giving a service, what should you do if you are exposed to blood?

    A. see your doctor
    B. wash exposed area with soap and water
    C. apply a topical disinfectant
    D. B and C only

32. If you accidently cut your client's neck and it bleeds, what should you do?

    A. put on disposable rubber gloves
    B. wash area with soap and water
    C. apply topical disinfectant to area
    D. all of the above

Poss.	Wrong	%	Right
32	0	100%	32
32	1	97%	31
32	2	94%	30
32	3	91%	29
32	4	88%	28
32	5	84%	27
32	6	81%	26
32	7	78%	25
32	8	75%	24
32	9	72%	23
32	10	69%	22
32	11	66%	21

3 SANITATION AND STERILIZATION PRE-TEST 3

28 Questions

1. Quaternary ammonium compound is used mainly in the school or salon as a(n)

    A. wave set
    B. disinfectant
    C. astringent
    D. soapy solution

2. Hair cutting implements are sanitized with

    A. 30% alcohol
    B. 30% formalin solution
    C. 40% alcohol
    D. 70% alcohol

3. A 5 percent formalin solution is used mainly to sanitize a(n)

    A. ultraviolet sanitizer
    B. tweezers
    C. cuticle scissors
    D. styling chair

___ 4. A soapy solution is used to remove foreign particles from

    A. brushes
    B. thinning shears
    C. a razor
    D. an ultraviolet sanitizer

___ 5. If the eye has been chemically burned, what should be done?

    A. flush eye with cool water
    B. flush eye with boric acid
    C. apply alcohol
    D. apply quats

___ 6. Rollers, combs, and brushes should be immersed in a 10 percent formalin solution for

    A. 5 minutes
    B. 10 minutes
    C. 15 minutes
    D. 20 minutes

___ 7. Ultraviolet rays are important sanitizers because they

    A. are the most effective physical method of sanitation
    B. have a germicidal effect
    C. kill most bacteria and some viruses
    D. all of the above

___ 8. Bacteria are also referred to as one-celled

    A. viruses
    B. inorganics
    C. microorganisms
    D. matter

___ 9. The basic procedure for sanitizing soiled implements, such as brushes, is to

    A. remove hair
    B. wash in soapy water
    C. place in wet sanitizer
    D. all of the above

___ 10. A common skin antiseptic would be

    A. 3% hydrogen peroxide
    B. 6% hydrogen peroxide
    C. 9% hydrogen peroxide
    D. 12% hydrogen peroxide

___ 11. Waste materials, such as hair removed from combs and brushes, should be put in a(n)

    A. closed container
    B. corner
    C. along side a waste basket
    D. neat pile

___ 12. Quats is used in the beauty salon as a(n)

    A. astringent
    B. deodorant
    C. disinfectant
    D. fumigant

___ 13. The sanitizing method most often used in the beauty salon is that of

    A. chemical disinfectants
    B. boiling
    C. baking in stoves
    D. washing with soap and water

___ 14. When a disinfectant solution is put in a receptacle with a cover, it is called a

    A. closed sanitizer
    B. dry sanitizer
    C. violet-ray sanitizer
    D. wet sanitizer

___ 15. When removing implements from a wet sanitizer, you should wear

    A. an operator-apron
    B. a hair net
    C. rubber gloves
    D. a neutralizing bib

___ 16. An effective chemical used in a wet sanitizer is

    A. soap
    B. quats
    C. alcohol
    D. alum

___ 17. Clean towels should be stored

    A. in a closed container
    B. on top of the styling station
    C. on the floor near the shampoo area
    D. in an open laundry basket

18. To be effective, a dry sanitizer should contain

    A. a fumigant
    B. alcohol
    C. a violet ray sanitizer
    D. a wet sanitizer

19. To be effectively sanitized, combs and brushes should be immersed in a solution that is

    A. a disinfectant
    B. a cleanser
    C. caustic
    D. a deodorant

20. All products poured from their original containers and used in the beauty salon should be

    A. tightly capped with a lid
    B. clearly labeled
    C. poured into clear bottles
    D. poured into glass bottles only

21. To be effective for sanitation, the strengths of the quats to be used should be at least

    A. 1:200
    B. 1:400
    C. 1:700
    D. 1:1000

22. An example of the chemical method of sanitization is

    A. steaming
    B. infrared rays
    C. quats
    D. boiling

23. A client trips in the shampoo area and falls down. You think the leg is broken. What should you do?

    A. pack the leg with ice compresses
    B. set the leg with splints
    C. call for medical assistance
    D. lift client to facial chair

24. What should the minimum strength hydrogen peroxide be to destroy the AIDS virus?

    A. 1%
    B. 2%
    C. 3%
    D. all of the above

25. When giving a service, what should you do if you accidently cut the client?

    A. see your doctor
    B. wash exposed area with soap and water
    C. apply a topical disinfectant
    D. B and C only

26. If you accidently cut your client's neck and it bleeds, what should you do?

    A. put on disposable rubber gloves
    B. wash area with soap and water
    C. apply a topical disinfectant to the area
    D. all of the above

27. When your newly sterilized scissors or comb is NOT in use, where should it be stored?

    A. wet sanitizer
    B. dry sanitizer
    C. your pocket
    D. your purse

28. Before washing your brushes and combs, what should be done to them first?

    A. put them in an ultraviolet sanitizer
    B. remove all hair and other foreign materials
    C. place them into a wet sanitzer
    D. soak them in a sanitizing agent

Poss.	Wrong	%	Right
28	0	100%	28
28	1	96%	27
28	2	93%	26
28	3	89%	25
28	4	86%	24
28	5	82%	23
28	6	79%	22
28	7	75%	21
28	8	71%	20
28	9	68%	19
28	10	64%	18

25 Questions

___ 1. The function of the hair is to

    A. adorn the body
    B. protect the skin
    C. adorn the head
    D. all of the above

___ 2. Hair is not found on the

    A. forearm and wrists
    B. forearm and nose
    C. knuckles of the hands
    D. soles of the feet

___ 3. Axillary hair is located

    A. under the chin
    B. on the scalp
    C. under the arms
    D. across the forehead

___ 4. Hair is referred to as an extension or

    A. addition of the skin
    B. addition of the nail
    C. appendage of the skin
    D. appendage of the nail

___ 5. A hot wax treatment would be used to remove superfluous hair in all of the following areas except one. Which one is the exception?

    A. upper lip
    B. lower jaw line
    C. eyebrow area
    D. underarms

___ 6. The protein molecules that are the building blocks of the hair are called

    A. amino alkalizers
    B. amino acids
    C. aspartic acids
    D. glutamic alkalizers

___ 7. The protein cross-bonds of the hair are called

    A. polypeptide bonds
    B. monopeptide bonds
    C. hydrogen bonds
    D. cystine bonds

___ 8. The physical wrapping of the hair during cold wave breaks the

    A. hydrogen bonds
    B. cystine bonds
    C. atomic bonds
    D. molecular bonds

___ 9. The center of the hair shaft which may or may not contain soft keratin is the

    A. medulla
    B. cortex
    C. cuticle
    D. follicle

___ 10. The natural coloring pigment found in the hair is called

    A. keratin
    B. melanin
    C. a tint
    D. a dye

___ 11. Goose bumps are caused by contraction of which muscle?

    A. cardiac
    B. arrector pili
    C. obicularis oris
    D. occipital

___ 12. The part of the follicle that contains the nerve and blood supply for the hair is the

    A. papilla
    B. capillary
    C. body
    D. none of the above

___ 13. Hair is an example of

    A. hard keratin
    B. soft keratin
    C. Henle's layer
    D. Huxley's layer

___ 14. The shape of a single hair shaft will be determined by the angle of the

    A. follicle
    B. cuticle
    C. hair shaft
    D. hair bulb

15. Scalp hair has a life expectancy of

   A. 1 to 2 months
   B. 1 to 1 1/2 years
   C. 1 1/2 to 1 3/4 years
   D. 2 to 5 years

16. When hair is in its resting cycle, and more likely to fall out, this stage is known as the

   A. terminal stage
   B. fall-out stage
   C. hair loss stage
   D. telogen stage

17. Clients with natural blonde hair will have about

   A. 90,000 scalp hairs
   B. 105,000 scalp hairs
   C. 109,000 scalp hairs
   D. none of the above

18. Scalp hair usually grows at a monthly rate of

   A. 1/4˝
   B. 1/2˝
   C. 3/4˝
   D. 1˝

19. Facial and scalp hair will grow faster if it is

   A. shaved
   B. plucked
   C. singed
   D. none of the above

20. Hair texture is determined by its

   A. diameter
   B. radius
   C. circumference
   D. perimeter

21. If a product has an acid pH, it affects the hair's porosity by

   A. increasing it
   B. decreasing it
   C. keeping it the same
   D. none of the above

22. The glands in the scalp that naturally lubricate the hair during brushing are called

   A. apocrine
   B. sebaceous
   C. sudoriferous
   D. eccrine

23. What is the name for the male hair loss due to the aging process?

   A. congenital alopecia
   B. male pattern baldness
   C. hair thinning
   D. routine hair loss

24. Which of the following would a dermatologist prescribe for men for regular hair loss?

   A. vitamin A
   B. minoxidal
   C. medicated shampoo
   D. creme rinse

25. What are some of the side effects of the drug for preventing hair loss?

   A. dizziness
   B. chest pain
   C. increased heart rate
   D. all of the above

Poss.	Wrong	%	Right
25	0	100%	25
25	1	96%	24
25	2	92%	23
25	3	88%	22
25	4	84%	21
25	5	80%	20
25	6	76%	19
25	7	72%	18
25	8	68%	17
25	9	64%	16
25	10	60%	15

25 Questions

___ 1. What general term below is used to describe any diseased condition of the hair?

    A. alopecia
    B. hirsutism
    C. trichosis
    D. trichorrhexis nodosa

___ 2. Hypertrichosis may appear in the form of excessive growth of

    A. the sebaceous glands
    B. the fingernails
    C. facial hair
    D. the axillary hair

___ 3. Alopecia areata affects the

    A. scalp
    B. eyebrows
    C. eyelashes
    D. all of the above

___ 4. Alopecia senilis refers to hair loss resulting from

    A. hereditary factors
    B. infection
    C. emotional problems
    D. onset of old age

___ 5. Depilatories in the form of a cream, paste, or powder are chemical products used to

    A. curl hair
    B. remove hair
    C. color hair
    D. straighten hair

___ 6. Before applying a chemical depilatory, how should the cosmetologist protect the client?

    A. buy only quality depilatories
    B. apply gauze to the area to be worked on
    C. give the client a skin test
    D. ask client to remove jewelry

___ 7. Tinea of the scalp is always treated by a

    A. doctor
    B. cosmetologist
    C. trichologist
    D. client at home

___ 8. Monilethrix is the technical term for hair that is

    A. coarse
    B. beaded
    C. overprocessed
    D. notched

___ 9. Cutting the superfacial hair is another form of

    A. depilation
    B. epilation
    C. expiration
    D. exaltation

___ 10. A person who uses a short-wave machine and a needle to permanently remove hair is called a(n)

    A. geologist
    B. cardiologist
    C. electrologist
    D. dermatologist

___ 11. Permanent hair removal, using the short-wave machine, should not be done on (in)

    A. nostrils
    B. ears
    C. eyelids
    D. all of the above

___ 12. Fine, lightly pigmented hair found all over the body is called

    A. vellus hair
    B. universal hair
    C. terminal hair
    D. total hair

___ 13. The technical name for eyebrow hair is

    A. capilli
    B. supercilia
    C. axillary
    D. cilia

___ 14. The brain is protected by the skull bone and

    A. axillary hair
    B. capilli hair
    C. cilia hair
    D. supercilia hair

___ 15. Hair is made up of a hard protein substance called

    A. carbon
    B. hydrogen
    C. keratin
    D. sulfur

___ 16. The smallest unit of any compound is a(n)

    A. atom
    B. radical
    C. molecule
    D. micron

___ 17. The chemical bonds broken during cold wave are the

    A. hydrogen bonds
    B. oxygen bonds
    C. cystine bonds
    D. ammonium bonds

___ 18. The cystine bonds are also referred to as

    A. cold waving bonds
    B. hydrogen bonds
    C. physical bonds
    D. disulfide bonds

___ 19. The layer of the hair in which the coloring pigment is found is the

    A. follicle
    B. medulla
    C. cortex
    D. cuticle

___ 20. The percentage of the hair shaft represented by the cortex layer is

    A. 15%
    B. 25%
    C. 50%
    D. 75%

___ 21. The slender, pocket-like depression in the skin from which the hair grows is the

    A. cuticle
    B. follicle
    C. arrector
    D. apocrine

___ 22. The root of the hair that is beneath the scalp is called the hair

    A. root
    B. bark
    C. trunk
    D. body

___ 23. What is the name for the male hair loss due to the aging process?

    A. congenital alopecia
    B. male pattern baldness
    C. hair thinning
    D. routine hair loss

___ 24. Which of the following would a dermatologist prescribe for men for regular hair loss?

    A. vitamin E
    B. minoxidal
    C. medicated shampoo
    D. creme rinse

___ 25. What are some of the side effects of the drug for preventing hair loss?

    A. dizziness
    B. rapid weight gain
    C. increased heart rate
    D. all of the above

Poss.	Wrong	%	Right
25	0	100%	25
25	1	96%	24
25	2	92%	23
25	3	88%	22
25	4	84%	21
25	5	80%	20
25	6	76%	19
25	7	72%	18
25	8	68%	17
25	9	64%	16
25	10	60%	15
25	11	56%	14

21 Questions

___ 1. Before using a hot wax depilatory, the cosmetologist should

   A. apply gauze to the work area
   B. give the client instructions
   C. check to be sure client is comfortable
   D. check the temperature of the wax

___ 2. A baby born with gray hair would have a condition described by the cosmetologist as

   A. acquired canities
   B. premature canities
   C. congenital canities
   D. prognosis canities

___ 3. When viewed under a microscope, cross-sections of wavy hair will usually appear

   A. flat
   B. semi-flat
   C. semi-oval
   D. round

___ 4. Generally, the rate of hair growth on different parts of the body will be

   A. the same everywhere
   B. faster above the waist
   C. faster below the waist
   D. different from area to area

___ 5. The technical term applied to the cyclical period when the hair begins to grow is the

   A. anagen stage
   B. terminal stage
   C. telogen stage
   D. origin stage

___ 6. A client with natural red hair color will have about

   A. 90,000 scalp hairs
   B. 91,000 scalp hairs
   C. 93,000 scalp hairs
   D. 95,000 scalp hairs

___ 7. If a client with natural red, black, brown, and blond hair colors, respectively, entered the school or salon, which color would normally have the greatest number of scalp hairs?

   A. red
   B. brown
   C. black
   D. blond

___ 8. Hair usually grows fastest in a climate that is

   A. warm
   B. cold
   C. moderate
   D. humid

___ 9. The condition of the hair is determined by its

   A. texture
   B. porosity
   C. elasticity
   D. all of the above

___ 10. When describing the amount of moisture the hair will absorb, we are referring to its

   A. appearance
   B. texture
   C. elasticity
   D. porosity

___ 11. Shaving is one way to remove hair from the

   A. palms
   B. armpits
   C. soles
   D. eyebrows

___ 12. When wet hair is stretched 50 percent longer than its original length, we are referring to the hair's

   A. flexibility
   B. longevity
   C. elasticity
   D. durability

13. What general prefix is used to describe most hair diseases?

    A. tricho
    B. tricko
    C. trio
    D. trigo

14. Hypertrichosis is a condition that is also called

    A. supercilia hair
    B. superfluous hair
    C. ringed hair
    D. twisted hair

15. When alopecia appears on the head, it looks like

    A. red, circular bald patches
    B. scaly, rectangular bald patches
    C. non-inflamed, oval bald patches
    D. oily scales and oval bald patches

16. Alopecia areata is nonscarring, and the hair loss is usually

    A. temporary
    B. permanent
    C. semipermanent
    D. universal

17. Tinea of the scalp is characterized by

    A. oily yellow scales
    B. silver and gray scales
    C. dry yellow scales
    D. brown and yellow scales

18. Trichorrhexis nodosa is the technical name for

    A. tied hair
    B. twisted hair
    C. stretched hair
    D. knotted hair

19. Pili annulati is a technical term for hair that is

    A. beaded
    B. knotted
    C. notched
    D. ringed

20. A permanent method for removing hair is

    A. analysis
    B. electrolysis
    C. encephalitis
    D. hydrolysis

21. If a short-wave machine is used for electrolysis, hair growth is stopped because of damage to the

    A. cortex
    B. medulla
    C. papilla
    D. cuticle

Poss.	Wrong	%	Right
21	0	100%	21
21	1	95%	20
21	2	90%	19
21	3	86%	18
21	4	81%	17
21	5	76%	16
21	6	71%	15
21	7	67%	14
21	8	62%	13
21	9	57%	12

5 SHAMPOOING PRE-TEST 1

19 Questions

1. What is the main purpose of shampooing the hair and scalp?

    A. conditioning
    B. cleansing
    C. coloring
    D. curling

2. The pH of a shampoo indicates the concentration of

    A. hydrogen
    B. oxygen
    C. nitrogen
    D. carbon

___ 3. The skin and hair have a natural pH in a range of

    A. 3.5–4.5
    B. 4.5–5.5
    C. 5.5–6.5
    D. 6.5–7.5

___ 4. Shampoos with a pH greater than seven (7) are called

    A. acid
    B. alkaline
    C. mild
    D. neutral

___ 5. Peroxide has a pH that is

    A. acid
    B. alkaline
    C. neutral
    D. none of the above

___ 6. When using a liquid-dry shampoo

    A. never allow the client to smoke cigarettes
    B. always wear an operator apron
    C. give an allergy test
    D. always wear a hair net

___ 7. An example of citric acid would be

    A. apple cider vinegar
    B. lemon juice
    C. creme rinse
    D. white vinegar

___ 8. Shampoos used on hair that has been permanently colored are called

    A. herbal
    B. medicated
    C. special
    D. none of the above

___ 9. Shampoos used for bedridden clients who do not have the use of water are called

    A. medicated
    B. conditioning
    C. powder dry
    D. super dry

___ 10. When a disease can easily be given to one person by another, it is called

    A. transient
    B. contagious
    C. infectious
    D. acute

___ 11. It is important to use a liquid-dry shampoo only

    A. before a permanent wave
    B. after the hair has been colored
    C. in a well-ventilated area
    D. in the hair drying area

___ 12. A short-term disease, such as influenza, is called

    A. chronic
    B. congenital
    C. acute
    D. acquired

___ 13. The outermost layer of skin on the head is called the

    A. dermis
    B. epidermis
    C. corium
    D. lucid

___ 14. An excessive number of dry, flat scales or flakes that fall from the head to the shoulders is known as

    A. pityriasis capitis simplex
    B. pityriasis steatoides
    C. psoriasis
    D. pediculosis

___ 15. Psoriasis of the scalp would appear as

    A. white oval bald patches
    B. red round bald patches
    C. inflamed (red) patches of overlapping white and yellow scales
    D. inflamed (red) patches of small overlapping white flakes

___ 16. If shampoo drips into the client's eye, what should you do?

    A. rinse with boric acid
    B. apply neutralizer to the eye
    C. flush with a lemon rinse
    D. flush with cool water

17. Scabies is an infestation of the scalp by
    A. the itch mite
    B. head lice
    C. ringworm
    D. tinea

18. An overly oily scalp is a disorder medically referred to as
    A. steatoma
    B. seborrhea
    C. asteatosis
    D. tinea

19. When rinsing the client's hair with hot water, how should you detect temperature changes in the water?
    A. watch for steam from the client's scalp
    B. little finger of hand held under nozzle of hose
    C. the color of the client's scalp turns bright pink
    D. the shampoo changes color

Poss.	Wrong	%	Right
19	0	100%	19
19	1	95%	18
19	2	89%	17
19	3	84%	16
19	4	79%	15
19	5	74%	14
19	6	68%	13

6 CONDITIONING PRE-TEST 1

10 Questions

1. Carefully read label directions on instant conditioners and setting aid conditioners because they are made in different
    A. bottles
    B. strengths
    C. tubes
    D. packets

2. Hair can be damaged by
    A. brush rollers
    B. heated rollers
    C. thermal curling irons
    D. all of the above

3. Elasticity is most directly related to the hair's
    A. porosity
    B. length
    C. texture
    D. tensile strength

4. The natural lubricant that gives hair a beautiful luster or sheen is called
    A. sebum
    B. seborrhea
    C. seconal
    D. permanent color

5. The differences in proteins used on the hair are mainly their size and
    A. weight
    B. origin
    C. color
    D. strength

6. The general types of conditioners include
    A. instant conditioners
    B. protein conditioners
    C. normalizing conditioners
    D. all of the above

7. Never attempt to sell the client
    A. a conditioner
    B. a necessary service
    C. an unneeded service
    D. all of the above

8. To preserve the hairstyle against humidity in the air, the conditioner should contain a(n)
    A. barrier coat
    B. shield cover
    C. wetting agent
    D. antihumectant

19

___ 9. The amount of water the hair can absorb is called

A. porosity
B. tension
C. elasticity
D. tone

Poss.	Wrong	%	Right
10	0	100%	10
10	1	90%	9
10	2	80%	8
10	3	70%	7
10	4	60%	6

___ 10. Hair with a hard glassy feel lacks

A. porosity
B. sebum
C. color
D. tone

---

7 SCALP TREATMENTS PRE-TEST 1

5 Questions

___ 1. You must not promise that scalp manipulations will

A. stimulate the scalp nerves
B. make the scalp look healthier
C. make the hair grow
D. increase blood circulation

___ 2. Scalp manipulations should not be given if the hair is going to be

A. cold waved
B. permanently colored
C. chemically lightened
D. all of the above

___ 3. Scalp conditioners are made for hair that is either oily or

A. long
B. dry
C. short
D. thin

___ 4. If overly tight, the scalp may be made more loose and pliable from a

A. scalp treatment
B. cold wave
C. shampoo
D. hair conditioner

___ 5. The usual benefit of a scalp treatment is that it helps normalize the

A. hair shaft
B. sebaceous glands
C. thyroid gland
D. pineal gland

Poss.	Wrong	%	Right
5	0	100%	5
5	1	80%	4
5	2	60%	3
5	3	40%	2
5	4	20%	1

---

8 FINGER WAVING PRE-TEST 1

10 Questions

___ 1. Semicircular designs combed into the hair are called

A. waves
B. base direction
C. shapings
D. arcs

___ 2. To make the hair more pliable and hold it in place when finger waving, you should use

A. creme rinse
B. setting lotion
C. hair lacquer
D. neutralizer

3. Before combing out the finger wave, the hair should be

   A. thoroughly dried
   B. thoroughly lubricated
   C. quite damp
   D. sprayed with lacquer

4. To determine the middle point at a curved line, you would bisect a

   A. 40 degree angle
   B. 45 degree angle
   C. 50 degree angle
   D. 90 degree angle

5. It is important to evenly distribute the setting lotion through the hair, so it will

   A. dry uniformly
   B. curl thoroughly
   C. color evenly
   D. comb completely

6. The main objective in finger waving the hair is to mold even

   A. curls and softness
   B. waves and ridges
   C. shaping and direction
   D. parts and shapes

7. To secure wave troughs for drying, the hair could be held in place with

   A. hairpins
   B. duckbill clips
   C. double prong clips
   D. single prong clips
   E. all of the above

8. When combing a finger wave, the comb and index finger should be

   A. parallel to each other
   B. angular to each other
   C. perpendicular to each other
   D. acute to each other

9. The shaping between two finger-wave ridges is called the wave

   A. direction
   B. trough
   C. arc
   D. curl

10. The wave and ridge for each finger-wave section of hair should be evenly

    A. curled
    B. cut
    C. matched
    D. clipped

Poss.	Wrong	%	Right
10	0	100%	10
10	1	90%	9
10	2	80%	8
10	3	70%	7
10	4	60%	6

9 SCULPTURE CURLS PRE-TEST 1

20 Questions

1. For the least amount of tightness when setting sculpture curls, you should use a

   A. no-stem curl
   B. half-stem curl
   C. quarter-stem curl
   D. long-stem curl

2. Removal of tangles from a mannequin begins in the

   A. nape section
   B. right side section
   C. top section
   D. crown section

3. If hair is hard to set because of texture, shortness, or lack of curl, you should use

A. end papers
B. cotton
C. wave crepe
D. a sanek strip

4. The section of the head that is closest to the neck is the

A. nape section
B. crown section
C. right side section
D. left side section

5. A line running across the page would be

A. diagonal
B. vertical
C. horizontal
D. octagonal

6. There are only two circular directions; they are

A. horizontal and vertical
B. parallel and perpendicular
C. clockwise and counterclockwise
D. half stem and no stem

7. A loose curl (one with the least strength) is produced by a

A. quarter-stem curl
B. half-stem curl
C. long-stem curl
D. no-stem curl

8. The kind of curl stem used to produce a curl of medium strength would be a

A. quarter-stem
B. half-stem
C. long-stem
D. no-stem

9. Hair may be stiff and gummy during the comb out if too much

A. setting lotion was used during setting
B. water was used during setting
C. hair spray was used during setting
D. balsam conditioner was used during setting

10. After the setting lotion has been applied, should the hair dry out during setting, spray more

A. filler on it
B. conditioner on it
C. water on it
D. setting lotion on it

11. To control difficult hair ends when making sculpture curls, or winding rollers, use

A. end papers
B. wax
C. roller clips
D. hair pins

12. Set sculpture curls within a shaping should

A. be separate
B. swing down
C. overlap
D. swing over

13. Very fine, limp hair may require the use of mostly

A. long-stem curls
B. half-stem curls
C. no-stem curls
D. full-stem curls

14. A large stand-up curl could also be called a barrel curl or

A. skipcurl
B. cascade curl
C. closed-end curl
D. clockwise curl

15. Alternating rows of sculpture curls and shapings used to form waves are known as

A. finger waving
B. triangle waving
C. skip waving
D. semi-waving

16. Stand-up curls may be made with bases that are square, rectangular, or

A. vertical
B. horizontal
C. triangular
D. diagonal

___ 17. One good way to obtain vertical or diagonal waves on the side of the head is to use a

A. barrel wave
B. skip wave
C. flair wave
D. stand-up wave

___ 18. When large strands of hair are used to make stand-up curls, they are called cascade curls or

A. wheel curls
B. barrel curls
C. sculpture curls
D. roller curls

___ 19. The pick-up point in the sculpture shaping is the place where the comb slices or

A. clips the curl
B. carves out the curl
C. turns the curl
D. shortens the curl

___ 20. If all the client's hair was set in pin curls and dried, but before the cosmetologist begins to comb it out, seven wet curls are discovered, what should be done?

A. air dry the curls with a fan
B. let friction from the brush dry the curls
C. reset curls and dry under hair dryer
D. dry curls with heat from hand

Poss.	Wrong	%	Right
20	0	100%	20
20	1	95%	19
20	2	90%	18
20	3	85%	17
20	4	80%	16
20	5	75%	15
20	6	70%	14

9 SCULPTURE CURLS PRE-TEST 2

20 Questions

___ 1. The part of the sculpture curl located between the base and the circle end is the

A. spiral
B. root
C. stem
D. strand

___ 2. When setting sculpture curls, where in the shaping should you begin?

A. closed end
B. center
C. open end
D. top

___ 3. The amount of tightness, mobility, and direction of the sculpture curl is determined by its

A. stem
B. curve
C. spiral
D. circle end

___ 4. The width and strength of a sculpture wave depends on the

A. size of the curl
B. size of the comb
C. setting lotion
D. drying method

___ 5. The half-stem curl allows the circle end to

A. move away from the base
B. move onto the base
C. spiral onto the stem
D. curl beyond the base

___ 6. When securing the sculpture curl with a clip, avoid disturbing the base of the

A. stem
B. shaping
C. root
D. shaft

23

7. The implement used to sculpture curls is a

   A. rake comb
   B. teasing comb
   C. styling comb
   D. pin-tail comb

8. A right angle is a

   A. 90 degree angle
   B. 45 degree angle
   C. 75 degree angle
   D. A and B

9. A line that is straight up and down is

   A. vertical
   B. horizontal
   C. octagonal
   D. diagonal

10. What angle do perpendicular lines make?

    A. 75 degree
    B. 90 degree
    C. 180 degree
    D. 360 degree

11. To get the strongest sculpture curls, you should use

    A. no-stem curls
    B. half-stem curls
    C. quarter-stem curls
    D. long-stem curls

12. Which of the following is not a part of the sculpture curl?

    A. body
    B. stem
    C. base
    D. end circle

13. The section of the head above the right ear is called

    A. the nape
    B. the crown
    C. the right side
    D. the left side

14. The section on the top of the head that goes from the front hairline back is the

    A. nape
    B. crown
    C. right side
    D. top

15. Another name for a sculpture curl is

    A. bob curl
    B. end curl
    C. pin curl
    D. base curl

16. The three parts of a sculpture curl are the circle, stem, and the

    A. strand
    B. base
    C. section
    D. curve

17. The more fixed part of the hair forming a sculpture curl that grows from the scalp is the

    A. strand
    B. circle
    C. base
    D. stem

18. Two lines alongside of each other with an equal amount of space between them are called

    A. arcs
    B. parallel
    C. perpendicular
    D. diagonal

19. When setting sculpture curls, comb in the shaping, then begin setting from the

    A. center
    B. closed end
    C. open end
    D. top

20. To avoid splits around the hairline and add strength to the comb-out, the cosmetologist should use which type of curls?

    A. triangular bases and no-stem curls
    B. square bases and half-stem curls
    C. rectangular bases and full-stem curls
    D. octangular bases and full-stem curls

24

Poss.	Wrong	%	Right
20	0	100%	20
20	1	95%	19
20	2	90%	18

20	3	85%	17
20	4	80%	16
20	5	75%	15
20	6	70%	14

10 SETTING THE HAIR WITH ROLLERS PRE-TEST 1

16 Questions

___ 1. Professional rollers are made of

A. plastic
B. nylon
C. wire mesh
D. all of the above

___ 2. The use of brush rollers to set the hair was discontinued in salons because they were

A. damaging the hair
B. slow drying
C. difficult to keep sanitized
D. A and C

___ 3. Short rollers are also referred to as

A. filler rollers
B. shortie rollers
C. stub rollers
D. spoolie rollers

___ 4. The ideal number of times hair is wrapped around a roller is

A. 1/2 to 1 times
B. 1 to 1-1/2 times
C. 1-1/2 to 2 times
D. 2-1/2 to 3 times

___ 5. To make a wave formation in the hair, the roller used should be large enough for the hair to go around it

A. less than 1 turn
B. 1 turn
C. 1-1/2 to 2 turns
D. more than 2 turns

___ 6. If you make a roller placement by holding the hair strand toward the front of the head, you are setting a

A. no-stem curl
B. half-stem curl
C. long-stem curl
D. tight-stem curl

___ 7. If you make a roller placement by holding the hair strand straight up or out from the head, you are setting a

A. no-stem curl
B. half-stem curl
C. long-stem curl
D. tight-stem curl

___ 8. To get the most amount of height or fullness, you should use a

A. no-stem curl
B. half-stem curl
C. long-stem curl
D. tight-stem curl

___ 9. The design must be combed into the hair

A. before setting
B. during setting
C. after setting
D. at any time

___ 10. The best time to correct a setting error is

A. during the comb out
B. after the hair is dried, but still in roller formation
C. before the hair is dried
D. when the client's hair is partially dried

___ 11. When putting a shaping into the hair, the hair should be

A. wet
B. damp
C. dry
D. moistened on the ends

___ 12. Plastic and nylon rollers are made in the shape of a

A. cylinder
B. cone
C. circle
D. A and B

25

___ 13. The distance around the outside of the roller is called

A. diameter
B. circumference
C. longitude
D. latitude

___ 14. To make a curve formation in the hair, the roller used should be large enough for the hair to go around the roller

A. 1 turn or less
B. 1-1/2 turns
C. 2 turns
D. none of the above

___ 15. To make a curly formation in the hair, the roller used should be large enough for the hair to go around the roller

A. less than 1 turn
B. 1-1/2 turns
C. 2 turns
D. more than two turns

___ 16. If you make a roller placement by holding the strand out, away, and toward the back of the head, you are setting a

A. no-stem curl
B. half-stem curl
C. long-stem curl
D. tight-stem curl

Poss.	Wrong	%	Right
16	0	100%	16
16	1	94%	15
16	2	88%	14
16	3	81%	13
16	4	75%	12
16	5	69%	11

---

11 SELECTING HAIRSTYLES PRE-TEST 1

17 Questions

___ 1. The standard or ideal facial shape is

A. oblong
B. round
C. oval
D. square

___ 2. The silhouette is the view of the head from

A. the back
B. the side
C. the front
D. any position

___ 3. To correct a diamond-shaped face, fullness is needed everywhere, except at the

A. cheekbones
B. eyebrows
C. forehead
D. jaw

___ 4. The text recommends a certain style for a heart-shaped face. The style is a

A. bubble
B. pageboy
C. French twist
D. shag

___ 5. The percentage of married women who work outside the home is at least

A. 20%
B. 30%
C. 40%
D. 50%

___ 6. One-third of the standard face would extend from the chin to the bottom of the

A. lower lip
B. eyebrows
C. eyelashes
D. nose

___ 7. The profile is the view of the head from the

    A. front
    B. back
    C. side
    D. face

___ 8. The problem with a diamond-shaped face is that it is narrow at the chin and

    A. eyebrows
    B. cheekbones
    C. jaws
    D. forehead

___ 9. To keep up with ever-changing hair fashion trends, it is important for the cosmetologist to

    A. improve hair porosity and elasticity
    B. know basic hairstyling techniques
    C. change hair colors often
    D. change hair shaping techniques often

___ 10. To design a hairstyle that is suitable for the client, the cosmetologist should consider

    A. shortening long hair
    B. lightening the hair to a pastel color
    C. the client's features, personality, and occupation
    D. setting the hair with sculptured curls

___ 11. When deciding on a hairstyle for the client, a side part or bangs will be determined by

    A. eye shape
    B. ear size
    C. hair length
    D. facial shape

___ 12. Round or square facial shapes are given a front parting to create the illusion of

    A. volume
    B. height
    C. width
    D. fullness

___ 13. The use of bangs will reduce the forehead area, which is desirable for the person with a(n)

    A. heart-shaped face
    B. oval-shaped face
    C. triangular-shaped face
    D. diamond-shaped face

___ 14. The problem with a heart-shaped face is that the chin is too narrow, and the width is at the

    A. eyebrows
    B. cheekbones
    C. jaw
    D. forehead

___ 15. The oval-shaped face is best characterized by a profile that is

    A. straight
    B. concave
    C. convex
    D. wavy

___ 16. An example of a physical imperfection would be

    A. a hangnail
    B. blue eyes
    C. brown eyes
    D. a scar

___ 17. What other factor(s) is considered in determining a hairstyle?

    A. hair cut
    B. hair color
    C. hair texture
    D. all of the above

Poss.	Wrong	%	Right
17	0	100%	17
17	1	94%	16
17	2	88%	15
17	3	82%	14
17	4	76%	13
17	5	71%	12
17	6	65%	11

26 Questions

___ 1. For a basic haircut, the cosmetologist would begin cutting the hair in the

A. top
B. side
C. crown
D. nape

___ 2. If too much bulk is removed from coarse hair, it tends to

A. look smooth and natural
B. stick out from the head
C. be super-curly
D. set more easily

___ 3. It is better to cut very fine guideline hairs with a

A. razor
B. thinning scissors
C. regular scissors
D. double-edge razor

___ 4. When shaping the hair, avoid thinning it within

A. 1-1/2–2″ from the scalp
B. 2-1/2–3″ from the scalp
C. 3-1/2–4″ from the scalp
D. 4-1/2–5″ from the scalp

___ 5. What draping supply is recommended for the client that is about to have a hair shaping only?

A. towel shampoo cape
B. shampoo cape
C. comb-out cape
D. neck strip and shampoo cape

___ 6. Double-notch hair cutting scissors are used on the hair to remove

A. color
B. taper
C. soil
D. bulk

___ 7. A low-elevation hair shaping means the hair is held and cut at an angle from the nape that does not exceed how many degrees from the head?

A. 45 degrees
B. 65 degrees
C. 85 degrees
D. none of the above

___ 8. When thinning coarse hair, avoid cutting too close to the

A. wave
B. scalp
C. strand
D. root

___ 9. If an area of hair that has been cut is stepped, then the hair is said to be

A. marked
B. struck
C. dropped
D. chunked

___ 10. Super-curly hair should be cut with a

A. clipper
B. scissors
C. razor
D. thinning shears

___ 11. When razor cutting, strokes that the cosmetologist should use are

A. firm and long
B. smooth and long
C. smooth and short
D. jerky and short

___ 12. Blunt cutting is called

A. hair designing
B. razor cutting
C. club cutting
D. angle cutting

13. To prevent the electric clipper blades from pulling the hair, what should you do?

    A. apply oil to them
    B. soak in alcohol
    C. apply ammonia to them
    D. dip them in peroxide

14. When hair in the top and side sections is cut to a length of 3 1/2–4 1/2 inches and styled away from the face, this is called

    A. edging
    B. feathering
    C. elevating
    D. contouring

15. When a man's hair is cut very short in the nape of the neck in a graduated way and seems to disappear into the neck, this is known as

    A. stepping
    B. feathering
    C. feather edge
    D. layering

16. For a hair shaping, the hair is sectioned off because the finished results tend to be more

    A. uniform
    B. uneven
    C. choppy
    D. individual

17. Double-notched scissors are used mainly to

    A. shorten the hair
    B. thin the hair
    C. elevate the hair
    D. all of the above

18. A razor used to cut the hair is called a

    A. shaper
    B. cutter
    C. slipper
    D. nipper

19. Proper storage of cutting implements is important to prevent

    A. over-use of implements
    B. injury to small children
    C. rust from forming
    D. the edges from becoming dull

20. The technique of holding the hair upward toward the crown or top of the head during a hair shaping is called

    A. low-elevation
    B. high-elevation
    C. feather edging
    D. stepping

21. What is the name given to one or more subsections of hair cut in the hairline or crown of the head that serve as a yardstick for cutting the rest of the hair?

    A. trendline
    B. radial line
    C. bias line
    D. guideline

22. You should not use an electric clipper if

    A. the client wants a trim
    B. the set screw has been adjusted
    C. it is noisy
    D. any teeth are broken

23. When cutting the hair with a shaper, it is important to

    A. cut using the guard
    B. thin toward the scalp
    C. use long, sliding strokes
    D. blunt all hair

24. What will happen if you submerge your electric clipper in a wet sanitizer while it is plugged into an outlet?

    A. the blades will slide
    B. the clipper won't cut correctly
    C. you will get an electric shock
    D. your clipper will vibrate

25. When the hair is cut straight across without any thinning, this is called

    A. slither cutting
    B. feathering
    C. blunt cutting
    D. effilating

___ 26. When razor cutting a client's hair, the hair should be

    A. damp
    B. thoroughly towel dried
    C. slightly moist
    D. wet

Poss.	Wrong	%	Right
26	0	100%	26
26	1	96%	25
26	2	92%	24
26	3	88%	23
26	4	85%	22
26	5	81%	21
26	6	77%	20
26	7	73%	19
26	8	69%	18
26	9	65%	17
26	10	62%	16
26	11	58%	15

12 HAIR SHAPING PRE-TEST 2

11 Questions

___ 1. Definite lines of demarcation that appear on the hair after a hair shaping are known as

    A. shingles
    B. elevations
    C. slices
    D. steps (marks)

___ 2. When hair is cut very short in the nape area of the head, this is known as

    A. feathering
    B. a tailored neckline
    C. sculpturing
    D. effilating

___ 3. When the hair is combed downward, what is the name for bottom lengths of hair on the hairstyle?

    A. sign line
    B. hanging length
    C. angle cut
    D. elevation line

___ 4. The slithering movement of the scissors used to shorten hair is also called

    A. elevating
    B. effilating
    C. thinning
    D. tapering

___ 5. Hair may be thinned with a razor, thinning shears, or

    A. finger tang
    B. regular scissors
    C. electric clipper
    D. hand clipper

___ 6. The hair can be shaped after a

    A. cold (chemical) wave
    B. permanent hair
    C. frosting
    D. all of the above

___ 7. When using the electric clipper, it is important not to

    A. clip the hair on the neck
    B. nick a mole
    C. cut the hair too fast
    D. notch the hair

___ 8. After each hair-shaping service, sanitize your scissors with

    A. 1% lemon rinse
    B. 2% hydrogen peroxide
    C. 70% ethyl alcohol
    D. 70% formalin

___ 9. Storing your scissors in your uniform pocket may result in

    A. a severe cut of your hand or wrist
    B. tarnishing of finish on the scissors
    C. dulling of blades of the scissors
    D. rust forming on the scissors

10. Which of the following hair-cutting implements is used to slither a dry hair strand?

    A. scissors
    B. razor
    C. tapering shears
    D. clipper

11. After cleaning the client's neck with a razor, what should be used to sanitize the blade of the razor?

    A. steel wool
    B. 70% alcohol
    C. rinse thoroughly with hot water
    D. wipe all hair off of it with a laundered towel

Poss.	Wrong	%	Right
11	0	100%	11
11	1	91%	10
11	2	82%	9
11	3	73%	8
11	4	64%	7

13 AIR-WAVING AND BLOW-DRYING PRE-TEST 1

17 Questions

1. Cooler air settings on an air waver are generally used on hair that is

    A. coarse
    B. bleached
    C. medium
    D. normal

2. Appliances for air waving may differ in their

    A. electrical power
    B. heating elements
    C. air velocity
    D. all of the above

3. Another term for air waving is

    A. iron waving
    B. press waving
    C. thermal waving
    D. blow waving

4. For quick-service hairstyling, use a(n)

    A. air clipper
    B. blow waver
    C. roller
    D. clamper

5. Heat is concentrated during blow waving through the use of attachments that are plastic or

    A. metal
    B. mineral
    C. organic
    D. vinyl

6. By rotating an air comb on the hair, the cosmetologist may achieve

    A. elasticity
    B. closeness
    C. height
    D. texture

7. The heat from the air waver should be directed

    A. away from the scalp
    B. toward the scalp
    C. at the ends
    D. toward the hair root

8. Hotter air settings on the air waver are generally used on hair that is

    A. normal
    B. coarse
    C. bleached
    D. tinted

___ 9. Quick-service hairstyling in the salon saves time for the

A. operator
B. client
C. supplier
D. A and B

___ 10. To insure safety, all hair wavers and blow dryers must be

A. set at low temperature settings
B. used on damp to dry hair
C. Underwriters Laboratories approved
D. inspected at time of purchase

___ 11. Wave set may be used in quick-service styling if it is

A. paste
B. liquid
C. gel
D. cream

___ 12. Extra care must be taken when blow waving long hair because it

A. may become hard to manage and curl
B. may dry too quickly and become oily
C. may be drawn into the air intake of the dryer
D. could stick to the brush and become straight

___ 13. When air waving, the cosmetologist should never place the blow comb on the

A. ends
B. scalp
C. sides
D. bangs

___ 14. By turning the brush of the blow comb into the strand near the scalp, this will help achieve

A. fullness
B. tone
C. elasticity
D. texture

___ 15. When air waving the hair, the head should be subdivided into strands that are the same size as those used for

A. cold waving
B. tint applications
C. roller setting
D. hair shaping

___ 16. On an electrical appliance, the abbreviation U.L. stands for the words

A. Under Load
B. Under Level
C. Union Label
D. Underwriters Laboratories

___ 17. To AVOID burning the client's scalp during a blow waving service, which direction should the flow of air be aimed?

A. toward the scalp
B. toward the bristles of the brush
C. toward the hand
D. away from the scalp toward the ear

Poss.	Wrong	%	Right
17	0	100%	17
17	1	94%	16
17	2	88%	15
17	3	82%	14
17	4	76%	13
17	5	71%	12
17	6	65%	11

13 AIR-WAVING AND BLOW-DRYING PRE-TEST 2

16 Questions

___ 1. Cooler air settings on an air waver are generally used on hair that is

A. coarse
B. bleached
C. medium
D. normal

___ 2. Appliances for air waving may differ in their

A. electrical power
B. heating elements
C. air velocity
D. all of the above

32

___ 3. Another term for air waving is

A. iron waving
B. press waving
C. thermal waving
D. blow waving

___ 4. For quick-service hairstyling, use a(n)

A. air clipper
B. blow waver
C. roller
D. clamper

___ 5. Heat is concentrated during blow waving through the use of attachments that are plastic or

A. metal
B. mineral
C. organic
D. vinyl

___ 6. By rotating an air comb on the hair, the cosmetologist may achieve

A. elasticity
B. closeness
C. height
D. texture

___ 7. The heat from the air waver should be directed

A. away from the scalp
B. toward the scalp
C. at the ends
D. toward the hair root

___ 8. Hotter air settings on the air waver are generally used on hair that is

A. normal
B. coarse
C. bleached
D. tinted

___ 9. Quick-service hairstyling in the salon saves time for the

A. operator
B. client
C. supplier
D. A and B

___ 10. To insure safety, all hair wavers and blow dryers must be

A. set at low temperature settings
B. used on damp to dry hair
C. Underwriters Laboratories approved
D. inspected at time of purchase

___ 11. Wave set may be used in quick-service styling if it is

A. paste
B. liquid
C. gel
D. cream

___ 12. Extra care must be taken when blow waving long hair because it

A. may become hard to manage and curl
B. may dry too quickly and become oily
C. may be drawn into the air intake of the dryer
D. could stick to the brush and become straight

___ 13. When air waving, the cosmetologist should never place the blow comb on the

A. ends
B. scalp
C. sides
D. bangs

___ 14. By turning the brush of the blow comb into the strand near the scalp, this will help achieve

A. fullness
B. tone
C. elasticity
D. texture

___ 15. When air waving the hair, the head should be subdivided into strands that are the same size as those used for

A. cold waving
B. tint applications
C. roller setting
D. hair shaping

33

16. On an electrical appliance, the abbreviation
U.L. stands for the words

    A. Under Load
    B. Under Level
    C. Union Label
    D. Underwriters Laboratories

Poss.	Wrong	%	Right
16	0	100%	16
16	1	94%	15
16	2	88%	14
16	3	81%	13
16	4	75%	12
16	5	69%	11

---

14 IRON CURLS PRE-TEST 1

15 Questions

___ 1. Poker curls are made in a spiral fashion from the

   A. ends to the scalp
   B. mid-strand to the ends
   C. ends to the mid-strand
   D. scalp to the ends

___ 2. Croquignole curling involves winding the hair strand from the

   A. ends to the scalp
   B. mid-strand to ends
   C. ends to mid-strand
   D. scalp to ends

___ 3. In order to heat evenly, thermal irons should be made of high quality

   A. brass
   B. steel
   C. aluminum
   D. B and C only

___ 4. As the iron is rolled toward the scalp, what does the cosmetologist use to protect the client's scalp?

   A. cotton
   B. towel
   C. comb
   D. an end paper

___ 5. Which of the following would be an example of a hairstyling implement for forming spiral curls in the hair?

   A. crimping iron
   B. marcel-style curling iron
   C. spring clamp-style curling iron
   D. B and C only

___ 6. Which of the following curling irons should be used to form a rippling effect in longer hair lengths?

   A. marcel-style curling iron
   B. crimp-style curling iron
   C. crimping iron
   D. pressing comb

___ 7. What is the name for the smallest diameter curling iron used for curling the hair?

   A. mini or midget curling iron
   B. C-size curling iron
   C. D-size curling iron
   D. quarter-size curling iron

___ 8. Which term describes the non-moveable hot part of the curling iron?

   A. barrel
   B. shell handle
   C. swivel base
   D. B and D only

___ 9. Which of the curling iron safety features allows the cord to remain untangled as the iron is rotated so you could avoid the possibility of an electrical shock?

   A. shell handle
   B. rod
   C. swivel base
   D. shell clamp

___ 10. What safety feature should be present on your curling iron that will allow you to regulate the temperature?

   A. circuit breaker
   B. thermostat
   C. rotating handle
   D. support clip

11. When iron curling, which of the following stem formations gives the hair the maximum amount of volume?

   A. no-stem curls
   B. half-stem curls
   C. full-stem curls
   D. none of the above

12. Which of the following is a safety feature that allows you to rest your curling iron on the top of the styling station?

   A. support clip
   B. rotating handle
   C. thermostat
   D. A and C only

13. During iron curling, what is the name for the curling method that curls the hair from the scalp to the ends?

   A. spiral curl
   B. poker curl
   C. croquignole curl
   D. candlestick curl

14. When thermal curling the hair, what condition will cause the hair to be scorched?

   A. over conditioning
   B. coloring the hair too dark
   C. rinsing with too much water
   D. curling wet hair

15. If your curling iron doesn't have a thermostat, and you determine that the temperature of your curling iron is too hot for the hair texture and condition of the strand you are going to curl, what should you do?

   A. blow on the iron
   B. wave the iron in the air
   C. towel cool the iron
   D. place barrel in a glass of water

Poss.	Wrong	%	Right
15	0	100%	15
15	1	93%	14
15	2	87%	13
15	3	80%	12
15	4	73%	11
15	5	66%	10

14 IRON CURLS PRE-TEST 2

20 Questions

1. As a safety precaution, what should you do before applying your curling iron to the client's hair?

   A. pretest the temperature
   B. towel cooling
   C. switch it off
   D. turn up the thermostat

2. What will determine the degree of curliness that will be achieved on your client's hair when using a curling iron?

   A. hair density; hair color
   B. hair color alone
   C. length of hair; size of barrel
   D. hair texture; size of the rod

3. Which of the following should be used to determine the temperature of the curling iron?

   A. watch for smoke
   B. use the pull test
   C. grab it in the palm of your hand
   D. clamp barrel across a white tissue

4. What type of shampoo cape should be used for the iron curling process?

   A. plastic cape
   B. floral plastic cape
   C. heat resistant cape
   D. no cape is needed

5. To achieve a larger wavy pattern on longer hair lengths, which curling iron size should you select?

   A. mini-size iron
   B. medium-size iron
   C. large-size iron
   D. micro-mini-size iron

6. Which curling iron size should be used for the shorter hair around the front hairline and nape?

   A. mini iron
   B. medium iron
   C. large iron
   D. A and C

7. What is one method used for testing curling iron temperature?

   A. watch for steam vapor to drift up from the iron
   B. use a piece of white paper
   C. smell the iron
   D. listen to the iron

8. When iron curling fine, thin hair, what size subsections should you use?

   A. large sections
   B. medium sections
   C. small sections
   D. razor thin sections

9. What method is used most often to heat your curling iron?

   A. electric power
   B. stove
   C. oven
   D. solar energy

10. What are the names for the chemicals used for sanitizing and cleaning your curling iron?

   A. shampoo
   B. alcohol
   C. alcohol and ammonia
   D. thio and ammonia

11. To achieve a curly hairstyle, which hair length will require the most rotations of the curling iron?

   A. short hair
   B. medium length hair
   C. long hair
   D. A and B only

12. Poker curls are made in a spiral fashion from the

   A. ends to the scalp
   B. mid-strand to the ends
   C. ends to the mid-strand
   D. scalp to the ends

13. If using your curling iron close to the client's scalp, what should be placed between the iron and the scalp to protect the client?

   A. aluminum foil
   B. an end wrap
   C. a comb
   D. a duck bill clip

14. If a client is severely burned with a curling iron, what should you do?

   A. take client to physician
   B. place a bandage on burn
   C. apply Gentian Violet jelly on burn
   D. cover wound with a clean towel

15. During the iron curling service, if the clamp is NOT kept moving in the proper direction, what damage will result on the hair?

   A. the hair will turn orange
   B. the hair will be scorched
   C. the hair will be overly curly
   D. the hair will be overly shiny

16. The term "clicking" used in connection with thermal curling methods refers to

   A. the sound of the iron as it heats up
   B. the opening/closing of the clamp as the iron is rotated
   C. the sound of the iron as it turns in the strand
   D. the opening/closing of the conditioner bottle during the curling process

17. When the hair is iron curled, what holds the hair against the barrel of the iron while the hair strand is being curled?

   A. shell clamp
   B. non-moveable handle
   C. rod
   D. the moveable handle

18. During the iron curling service, if the clamp is NOT kept moving, what damage will result on the hair?

   A. the hair will turn orange
   B. the hair will be scorched
   C. the hair will be overly curly
   D. the hair will be overly shiny

19. To achieve a curly hairstyle, which hair length will require the maximum rotations of the curling iron?

   A. short hair
   B. medium length hair
   C. long hair
   D. A and B only

20. If using your curling iron close to the client's scalp, what should be placed between the iron and the scalp to protect the client?

   A. aluminum foil
   B. an end wrap
   C. a comb
   D. a duck bill clip

Poss.	Wrong	%	Right
20	0	100%	20
20	1	95%	19
20	2	90%	18
20	3	85%	17
20	4	80%	16
20	5	75%	15
20	6	70%	14

15, 16, 17 HAIR COLOR PRE-TEST 1

27 Questions

1. When doing a tint retouch, apply the tint only to the

   A. hair root
   B. hair ends
   C. cold shaft
   D. new growth

2. To prevent overlapping on a tint retouch, the tint is applied from the scalp to about

   A. 1/16 up to the tinted hair
   B. 1/16 over the already tinted hair
   C. 1/4 up to the tinted hair
   D. 1/2 over the tinted hair

3. One disadvantage of using temporary rinses is that the color

   A. rubs off on clothing
   B. completely covers gray hair
   C. will lighten natural pigment
   D. requires a patch test

4. Semipermanent colors are also referred to as

   A. semipermanent rinses
   B. permanent rinses
   C. permanent tints
   D. shampoo-in hair colors

5. A one-process permanent tint contains

   A. aniline derivative dye
   B. metallic dye
   C. vegetable dye
   D. henna dye

6. Before applying an aniline derivative tint, omit

   A. hair brushing
   B. the patch test
   C. the strand test
   D. the metallic salt test

___ 7. Just before applying a hair tint, it would be a good safety precaution to

    A. put cotton on the hairline
    B. put cotton around the client's neck
    C. check again for scalp abrasions
    D. clean combs and brushes

___ 8. Semipermanent tints usually do not require

    A. a predisposition test
    B. aniline derivative tint
    C. hydrogen peroxide
    D. processing times

___ 9. Semipermanent colors contain

    A. water
    B. certified vegetable dye
    C. azo dye
    D. all of the above

___ 10. Synthetic, or organic hair colors are found in

    A. vegetable tints
    B. aniline derivative tints
    C. certified vegetable tints
    D. metallic tints

___ 11. One of the main chemicals in aniline derivative tints is

    A. sulfonated oil
    B. ammonium thioglycolate
    C. cystine disulfide
    D. para-phenylene-diamine

___ 12. One disadvantage for the cosmetologist in giving a permanent hair color is that it

    A. brings repeat business
    B. costs the client more
    C. creates self-satisfaction
    D. requires more time

___ 13. A predisposition test is required before applying a(n)

    A. vegetable derivative tint
    B. animal derivative tint
    C. metallic derivative tint
    D. aniline derivative tint

___ 14. Before applying an aniline derivative tint, the cosmetologist is required to give the client a

    A. test curl
    B. test wave
    C. patch test
    D. strand test

___ 15. In selling the client semipermanent hair color, the cosmetologist would specify that

    A. semipermanent color does not rub off
    B. retouching is eliminated
    C. the color will last 4-6 shampoos
    D. all of the above

___ 16. Aniline derivative tints color the hair because they are

    A. penetrating tints
    B. metallic dyes
    C. henna dyes
    D. vegetable tints

___ 17. The basic chemical found in aniline derivative tint is

    A. ammonia
    B. coal tar
    C. metallic
    D. vegetable

___ 18. The chemical symbol for hydrogen peroxide is

    A. H_2O
    B. H_2O_2
    C. H_2O_3
    D. H_2O_4

___ 19. A single application tint is prepared by mixing the required tint with

    A. hard water
    B. 10-volume peroxide
    C. ammonia water
    D. 20-volume peroxide

20. A client is sitting in the cosmetologist's styling chair for a scheduled virgin tint. After getting the coloring product from the dispensary, the cosmetologist discovers there is no developer anywhere in the salon. The cosmetologist should

A. use water for the developer and give the tint
B. use cold wave neutralizer
C. use shampoo for developer
D. reschedule the appointment

21. If the client reacts positively to a patch test for a hair color, the condition on the skin is called dermatitis

A. venenata
B. lesion
C. abrasion
D. scrape

22. Aniline derivative tints are made of

A. compound dye
B. metallic dye
C. synthetic, organic dye
D. vegetable dye

23. The cosmetologist selects the proper shade in semipermanent hair color by using the

A. cosmetology text
B. color chart
C. client's present hair color
D. B and C

24. The name given to the process that explains the chemical reaction of mixing hydrogen peroxide and an aniline derivative tint is

A. hydrolization
B. oxidation
C. softening
D. filling

25. The general term used to describe a bleach and toner is

A. separate application
B. single application
C. double application
D. triple application

26. The word used to describe the coloring of the new growth of hair that is already tinted is

A. toner
B. retouch
C. tone-up
D. regrowth

27. Using hair color theory, what is the term used to describe differences in a particular hair color?

A. stars
B. levels
C. variances
D. reflections

Poss.	Wrong	%	Right
27	0	100%	27
27	1	96%	26
27	2	93%	25
27	3	89%	24
27	4	85%	23
27	5	81%	22
27	6	78%	21
27	7	74%	20
27	8	70%	19
27	9	67%	18
27	10	63%	17
27	11	59%	16

15, 16, 17 HAIR COLOR PRE-TEST 2

26 Questions

1. Terms such as cool, drab, and warm, describe

A. tones of a hair color
B. shades of a hair color
C. brightness of a hair color
D. depth of a hair color

2. It is best to stay away from giving an aniline derivative tint if there are

A. dry hair ends
B. dandruff scales
C. many gray hairs
D. scalp abrasions

___ 3. During hair tinting, the hydrogen peroxide acts as a catalyst when mixed with a(n)

    A. vegetable color
    B. aniline derivative color
    C. henna color
    D. metallic powder

___ 4. Hair tinting affects the hair by

    A. adding natural color to it
    B. removing all pigment from it
    C. adding an artificial color to it
    D. bleaching all pigment from it

___ 5. Before each aniline derivative tint, the client's patch test must be

    A. negative
    B. positive
    C. neutral
    D. acid

___ 6. The volume of the peroxide commonly used to soften and swell the hair when tinting is

    A. 10 volume
    B. 20 volume
    C. 30 volume
    D. 40 volume

___ 7. Temporary rinses should be combed evenly over the entire hair

    A. bulb
    B. cortex
    C. shaft
    D. root

___ 8. A streak caused by overlapping color on previously tinted hair is called a line of

    A. demarcation
    B. separation
    C. sensitivity
    D. discoloration

___ 9. Prior to the tint application, the hair must be divided into how many equal sections?

    A. one
    B. four
    C. six
    D. eight

___ 10. A tint that lightens and colors the hair in one application (one step) is the

    A. single-application tint
    B. double-application tint
    C. triple-application tint
    D. henna tint

___ 11. The usual area on the skin to give a patch test is the bend of the elbow, or behind the

    A. shoulder
    B. knee
    C. wrist
    D. ear

___ 12. Before the application of an aniline derivative tint, the patch test must remain on the skin for at least

    A. 16 hours
    B. 24 hours
    C. 32 hours
    D. 48 hours

___ 13. How many hours before giving a semipermanent hair color would the cosmetologist give a predisposition test?

    A. 18 hours
    B. 24 hours
    C. 30 hours
    D. 36 hours

___ 14. The medical term for the positive reaction to a skin test is dermatitis

    A. nodosa
    B. senilis
    C. venenata
    D. corona

___ 15. The general term used to describe a penetrating, single-application permanent hair color is a

    A. shampoo tint
    B. single-application tint
    C. double-process tint
    D. highlighting tint

16. A highlighting aniline shampoo tint is known as a

   A. single-step bleach
   B. single-step rinse
   C. semi-rinse
   D. soap cap

17. Egyptian henna is an example of a tint made from a

   A. salt
   B. metal
   C. vegetable
   D. mineral

18. When doing a tint retouch, the color is only applied to the hair

   A. papilla
   B. new growth
   C. bulb
   D. follicle

19. Single-application tints lighten the hair, and also

   A. bleach it
   B. deposit toner
   C. deposit color
   D. deposit peroxide

20. The physical action that causes the temporary color to adhere to the hair shaft is referred to as

   A. highlighting
   B. absorption
   C. penetrating
   D. coating

21. Temporary rinses require a predisposition test

   A. at all times
   B. before each application
   C. when specified by the manufacturer
   D. once a week

22. Hair that has not had chemicals applied to it is called

   A. primary hair
   B. tertiary hair
   C. virgin hair
   D. vellus hair

23. The term used for a tint diluted with shampoo is

   A. permanent shampoo
   B. shampoo-in color
   C. soap cap
   D. retouch shampoo

24. When selling a semipermanent rinse, the client should be made aware that the color is applied to all of the hair and that there will be some degree of fading after several shampoos, so there is no need for a

   A. patch test
   B. retouch
   C. strand test
   D. conditioning treatment

25. A patch test is required before the application of a

   A. cold wave
   B. one-process tint
   C. rinse
   D. conditioner

26. A single-application tint begins working when mixed with

   A. 20-volume peroxide
   B. oil bleach
   C. ammonium
   D. distilled water

Poss.	Wrong	%	Right
26	0	100%	26
26	1	96%	25
26	2	92%	24
26	3	88%	23
26	4	85%	22
26	5	81%	21
26	6	77%	20
26	7	73%	19
26	8	69%	18
26	9	65%	17
26	10	62%	16
26	11	58%	15

24 Questions

___ 1. To test the strength of hydrogen peroxide, you would use which instrument?

    A. barometer
    B. hydrometer
    C. odometer
    D. chronometer

___ 2. Natural hair color is determined by its

    A. porosity
    B. pigment
    C. medulla
    D. cuticle

___ 3. If a strand of hair was tested and found to have a metallic dye on it, the strand would look

    A. coarse
    B. discolored
    C. hardened
    D. stripped

___ 4. Semipermanent hair color partially penetrates the

    A. cuticle
    B. cortex
    C. medulla
    D. follicle

___ 5. After what number of shampoos will semipermanent hair color wash out of the hair?

    A. 2 to 3
    B. 4 to 6
    C. 5 to 6
    D. 7 to 8

___ 6. The pH of a semipermanent color falls in the range of

    A. 4 to 6
    B. 5 to 6
    C. 7 to 9
    D. 9 to 10

___ 7. In choosing a semipermanent hair color for your client, the factor to be considered is the

    A. color rub off
    B. coating quality
    C. color penetration
    D. all of the above

___ 8. Hair colors that have no red or gold tones are classified as

    A. toners
    B. auburn
    C. highlighted
    D. drab

___ 9. Hair ends may turn darker when using an oxidizing tint if those ends are extremely

    A. straight
    B. over-porous
    C. resistant
    D. curly

___ 10. Before tinting, extremely porous hair ends should be treated with a

    A. cold wave
    B. color filler
    C. toner
    D. rinse

___ 11. As a safety measure when giving a permanent hair color, it is required by federal law that the cosmetologist give a predisposition test

    A. once very other year
    B. twice a year
    C. before each monthly application
    D. before each weekly application

___ 12. To prevent a line of demarcation during a tint retouch, it is important to avoid

    A. rotating a bottle
    B. overlapping the tint
    C. mixing tint
    D. rubbing the scalp

13. The oxidizing agent for an aniline derivative tint is

   A. hydrogen peroxide
   B. metallic salts
   C. sodium bromate
   D. sodium hydroxide

14. Since some toners are aniline derivative tints, they require a

   A. strand test
   B. patch test
   C. color test
   D. test curl

15. Terms such as cool, drab, and warm describe

   A. tones of a hair color
   B. shades of a hair color
   C. brightness of a hair color
   D. depth of a hair color

16. To achieve a permanent hair color, the color molecules must penetrate into the

   A. cuticle
   B. cortex
   C. medulla
   D. follicle

17. If the site of the patch test is positive, for example burning, swollen, and inflamed, this condition is known as

   A. dermatitis acne
   B. dermatitis freckles
   C. dermatitis venenata
   D. dermatitis pimple

18. Semipermanent rinses seldom, if ever, are mixed with

   A. hydrogen peroxide
   B. bleach
   C. aniline tints
   D. aniline toners

19. Temporary hair colors contain

   A. aniline tint
   B. bleach
   C. certified color
   D. peroxide

20. Temporary hair colors are removed by

   A. bleaching
   B. stripping
   C. shampooing
   D. rinsing

21. An example of a secondary color is

   A. blue
   B. red
   C. violet
   D. yellow

22. By law, a predisposition test must be given before each

   A. oxidation tint
   B. bleach
   C. temporary rinse
   D. conditioning treatment

23. What is the chemical that causes an aniline tint to oxidize, and penetrate into the hair shaft?

   A. color base
   B. soap cap
   C. peroxide
   D. water

24. If you are unsure what results to expect before applying a permanent hair color to your client, what should you do?

   A. give a pull test
   B. give a porosity test
   C. give a strand test
   D. give an elasticity test

Poss.	Wrong	%	Right
24	0	100%	24
24	1	96%	23
24	2	92%	22
24	3	88%	21
24	4	83%	20
24	5	79%	19
24	6	75%	18
24	7	71%	17
24	8	67%	16
24	9	63%	15

22 Questions

___ 1. The medical term for the positive reaction to a skin test is

A. nodosa
B. senilis
C. venenata
D. corona

___ 2. Over-porous hair ends can be prevented from absorbing too much tint by applying a

A. cold wave solution
B. temporary rinse
C. color filler
D. acid shampoo

___ 3. When explaining the advantages of the use of a temporary hair color, the hairdresser would inform the client that the color will

A. highlight the natural color
B. be removed with a shampoo
C. not change the condition of the hair
D. all of the above

___ 4. Since there are metallic salts in compound dyes, hair colored with them is unfit for

A. cold waving
B. shampooing
C. rinsing
D. cutting

___ 5. Rinses made to last from 4-6 weeks are known as

A. semipermanent hair colors
B. temporary hair colors
C. toners
D. fillers

___ 6. An advantage for the cosmetologist in giving a permanent hair color is that it

A. can be shampooed
B. guarantees the return of the client
C. requires a patch test
D. requires more time

___ 7. To lighten the hair, how far away from the scalp is a virgin color applied?

A. 1/4 to 1/8"
B. 1/2" to 1""
C. 1-1/2 to 2"
D. 2"

___ 8. When giving a tint retouch, the tint is applied first to the

A. hair ends
B. hair roots
C. new growth
D. hairline

___ 9. The tint service record should be completed

A. for each tint that is given
B. only for the first patch test
C. only when damage occurs
D. only if the hair was given a cold wave

___ 10. During tinting, the part of the hair that absorbs the tint the fastest is the

A. hair most difficult to tint
B. middle of the hair shafts
C. hair next to the scalp
D. hair ends

___ 11. The hydrogen peroxide used for tinting is made of water, and

A. 2% hydrogen peroxide
B. 4% hydrogen peroxide
C. 6% hydrogen peroxide
D. 8% hydrogen peroxide

___ 12. If a client has a yellowish hue in her hair, what tertiary color base in a weekly rinse would neutralize the yellow?

A. blue-violet
B. red-orange
C. yellow-green
D. red-violet

___ 13. Temporary color rinses contain

A. distilled color
B. certified color
C. aniline color
D. coal-tar color

14. Temporary hair colors remain in the hair for
    A. one shampooing
    B. four weeks
    C. six weeks
    D. eight weeks

15. Bleach or tint mixed with peroxide must be discarded because of
    A. relaxation
    B. oxidation
    C. presoftening
    D. hardening

16. Two secondary colors that neutralize each other are
    A. violet-blue
    B. blue-green
    C. yellow-violet
    D. none of the above

17. Certified colors used in temporary rinses are regulated by which of the following agencies?
    A. The American Medical Association
    B. The Department of Hair Coloring
    C. The Federal Food and Drug Administration
    D. The National Pharmaceutical Board

18. Egyptian henna is an example of a(n)
    A. progressive dye
    B. metallic tint
    C. aniline derivative tint
    D. semipermanent color

19. A compound dye is a combination of a vegetable hair tint with
    A. an aniline derivative tint
    B. metallic salts
    C. a color rinse
    D. a shampoo tint

20. When peroxide and tint are mixed, they should be mixed only in a
    A. metal dish
    B. metal pan
    C. glass or plastic container
    D. iron bowl

21. If tinted hair is reconditioned, the conditioning will be directed to
    A. the entire hair length
    B. all hair follicles
    C. the hair bulb
    D. the entire papilla

22. Before using a dye remover on hair thought to have a metallic tint on it, the cosmetologist should test for
    A. sodium salts
    B. chlorinated water
    C. metallic salts
    D. hard water

Poss.	Wrong	%	Right
22	0	100%	22
22	1	95%	21
22	2	91%	20
22	3	86%	19
22	4	82%	18
22	5	77%	17
22	6	73%	16
22	7	68%	15
22	8	64%	14
22	9	59%	13
22	10	55%	12

24 Questions

___ 1. How many stages does black hair go through to become pale blonde?

    A. four
    B. five
    C. six
    D. seven

___ 2. Powder bleaches should not be applied to the

    A. lashes
    B. scalp
    C. nape
    D. crown

___ 3. A toner with a yellow base would be described by the manufacturer as having

    A. lemon tones
    B. maize tones
    C. orange tones
    D. gold tones

___ 4. Which of the following is the best definition of a permanent color toner?

    A. an aniline derivative tint in pastel colors
    B. an aniline tint having a gold base
    C. para-phenylene-diamine dyes
    D. color that cannot be removed

___ 5. If you overlap bleach when doing a bleach retouch, it will result in

    A. more elasticity
    B. less elasticity
    C. breakage
    D. hair yellowing

___ 6. When a cap is used, and strands of hair all over the head are lightened, this is known as

    A. tinting
    B. frosting
    C. streaking
    D. painting

___ 7. The three basic bleach classifications are oil, cream, and

    A. moist
    B. powder
    C. liquid
    D. dry

___ 8. The lightest toner can only be applied to hair bleached to the

    A. brown stage
    B. red-gold stage
    C. pale yellow stage
    D. red stage

___ 9. A hair lightener should never be applied to a scalp that has

    A. scratches and abrasions
    B. a small lump
    C. a bump
    D. an old scar

___ 10. The process of lightening and toning the hair is also known as a double

    A. timer
    B. service
    C. process
    D. stripping

___ 11. Lightening the hair begins with the application of a

    A. stripping agent
    B. toning agent
    C. moisturizing agent
    D. bleaching agent

___ 12. Decolorization takes place in which layer of the hair?

    A. cuticle
    B. cortex
    C. medulla
    D. all of the above

13. Which lightener should you use for a lightener retouch and toner?

    A. cream lightener
    B. powder lightener
    C. oil lightener
    D. frosting bleach

14. The lightest stage that hair can be bleached is

    A. gold
    B. pale yellow
    C. pale red-gold
    D. pale orange

15. Lightening small strands of hair toward the front of the head is known as

    A. retouching
    B. tipping
    C. a soap cap
    D. a filler

16. Lightening larger strands of hair toward the front of the head is called

    A. tipping
    B. streaking
    C. frosting
    D. toning

17. Sulfonated oil bleaches are activated using

    A. ammonium thioglycolate
    B. sodium hydroxide
    C. sodium bromate
    D. hydrogen peroxide

18. The length of time the hair lightener remains on the hair varies with hair porosity, condition, and

    A. desired toner shade
    B. time scheduled
    C. amount of bleach used
    D. amount of peroxide used

19. Hydrogen peroxide (20 volume) added to the bleaching agent acts as a

    A. booster
    B. stripper
    C. catalyst
    D. protinator

20. Bleaching decolorizes pigments that are brown, red, and

    A. blue
    B. gray
    C. green
    D. yellow

21. Before giving a lightener retouch, what should you do?

    A. a predisposition test
    B. brush the hair vigorously
    C. examine scalp for cuts and abrasions
    D. give the client a strand test

22. During lightening, the condition of the hair becomes more

    A. elastic
    B. spongy
    C. stringy
    D. porous

23. When lightening and toning the hair, you should wear

    A. protective shoes
    B. a hair net
    C. an operator apron
    D. protective gloves

24. Where along the hair strand should you begin the application of a virgin bleach?

    A. 1/2″ away from the scalp
    B. 1″ from scalp
    C. from the ends to the center of the hair strand
    D. from the ends down to the scalp

Poss.	Wrong	%	Right
24	0	100%	24
24	1	96%	23
24	2	92%	22
24	3	88%	21
24	4	83%	20
24	5	79%	19
24	6	75%	18
24	7	71%	17
24	8	67%	16
24	9	63%	15

25 Questions

___ 1. When an aniline toner is used, what test must be given first?

A. shampoo
B. strand
C. patch
D. elasticity

___ 2. The chemical process of bleach on the hair is (known as)

A. stimulation
B. neutralization
C. evaporation
D. oxidation

___ 3. Full-strength bleach on the scalp MAY cause

A. stinging
B. irritation
C. blistering
D. all of the above

___ 4. Before applying a toner to gray or white hair, it is necessary to prelighten the hair in order to make the hair

A. resistant enough
B. porous enough
C. lower in pH
D. lower in alkaline

___ 5. A creme bleach continues to lighten because it remains

A. moist
B. thick
C. thin
D. dry

___ 6. When giving a lightener retouch, what would be the results if the mixture is overlapped?

A. nothing
B. a gold band
C. incomplete bleaching
D. breakage

___ 7. A drastic color change from dark to very light hair color requires

A. pretoning
B. prelightening
C. pretipping
D. prefrosting

___ 8. Applying bleach to selected strands of hair is known as

A. weaving
B. streaking
C. tipping
D. painting

___ 9. Containers used for mixing bleach should be made of

A. ceramic
B. wood
C. metal
D. glass

___ 10. When the proper stage of streaking is reached, which shampoo is BEST to remove bleach?

A. mild
B. medicated
C. non-stripping (acid)
D. alkaline

___ 11. The process of lightening the hair around the hairline is called

A. retouching
B. framing
C. overlapping
D. shelling

___ 12. To keep all sections separated and to assure that all bleached areas process evenly, apply

A. a neutralizing cape
B. a plastic cap
C. duck bill clips
D. aluminum foil

13. During the frosting service, avoid pulling strands of hair through the cap from the

   A. crown
   B. hairline
   C. ears
   D. nape

14. When lightening and toning the hair, you should wear

   A. protective shoes
   B. a hair net
   C. an operator apron
   D. protective gloves

15. When giving a virgin bleach to medium brown hair, the cosmetologist should begin applying the lightener

   A. 1/2˝ from scalp up to ends
   B. from scalp to ends
   C. from ends to scalp
   D. from center of hair shaft to ends

16. Applying tint or lightener to small, unevenly colored strands of hair missed during the first application of a tint or bleach is called spot bleaching, or spot

   A. smoothing
   B. tinting
   C. blending
   D. lathering

17. Pre-bleaching (lightening) is required before the application of a

   A. semipermanent rinse
   B. one-process tint
   C. toner
   D. temporary rinse

18. The removal of a penetrating tint from the hair is called

   A. relaxing
   B. a soap cap
   C. stripping
   D. tinting

19. To equalize the porosity of the hair, use a

   A. steamer
   B. stripper
   C. filler
   D. equalizer

20. Hair coloring formulas and their results are recorded on a

   A. comparison chart
   B. salon appointment book
   C. client record card
   D. color mixing chart

21. A lightening and toning service is also called a

   A. double play
   B. two-bottle color
   C. double lightener
   D. double-application service

22. Lightening the hair means the same as

   A. rinsing it
   B. toning it
   C. decolorizing it
   D. dying it

23. Bleach SHOULD BE applied to hair that is

   A. wet
   B. dry
   C. shampooed
   D. brushed

24. If you overlap bleach when doing a bleach retouch, it will result in

   A. more elasticity
   B. less elasticity
   C. breakage
   D. hair yellowing

25. What is the chemical agent that acts as a CATALYST when added to the bleach and activator that causes the mixture to lighten the hair?

   A. energizer
   B. protinator
   C. packet
   D. peroxide

Poss.	Wrong	%	Right
25	0	100%	25
25	1	96%	24
25	2	92%	23
25	3	88%	22
25	4	84%	21

25	5	80%	20
25	6	76%	19
25	7	72%	18
25	8	68%	17
25	9	64%	16
25	10	60%	15

19 CREATIVE LIGHTENING AND TONING PRE-TEST 2

16 Questions

___ 1. Dry, brittle, fragile hair may result from excessive use of hydrogen peroxide and

A. lightener
B. rinse
C. semipermanent rinse
D. henna rinse

___ 2. The process of applying bleach through selected strands of hair is known as

A. bleaching
B. framing
C. streaking
D. stranding

___ 3. Applying a normalizing lotion to bleached hair will lower the hair's

A. alkalinity
B. affinity
C. chemistry
D. acidity

___ 4. Removing artificial color from the hair requires the use of a

A. stripper
B. steamer
C. dye solvent
D. bleach

___ 5. A retouch hair lightener is applied to the

A. new growth of hair
B. entire hair shaft
C. the ends only
D. cold shaft only

___ 6. The use of foil on bleach strands accelerates

A. breaking
B. swelling
C. stretching
D. decolorizing

___ 7. When hair is pulled through a rubber or plastic cap, which bleach is recommended?

A. paste
B. oil
C. creme
D. powder

___ 8. Before giving a lightener retouch, what should you do?

A. a predisposition test
B. brush the hair vigorously
C. examine the scalp for cuts and abrasions
D. give the client a strand test

___ 9. The client has just received a frosting and complains that there are too many frosted strands of hair. How could the cosmetologist reduce the amount of frosted hair?

A. apply tint all over the head
B. give client a tintback
C. apply a filler
D. give client a reverse frosting

___ 10. Bleach can be kept moist during frostings by using

A. an over-cap
B. warm water
C. a hot towel
D. a dry towel

___ 11. If bleach drips onto the skin, the bleach should be removed using

A. cold-cool water
B. tepid-hot water
C. hot water only
D. very hot water

12. When hydrogen peroxide is mixed with sulfonated oil (sodium persulfates) the result is an oil

    A. lightener
    B. rinse
    C. relaxer
    D. neutralizer

13. When changing the color of the hair to a much lighter color, it is required that the hair be

    A. preneutralized
    B. prelightened
    C. prehardened
    D. preshaded

14. Which bleach is recommended for frosting and streaking?

    A. creme
    B. paste
    C. oil
    D. powder

15. The alkalinity of bleach is neutralized by applying a

    A. rinse
    B. normalizer
    C. conditioner
    D. neutralizer

16. An effect achieved by placing a plastic or rubber cap on the client's hair and pulling strands through the cap is known as

    A. painting
    B. streaking
    C. frosting
    D. tipping

Poss.	Wrong	%	Right
16	0	100%	16
16	1	94%	15
16	2	88%	14
16	3	81%	13
16	4	75%	12
16	5	69%	11

19 CREATIVE LIGHTENING AND TONING PRE-TEST 3

24 Questions

1. When an aniline toner is used, what test must be given first?

    A. shampoo
    B. strand
    C. patch
    D. elasticity

2. The chemical process of bleach on the hair is (known as)

    A. stimulation
    B. neutralization
    C. evaporation
    D. oxidation

3. Full strength bleach on the scalp MAY cause

    A. stinging
    B. irritation
    C. blistering
    D. all of the above

4. Before applying a toner to gray or white hair, it is necessary to pre-lighten the hair in order to make the hair

    A. resistant enough
    B. porous enough
    C. lower in pH
    D. lower in alkaline

5. A cream bleach continues to lighten because it remains

    A. moist
    B. thick
    C. thin
    D. dry

6. When giving a lightener retouch, what would be the results if the mixture is overlapped?

    A. nothing
    B. a gold band
    C. incomplete bleaching
    D. breakage

___ 7. A drastic color change from dark to very light hair color requires

A. pre-toning
B. pre-lightening
C. pre-tipping
D. pre-frosting

___ 8. Applying bleach to selected strands of hair is known as

A. weaving
B. streaking
C. tipping
D. painting

___ 9. Containers used for mixing bleach should be made of

A. ceramic
B. wood
C. metal
D. glass

___ 10. When the proper stage of streaking is reached, which shampoo is BEST to remove bleach?

A. mild
B. medicated
C. non-stripping (acid)
D. alkaline

___ 11. The process of lightening the hair around the hairline is called

A. retouching
B. framing
C. overlapping
D. shelling

___ 12. To keep all sections separated and to assure that all bleached areas process evenly, apply

A. a neutralizing cape
B. a plastic cap
C. duck bill clips
D. aluminum foil

___ 13. During the frosting service, avoid pulling strands of hair through the cap from the

A. crown
B. hairline
C. ears
D. nape

___ 14. When lightening and toning the hair, you should wear

A. protective shoes
B. a hair net
C. an operator apron
D. protective gloves

___ 15. When giving a virgin bleach to medium brown hair, the cosmetologist should begin applying the lightener

A. 1/2″ from scalp up to ends
B. from scalp to ends
C. from ends to scalp
D. from center of hair shaft to ends

___ 16. Applying tint or lightener to small, unevenly colored strands of hair missed during the first application of a tint or bleach is called spot bleaching, or spot

A. smoothing
B. tinting
C. blending
D. lathering

___ 17. Pre-bleaching (lightening) is required before the application of a

A. semipermanent rinse
B. one process tint
C. toner
D. temporary rinse

___ 18. The removal of a penetrating tint from the hair is called

A. relaxing
B. a soap cap
C. stripping
D. tinting

___ 19. To equalize the porosity of the hair, use a

A. steamer
B. stripper
C. filler
D. equalizer

___ 20. Hair coloring formulas and their results are recorded on a

A. comparison chart
B. salon appointment book
C. client record card
D. color-mixing chart

_____ 21. A lightening and toning service is also called

    A. double play
    B. two-bottle color
    C. double lightener
    D. double-application service

_____ 22. Lightening the hair means the same as

    A. rinsing it
    B. toning it
    C. decolorizing it
    D. dying it

_____ 23. Bleach SHOULD BE applied to hair that is

    A. wet
    B. dry
    C. shampooed
    D. dark

_____ 24. If you overlap bleach when doing a bleach retouch, it will result in

    A. more elasticity
    B. less elasticity
    C. breakage
    D. hair yellowing

Poss.	Wrong	%	Right
24	0	100%	24
24	1	96%	23
24	2	92%	22
24	3	88%	21
24	4	83%	20
24	5	79%	19
24	6	75%	18
24	7	71%	17
24	8	67%	16
24	9	63%	15

20 PERMANENT WAVE PRE-TEST 1

23 Questions

_____ 1. Which of the following terms is not used in the test to describe a chemical (cold) wave?

    A. body wave
    B. support wave
    C. structure wave
    D. texture wave

_____ 2. If the elastic strap of the cold wave rod is twisted, or stretched too tightly across the base of the hair, it may cause

    A. hair breakage
    B. curl relaxation
    C. frizzy curls
    D. straight curls

_____ 3. If too much tension is used during cold wave wrapping, this may cause the processing time to be

    A. stopped
    B. increased
    C. retarded
    D. accelerated

_____ 4. The most successful cold wave can only be given to hair that has been properly

    A. lubricated
    B. brightened
    C. lightened
    D. shaped

_____ 5. The pH range for acid waves is

    A. 2.5–4.5
    B. 5.8–6.8
    C. 7.9–8.8
    D. 9.0–9.7

_____ 6. One disadvantage of an acid wave is that it is

    A. difficult to time
    B. slow processing
    C. harder on the skin
    D. drying to the hair

_____ 7. A self-timing permanent wave is one in which the manufacturer recommends that you

    A. test curl every 3 minutes
    B. towel blot each rod
    C. process for a set period of time
    D. place client under a dryer

___ 8. The strength of the cold waving solution to be used is determined by the hair texture and

A. color
B. condition
C. density
D. viscosity

___ 9. Cold waving solution causes the hair shaft to

A. soften and contract
B. soften and swell
C. harden and contract
D. harden and swell

___ 10. Blocking and winding the hair at the beginning of a cold wave may begin in the

A. nape area
B. ear area
C. eye area
D. nose area

___ 11. When inspecting a wrapped cold wave, the smallest rods would usually be in the

A. crown section
B. nape section
C. eye section
D. ear section

___ 12. If the hair was vigorously brushed before a cold wave, the result could be

A. scalp irritations
B. alopecia areata
C. nail scratches
D. scalp tightening

___ 13. Before a cold wave, gentle scalp manipulations follow the application of a

A. chemical relaxer
B. mild shampoo
C. strong shampoo
D. neutralizing shampoo

___ 14. Machine, preheat, and machineless permanent waves curled the hair using two physical principles. What were they?

A. winding and stretching
B. stretching and cooling
C. winding and heating
D. stretching and softening

___ 15. To achieve a good curl when permanent waving, how much tension should be applied to the hair as it is wound on the rods?

A. very firm tension
B. very little tension
C. moderate-firm even tension
D. no tension

___ 16. When sodium bromate fumes and ammonia fumes mix together in an open towel hamper, what could result?

A. a fire
B. a strong acid smell
C. discoloration of towels
D. stain in the hamper

___ 17. Better saturation of the cold waving solution into the hair is achieved when it is

A. wrapped correctly
B. analyzed accurately
C. curled properly
D. pressed thoroughly

___ 18. The greatest risk of hair damage during cold waving is presented by hair that is

A. conditioned
B. retouched
C. over lightened
D. tinted

___ 19. Before a cold wave is wrapped the hair is usually dried using a

A. blow comb
B. hand dryer
C. towel
D. rat-tail comb

___ 20. When giving a cold wave always read and follow the

A. manual's instructions
B. textbook's instructions
C. workbook's instructions
D. manufacturer's instructions

21. When permanent waving very sparse (thin) hair, what size rods and subsections will give the most curl?

   A. small rods, large subsections
   B. small rods, small subsections
   C. large rods, large subsections
   D. none of the above

22. When permanent waving the hair, how many turns must the hair be wound around the rod in order to achieve a curl pattern?

   A. once
   B. twice
   C. four turns
   D. five turns

23. After processing a perm, what can you do to prevent the rods from being forced from the hair during rinsing?

   A. tighten them up
   B. use low water pressure
   C. put on a hair net
   D. rinse with cool water

Poss.	Wrong	%	Right
23	0	100%	23
23	1	96%	22
23	2	91%	21
23	3	87%	20
23	4	83%	19
23	5	78%	18
23	6	74%	17
23	7	70%	16
23	8	65%	15
23	9	61%	14

20 PERMANENT WAVE PRE-TEST 2

24 Questions

1. Before cold waving the entire head, the degree to which the hair will curl can be determined by using

   A. concave curls
   B. convex curls
   C. test curls
   D. pin curls

2. The PH value of the cold wave solution would be

   A. oxygen
   B. alkaline
   C. neutral
   D. acid

3. Cotton is placed around the hairline before applying the cold waving solution; it should be

   A. removed after it is applied
   B. allowed to remain until the neutralizer is applied
   C. removed following the neutralizer
   D. removed when the rods are taken out

4. The elastic strap of the cold wave rod is normally fastened

   A. along the very bottom of the section
   B. next to the top parting of the section
   C. along the vertical parting of the curl
   D. across the top of the curl

5. If the cosmetologist is NOT careful when drying the hair after a curly permanent wave the hair can be burned with the

   A. setting lotion
   B. infra-red lamp
   C. tint mixture
   D. hydrogen

6. In which of the following conditions should the cosmetologist REFUSE to give the client a cold wave

   A. a scar on the scalp
   B. a cranial surgical wound
   C. a scalp freckle
   D. an ulna surgical wound

___ 7. During a wrapping procedure using waving solution, breakages can occur if too much tension is placed on the

    A. hair
    B. comb
    C. end wrap
    D. rod

___ 8. To remove dripping cold waving solution, use a piece of cotton or the corner of a towel saturated with

    A. cold water
    B. warm water
    C. tepid water
    D. hot water

___ 9. If a couple of small areas of the hair do not have enough curl one week after the wave process, the cosmetologist should give the client

    A. a refund check
    B. another cosmetologist
    C. some pickup curls
    D. another chemical wave

___ 10. When wrapping a ponytail cold wave, it is better to begin wrapping in the

    A. bottom section
    B. top section
    C. middle section
    D. front section

___ 11. The action of cold waving solution on the hair is one of

    A. softening
    B. hardening
    C. shrinking
    D. contracting

___ 12. When processing the cold wave, the hair tends to swell, or

    A. expand
    B. contract
    C. harden
    D. shrink

___ 13. Cold waving resistant hair would usually require a

    A. longer processing time
    B. shorter processing time
    C. conditioner
    D. toner

___ 14. If a plastic cap is used to cover the permanent waving rods during processing, what should you be careful NOT to do?

    A. allow too much heat to collect
    B. tighten the cap too much
    C. allow too much air to escape
    D. clip the cap in the front section

___ 15. When relaxing a permanent wave that is too curly, where should you begin your application?

    A. the nape section
    B. the top section
    C. the side section
    D. the crown section

___ 16. When sodium bromate fumes and ammonia fumes mix together in a open towel hamper, what could result?

    A. fire
    B. strong acid smell
    C. discoloration of towels
    D. stain in the hamper

___ 17. When rinsing a permanent wave, what can you do to prevent water from running down the client's neck and back?

    A. ask the client to raise her head
    B. use low water pressure
    C. use a neutralizing bib
    D. place foil around the neck

___ 18. If your permanent wave is not processing in a normal amount of time, what should you do?

    A. resaturate the hair
    B. mist with a water bottle
    C. cover hair with aluminum foil
    D. all of the above

___ 19. During the processing of a permanent wave, what would cause the waving lotion to evaporate?

A. rod size
B. body heat
C. temperature of work area
D. B and C only

___ 20. When your permanent wave test curl shows little or no curl development, what should you do?

A. place client under a hot dryer
B. cover rods with cellophane
C. resaturate with the same or stronger waving lotion
D. rinse and dry with a dryer before neutralizing

___ 21. Should permanent wave lotion accidently drip into the client's eye, what should you do?

A. stop action by applying neutralizer to eye
B. flush eye with lots of water and take client to doctor
C. blot chemical and apply hot water to eye
D. mist eye with bottle of warm water

___ 22. One of the most important things to remember when giving clients a permanent wave is

A. always give them a piece of cotton
B. never leave them unattended
C. shampoo three times before wrapping hair
D. brush hair thoroughly before shampooing

___ 23. When wrapping an acid permanent wave on hair that is normal in texture and condition, how much tension should be used during the wrapping procedure?

A. moderate, even tension
B. limp, no tension
C. firm, maximum tension
D. as tight as you can

___ 24. If you need to use a plastic overcap during the processing of a permanent wave, what will occur if the elastic band is too tight around the hairline by the rods?

A. the elastic band will push the rods out
B. the tension will cause hair breakage
C. it should be removed from all caps
D. it is made so that it is never too tight

Poss.	Wrong	%	Right
24	0	100%	24
24	1	96%	23
24	2	92%	22
24	3	88%	21
24	4	83%	20
24	5	79%	19
24	6	75%	18
24	7	71%	17
24	8	67%	16
24	9	63%	15

20 PERMANENT WAVE PRE-TEST 3

23 Questions

___ 1. The solution that processes a cold wave contains

A. quats
B. ammonium carbonate
C. ammonium thioglycolate
D. hydrogen peroxide

___ 2. The waveability of hair during a cold wave depends upon its

A. condition
B. color
C. growing cycle
D. density

3. Chemical (cold) waving is more popular today because the cosmetologist receives better training, and the waves are

   A. frizzier
   B. straighter
   C. improved
   D. natural

4. When relaxing naturally curly hair or an over-curly permanent wave, what should you do if the hair is processing slowly and you want to speed up the processing?

   A. reapply the relaxing mixture
   B. place cap over hair and seat client under a warm hair dryer
   C. rinse relaxer, dry hair with a dryer, and reapply mixture
   D. use ultra-violet lamp to speed up processing

5. In order for an acid permanent wave to curl the hair, what must be applied?

   A. gel
   B. heat
   C. over-cap
   D. water

6. When applying the waving solution as part of the permanent waving process, the cosmetologist sees that there is a purple discoloration of the solution on the client's towel. What should the cosmetologist do?

   A. stop and rinse the hair with water
   B. apply neutralizer immediately
   C. continue to give the permanent
   D. apply a different waving solution

7. A permanent wave using heat created by mixing a chemical with the waving lotion, is called what type of permanent wave?`

   A. strongly alkaline wave
   B. neutral wave
   C. cold wave
   D. exothermic

8. After processing, the cold waving lotion is usually removed from the hair by

   A. shampooing
   B. neutralizing
   C. rinsing
   D. toning

9. During neutralizing, the weight of the client's head against the neck of the shampoo bowl could cause

   A. discoloration of the bowl
   B. discoloration of the hair
   C. hair breakage
   D. rod breakage

10. When giving a ponytail chemical wave, the cosmetologist has to be careful in using the rubber binders because too much tension will cause

    A. the binder to break
    B. rod breakage
    C. hair breakage
    D. wave breakage

11. Before a cold wave, a test curl may be given in order to determine the approximate

    A. section size
    B. processing time
    C. degree of color
    D. rod tension

12. Cold waving end wraps (papers) must be

    A. water repellent
    B. waxed
    C. porous
    D. waterproof

13. When giving a cold wave, saturated cotton is removed from the hairline to prevent

    A. discoloration
    B. irritation
    C. corrugations
    D. inundations

14. When the cold wave rod subsections are too large, they will

    A. prevent thorough penetration of the solution
    B. improve the porosity of the hair
    C. cause over-processing
    D. cause under-processing

15. When giving a permanent wave, the cosmetologist notices the waving solution turns purple after it is applied to the hair. What does this indicate?

    A. minerals are present in the hair
    B. the client has been tinting her hair at home
    C. a recent illness in the client's home
    D. no one knows why this happens

16. When giving a cold wave, the cosmetologist is about to neutralize the perm, but discovers there is no neutralizer anywhere in the salon. What should the cosmetologist do to keep the most curl in the hair?

    A. rinse the hair and remove the rods
    B. blot the hair and apply 20 volume hydrogen peroxide
    C. blot rods with damp towel and air dry
    D. rinse rods and place under dryer

17. In which of the following conditions should the cosmetologist REFUSE to give the client a cold wave?

    A. a scar on the scalp
    B. a cranial surgical wound
    C. a scalp freckle
    D. an ulna surgical wound

18. The best way to hold a strand of hair for winding a cold wave is

    A. toward the face
    B. against the crown
    C. against the neck
    D. up and down from the scalp

19. A milder strength cold waving solution should be used on hair that is

    A. coarse
    B. normal
    C. tinted
    D. wiry

20. Fishhook ends are prevented by the correct use of

    A. conditioners
    B. end papers
    C. test papers
    D. texturizers

21. After processing a perm, what can you do to prevent the rods from being forced from the hair during rinsing?

    A. tighten them up
    B. use low water pressure
    C. put hair net over rods
    D. rinse with cool water

22. During cold waving, the hair is parted off into small subdivisions before wrapping. The shape of these subdivisions is

    A. rectangular
    B. square
    C. triangular
    D. circular

23. If the cosmetologist is NOT careful when drying the hair after a curly permanent wave, the hair can be burned with the

    A. setting lotion
    B. infra-red lamp
    C. tint mixture
    D. hydrogen

Poss.	Wrong	%	Right
23	0	100%	23
23	1	96%	22
23	2	91%	21
23	3	87%	20
23	4	83%	19
23	5	78%	18
23	6	74%	17
23	7	70%	16
23	8	65%	15
23	9	61%	14

26 Questions

___ 1. The most popular basic chemical used for relaxing super-curly hair is sodium

A. bromate
B. hydroxide
C. bicarbonate
D. sulfur

___ 2. Chemical relaxers are also called

A. curl straighteners
B. thermal pressures
C. perms
D. presses

___ 3. The base in a no-base chemical relaxer is used to

A. straighten the hair
B. protect the scalp
C. protect the hair
D. neutralize the relaxer

___ 4. The straightening action is stopped during a chemical relaxer by using a

A. stabilizing creme
B. neutralizing creme
C. neutralizing shampoo
D. stabilizing rinse

___ 5. The process of chemically straightening super-curly hair is called chemical hair

A. normalizing
B. relaxing
C. crimping
D. stabilizing

___ 6. The action of a chemical hair straightener causes the hair to

A. shrink and harden
B. shift and mold
C. shape and curl
D. soften and swell

___ 7. Before applying a chemical relaxer, analyze the hair for porosity, texture, and elasticity; then examine the

A. fingernails
B. scalp
C. hairline
D. relaxing kit

___ 8. For chemically straightening the hair, use a chemical relaxer, and a(n)

A. conditioner
B. pre-creme
C. stabilizer
D. setting lotion

___ 9. Before using a chemical hair straightener, the cosmetologist would not

A. brush the hair
B. analyze the hair
C. examine the scalp
D. read label directions

___ 10. A thio relaxer affects the hair shaft by causing it to

A. harden and swell
B. harden and shrink
C. soften and shrink
D. soften and swell

___ 11. The best shampoo to use after a chemical relaxer is a shampoo that has a(n)

A. oil base
B. acid pH
C. alkaline pH
D. neutral base

___ 12. Before applying a chemical relaxer, the hair and scalp must be

A. shampooed
B. brushed
C. examined
D. tinted

13. To stop the action of the sodium hydroxide and remove it from the hair, the cosmetologist

    A. rinses and shampoos the hair
    B. conditions, then rinses the hair
    C. combs, then shampoos the hair
    D. air neutralizes the hair

14. If unsure which strength chemical relaxer should be used, the cosmetologist should take a(n)

    A. patch test
    B. strand test
    C. skin test
    D. allergy test

15. If super-curly hair has been thermal pressed, or is otherwise very damaged, the cosmetologist should

    A. use a mild-strength relaxer
    B. advise a tint to even the hair porosity
    C. refuse the chemical relaxer
    D. refer the person to another salon

16. As in cold waving, chemical relaxers work faster on hair that is

    A. wiry
    B. coarse
    C. porous
    D. non-porous

17. Before a chemical relaxer, the skin and scalp can be protected from chemical burns by applying a

    A. neutralizer
    B. stabilizer
    C. base
    D. jelly

18. Chemical relaxers are packaged in a

    A. carton
    B. unit
    C. set
    D. kit

19. If the client has a little spot on the scalp that is burning during the processing of a chemical hair relaxer on super-curly hair, what should you do?

    A. rinse all relaxer from hair immediately
    B. apply an astringent to the spot
    C. apply petrolatum to the spot
    D. spray spot with cool water

20. If you live in a very warm climate and your client arrives perspiring before having a chemical hair relaxer, what should you do?

    A. thoroughly shampoo the hair
    B. place client under cool dryer
    C. wait while client cools off
    D. blot moisture from scalp before starting

21. A term often used in connection with sodium hydroxide is

    A. neutral
    B. acid
    C. alkaline
    D. caustic

22. The main chemical used to stop the relaxer is

    A. ammonium thioglycolate
    B. hydrogen peroxide
    C. sodium bromate
    D. sodium hydroxide

23. The difference between a base and no-base relaxer is that the no-base

    A. does not require application of the base
    B. always requires the use of protective gloves
    C. is safer to use, but requires more time
    D. is more dangerous to use, but requires more time

24. Should a chemical relaxer accidently drip into the client's eye, what should you do?

    A. stop action by applying neutralizer to eye
    B. flush eye with lots of water and take client to doctor
    C. blot chemical and apply hot water to eye
    D. mist eye with bottle of warm water

___ 25. Before giving a retouch chemical relaxer, what should be applied to the previously relaxed hair first?

A. water
B. protective conditioner
C. presoftening rinse
D. prerelax shampoo

___ 26. Where along the hair strand should the application of a chemical relaxer on virgin hair begin and end?

A. 1/2″ from scalp up to 1/2″ in from end of strand
B. scalp up to the middle of hair strand
C. middle of hair strand to end of hair strand
D. scalp to very end of hair strand

Poss.	Wrong	%	Right
26	0	100%	26
26	1	96%	25
26	2	92%	24
26	3	88%	23
26	4	85%	22
26	5	81%	21
26	6	77%	20
26	7	73%	19
26	8	69%	18
26	9	65%	17
26	10	62%	16
26	11	58%	15

---

21 CHEMICAL HAIR RELAXING PRE-TEST 2

26 Questions

___ 1. Since all relaxers are basically the same, reading label directions is necessary

A. sometimes
B. seldom
C. never
D. always

___ 2. If you use all of a particular relaxer cream, but are in need of more to complete the service, it is best to

A. add water to what is on the hair
B. add water to what is left in the jar, then apply to the hair
C. add a relaxer made by another company
D. neutralize the hair and continue when there is enough material to finish

___ 3. The application of a base or no-base relaxer would begin in the

A. nape section
B. left side section
C. right side section
D. crown section

___ 4. After a sodium hydroxide relaxer has processed, but before it is shampooed, the hair should be thoroughly

A. combed
B. conditioned
C. rinsed
D. brushed

___ 5. After chemically relaxing the hair for a client with super-curly hair, what service should NOT be given to the client?

A. roller set
B. regular electric curling iron set
C. pressing comb/thermal iron set
D. pick out style after hair has been dried

___ 6. Hair should be conditioned after a sodium hydroxide relaxer to prevent

A. breakage during combing and setting
B. dry, scaly scalp
C. red, irritated scalp
D. breakage during thermal pressing

___ 7. The neutralizing shampoo used in the chemical relaxing service is also called a

A. stabilizer
B. cleaner
C. conditioner
D. filler

8. After a chemical relaxer, a conditioner should be applied

    A. after the hair is set
    B. just before the comb-out
    C. before the hair is styled with rollers
    D. after the comb-out

9. The stabilizer used in chemical hair relaxing is also called a(n)

    A. normalizer
    B. fixative
    C. acid
    D. controller

10. The process of permanently changing the structural bonds of super-curly hair into a straight position is called

    A. bond straightening
    B. decurling
    C. chemical relaxing
    D. uncurling

11. Hair is chemically straightened with thio, or

    A. sodium hydroxide
    B. hydrogen peroxide
    C. borax
    D. formalin

12. Cosmetologists avoid giving a chemical relaxer when the scalp examination reveals the presence of

    A. firm, tight scalp
    B. abrasions and scratches
    C. oily scalp and hair
    D. loose, pliable scalp

13. When giving a chemical relaxer, the cosmetologist must wear

    A. a coverall apron
    B. safety glasses
    C. protective gloves
    D. thick-soled shoes

14. Just before applying the relaxer, the hair is subdivided into

    A. two sections
    B. four sections
    C. six sections
    D. eight sections

15. When subsectioning the hair around the face for application of the relaxer, it is best to part the hair

    A. horizontally
    B. vertically
    C. up and down
    D. diagonally

16. If too much pressure is applied during the relaxing service, the hair will

    A. break
    B. dissolve
    C. stretch
    D. revert to curl

17. During neutralizing, the hair should be shampooed at least how many times?

    A. 1 to 2
    B. 2 to 3
    C. 3 to 4
    D. as many as needed

18. The suggested implement to use for cutting hair that has been chemically relaxed is the

    A. scissors
    B. razor
    C. thinning shears
    D. electric clipper

19. Chemical relaxers should be used carefully because the hair may

    A. dissolve
    B. stretch
    C. become porous
    D. become oily

20. The chemical relaxer begins to work when what is applied?

    A. hot water and shampoo
    B. cold water and stabilizer
    C. heat and friction
    D. medium-heat hair dryer

21. When relaxing virgin hair, the relaxer is always combed through the

    A. scalp hair right away
    B. ends of each strand right away
    C. entire length of the strand
    D. none of the above

___ 22. It is harmful to the hair to leave a chemical relaxer on it longer than

    A. 10 minutes
    B. 15 minutes
    C. 20 minutes
    D. 25 minutes

___ 23. When giving a chemical relaxer, which areas of the head are the most fragile and most likely to be damaged?

    A. crown and top sections
    B. front hairline and nape sections
    C. crown and front hairline sections
    D. crown and nape sections

___ 24. After instruction and practice, what is the ideal amount of time for applying and processing a chemical relaxer?

    A. 4 minutes
    B. 6 minutes
    C. 15 minutes
    D. 20 minutes

___ 25. When applying a chemical relaxer, it is important that you AVOID

    A. misting the hair with water
    B. using small sections
    C. tugging on the hair
    D. timing your application

___ 26. When rinsing the chemical relaxer from the hair, to avoid tangling, it is important to use

    A. low to medium water pressure
    B. high water pressure
    C. hot water at all times
    D. an alkaline shampoo

Poss.	Wrong	%	Right
26	0	100%	26
26	1	96%	25
26	2	92%	24
26	3	88%	23
26	4	85%	22
26	5	81%	21
26	6	77%	20
26	7	73%	19
26	8	69%	18
26	9	65%	17
26	10	62%	16
26	11	58%	15

22 THERMAL PRESSING PRE-TEST 1

20 Questions

___ 1. Thermal pressing usually begins in the

    A. nape section
    B. crown section
    C. side section
    D. top section

___ 2. The metal part of a pressing comb is made of

    A. aluminum and iron
    B. copper and brass
    C. brass and pewter
    D. aluminum and stainless steel

___ 3. During pressing, the hair is protected by

    A. foil
    B. a cap
    C. oil
    D. gel

___ 4. Round curling involves winding the hair strand from the

    A. ends to the scalp
    B. mid-strand to the ends
    C. ends to the mid-strand
    D. scalp to the ends

___ 5. Poker curls are made in a spiral fashion from the

    A. ends to the scalp
    B. mid-strand to the ends
    C. ends to the mid-strand
    D. scalp to the ends

___ 6. During a salon service, when should the hair be pressed?

    A. after shampooing
    B. after chemical relaxing
    C. before the perm
    D. before the hair cut

___ 7. A pressing comb is heated using a(n)

    A. electric heater
    B. oil heater
    C. solar heater
    D. core heater

___ 8. If you are pressing gray or blonde hair, you should use light pressure, and

    A. more heat
    B. maximum heat
    C. less heat
    D. very intense heat

___ 9. Croquignole curling involves winding the hair strand from the

    A. ends to the scalp
    B. mid-strand to ends
    C. ends to mid-strand
    D. scalp to ends

___ 10. Hair is pressed only when it is

    A. wet
    B. towel-dried
    C. dryer-dried
    D. damp

___ 11. When pressing the hair, the hot comb is usually brought through the

    A. top of the strand only
    B. bottom of the strand only
    C. top and bottom of each strand
    D. center of each strand

___ 12. Hair pressing is usually done using

    A. 1/4" partings
    B. 1/2" partings
    C. 1" partings
    D. 1-1/2" partings

___ 13. What does the thermal pressing service do to the hair?

    A. colors the hair
    B. straightens the hair temporarily
    C. curls the hair permanently
    D. crimps the hair permanently

___ 14. Once heated for use, the temperature of thermal irons is tested on

    A. the touch of the hand
    B. a piece of white tissue
    C. a damp sponge
    D. the client's hair

___ 15. When thermal pressing the hair, which area of the head is the hair usually most fragile and subject to breakage?

    A. hairline
    B. crown
    C. top-crown sections
    D. crown into the side sections

___ 16. As the iron is rolled toward the scalp, what does the cosmetologist use to protect the client's scalp?

    A. cotton
    B. towel
    C. comb
    D. an end paper

___ 17. If the hair is smoking too much during a thermal press, what should you do?

    A. use more pressing oil
    B. use less pressing oil
    C. use more heat
    D. use more conditioner

___ 18. When thermal pressing fine hair, you would

    A. use less pressure and heat
    B. use more pressure and heat
    C. use less pressure, but more heat
    D. use more pressure, but less heat

___ 19. It is usually more difficult to press which of the following hair textures?

    A. fine hair
    B. medium hair
    C. gray hair
    D. coarse, wiry hair

___ 20. You should use less pressure and heat in which of the following situations?

A. lightened hair
B. tinted hair
C. coarse hair
D. A and B only

Poss.	Wrong	%	Right
20	0	100%	20
20	1	95%	19
20	2	90%	18
20	3	85%	17
20	4	80%	16
20	5	75%	15
20	6	70%	14

22 THERMAL PRESSING PRE-TEST 2

23 Questions

___ 1. After the hair is pressed, the thermal iron forms the curl by rotating the iron using a(n)

A. clicking action
B. sliding action
C. oval action
D. back and forth action

___ 2. After a thermal wave, the hair is brushed and combed into a hairstyle

A. after the lanolin has been applied
B. while the hair is still hot
C. when the hair has been cooled
D. while the hair is lukewarm

___ 3. When thermal waving the hair, fine, short hairs around the hairline are best curled with

A. some pin curls
B. a smaller iron
C. a crimper
D. some perm rods

___ 4. The clicking referred to when thermal waving means how the iron is

A. heated
B. cleaned
C. cooled
D. opened and closed

___ 5. Once the hair strand has been scorched (burned) during a thermal pressing service, how can it be repaired?

A. reconditioning
B. use of a filler
C. cutting the hair
D. applying more oil

___ 6. Before thermal waving super-curly hair, the cosmetologist should

A. color it
B. press it
C. shape it
D. comb it

___ 7. What is the name for the service in which the hair is pressed twice on the top of the strand, and once on the underside?

A. one press
B. light press
C. comb press
D. soft press

___ 8. When pressing the hair, hair texture has to be considered, as well as the

A. temperature of the comb
B. chemicals to be used
C. setting pattern
D. cutting method

___ 9. Before pressing the hair, it should be

A. combed and brushed
B. shampooed and dried
C. shampooed and marcelled
D. dried and curled

___ 10. If the hair is pressed twice on each side of the strand before it is curled, this press is called a

A. soft press
B. hard press
C. firm press
D. double press

11. Temporarily straightening the hair with the hot comb is called hair

A. crimping
B. straightening
C. pressing
D. molding

12. To adequately straighten the hair, the pressing comb should be

A. perfectly even
B. hot enough
C. curved enough
D. heavy enough

13. Hair that has been chemically relaxed cannot be silked, or

A. set
B. curled
C. brushed
D. pressed

14. The temperature of the pressing comb is determined by its reaction to the

A. touch
B. tissue
C. client
D. litmus paper

15. What would be the results of thermal pressing hair that was NOT thoroughly dried?

A. it would be scorched
B. it would be shiny
C. it would be slightly curly
D. it would be very curly

16. Before thermal pressing the hair, what should be done first?

A. shampoo and condition it
B. shampoo and dry it thoroughly
C. shampoo, condition, then dry it thoroughly
D. nothing, just press it

17. Should you accidently burn the client's scalp during a thermal pressing service, what should you apply to the burn?

A. Neosporin ointment
B. violet jelly
C. butter coating
D. alcohol solution

18. When giving a pressing service, the cosmetologist should use

A. moderate pressure and heat
B. moderate pressure and intense heat
C. firm pressure and intense heat
D. B and C only

19. As a safety consideration, before pressing the hair, the practitioner should check the scalp for

A. flakes
B. abrasions
C. discoloration
D. oiliness

20. How can gradual breakage of the hair happen as the result of thermal hair pressing?

A. too much oil
B. too much brushing
C. having the hair pressed too often
D. having the hair shampooed too often

21. What is used to remove carbon build-up from your thermal iron?

A. sand paper
B. steel wool
C. an emery board
D. all of the above

22. If the hair has been pressed, but the desired result was not achieved, what happened?

A. not enough heat
B. not enough pressure
C. not enough curl
D. A and B only

___ 23. Which of the following hair textures will be difficult to press?

A. fine, curly hair
B. coarse, wiry hair
C. medium hair
D. fine, gray, curly hair

Poss.	Wrong	%	Right
23	0	100%	20
23	1	95%	19
23	2	90%	18
23	3	85%	17
23	4	80%	16
23	5	75%	15
23	6	70%	14

---

22 THERMAL PRESSING PRE-TEST 3

17 Questions

___ 1. The temperature of the pressing comb is determined by its reaction to the

A. touch
B. tissue
C. client
D. litmus paper

___ 2. Hair that has been chemically relaxed cannot be silked, or

A. set
B. curled
C. brushed
D. pressed

___ 3. To adequately straighten the hair, the pressing comb should be

A. perfectly even
B. hot enough
C. curved enough
D. heavy enough

___ 4. Thermal pressing usually begins in the

A. nape section
B. crown section
C. side section
D. top section

___ 5. Temporarily straightening the hair with the hot comb is called hair

A. crimping
B. straightening
C. pressing
D. molding

___ 6. If the hair is pressed twice on both sides of the strand before it is curled, this press is called a

A. soft press
B. hard press
C. firm press
D. double press

___ 7. Before pressing the hair, it should be

A. combed and brushed
B. shampooed and dried
C. shampooed and marcelled
D. dried and curled

___ 8. When pressing the hair, hair texture has to be considered, as well as the

A. temperature of the comb
B. chemicals to be used
C. setting pattern
D. cutting method

___ 9. A single hair-pressing treatment with the hot comb is known as a

A. one press
B. light press
C. comb press
D. soft press

___ 10. Before thermal waving super-curly hair, the cosmetologist should

A. color it
B. press it
C. shape it
D. comb it

11. The styling comb used in thermal waving should be made of

    A. aluminum
    B. steel
    C. hard rubber
    D. soft rubber

12. The clicking referred to when thermal waving means how the iron is

    A. heated
    B. cleaned
    C. cooled
    D. opened and closed

13. When thermal waving the hair, fine, short hairs around the hairline are best curled with

    A. pin curls
    B. a smaller iron
    C. a crimper
    D. perm rods

14. After a thermal wave, the hair is brushed and combed into a hairstyle

    A. after the lanolin has been applied
    B. while the hair is still hot
    C. when the hair has been cooled
    D. while the hair is lukewarm

15. When pressing the hair, what does the use of a pressing oil prevent?

    A. scorching
    B. breaking
    C. burning
    D. all of the above

16. After the hair has been thermal pressed, what will cause the hair to revert back to its natural curliness?

    A. heat
    B. moisture
    C. hairspray
    D. all of the above

17. Which of the following hair textures would most likely be given a hard press?

    A. fine hair
    B. medium hair
    C. coarse hair
    D. all of the above

Poss.	Wrong	%	Right
17	0	100%	17
17	1	94%	16
17	2	88%	15
17	3	82%	14
17	4	76%	13
17	5	71%	12
17	6	65%	11

23 RECURLING PRE-TEST 1

19 Questions

1. The double-application service in which super-curly hair is straightened then curled on permanent wave rods is called a(n)

    A. recurl
    B. structuring
    C. Afro-pick
    D. none of the above

2. To be successful, what size rod subsections should the cosmetologist use when doing a curl reformation?

    A. small subsections
    B. medium subsections
    C. large subsections
    D. none of the above

3. When giving a curl reformation, it is very important to wear

    A. a hair net
    B. an operator apron
    C. protective shoes
    D. none of the above

4. What is the main chemical used in the neutralizer of most curl reformation products?

    A. hydrogen peroxide
    B. sodium bromate
    C. ammonium thioglycolate
    D. sodium chloride

69

_____ 5. If the client is scheduled for a curl reformation and tells you that he/she had a chemical hair relaxer last month, what should you do?

A. give the service
B. condition the hair, then give the service
C. give the service, then condition the hair
D. refuse to give the service

_____ 6. Which of the following is part of the curl reformation service?

A. place cap over hair during processing
B. test curl strand
C. apply curl booster
D. all of the above

_____ 7. During a curl reformation, how much tension is used to wrap the hair on the rods?

A. no tension
B. moderate tension
C. slight tension
D. firm tension

_____ 8. What is the name for the product that straightens the hair in the curl reformation service?

A. chemical relaxer
B. chemical rearranger
C. hair straightener
D. hair filler

_____ 9. When giving a curl reformation, how many turns is the rod unwound in order to test curl the strand?

A. 1-1/2 - 2 turns
B. 2-1/2 - 3 turns
C. 3-1/2 - 4 turns
D. 4-1/2 - 5 turns

_____ 10. What is one thing to watch out for when you are about to give a curl reformation?

A. too many test curls
B. client allergies
C. using too many rods
D. tangled hair

_____ 11. Which type of hair will curl the fastest?

A. coarse hair
B. hair with elasticity
C. porous hair
D. fine hair

_____ 12. Before applying a curl reformation straightener, what should you do?

A. make a client record
B. apply the neutralizer to the nape
C. apply a base to hairline
D. give a scalp treatment

_____ 13. When applying the curl rearranger, you should wear

A. gloves
B. an operator apron
C. protective sleeves
D. all of the above

_____ 14. When doing a curl reformation, how often should the rearranger be tested?

A. 1 - 2 minutes
B. 3 - 5 minutes
C. 6 - 8 minutes
D. 9 - 10 minutes

_____ 15. During a curl reformation, the hair dries out while you are wrapping the hair on the rods. What should you do?

A. apply more waving solution
B. apply water to dry strands
C. use spray-on conditioner
D. use two end wraps

_____ 16. Before applying the neutralizer to the rods when doing a curl reformation, the hair should be rinsed with

A. conditioner
B. hot water
C. tepid water
D. cold water

17. The client is receiving a curl reformation. The rearranger has been applied, capped, and put under the dryer. How often should the processing be checked for relaxation?

    A. every 5 minutes
    B. every 10 minutes
    C. every 15 minutes
    D. it doesn't need to be checked

18. To protect the skin during the processing and neutralizing of a soft curl, it is very important to

    A. wipe off the shampoo bowl
    B. frequently change the neck towel
    C. wear protective sleeves
    D. all of the above

19. When giving a soft curl, how many times should the hair strand go around the rod to obtain a good curl formation?

    A. 1 turn
    B. 2 turns
    C. 3 turns
    D. 4-1/2 turns

Poss.	Wrong	%	Right
19	0	100%	19
19	1	95%	18
19	2	89%	17
19	3	84%	16
19	4	79%	15
19	5	74%	14
19	6	68%	13

24 DESCRIBING THE SKIN PRE-TEST 1

23 Questions

1. The sweat and oil glands are located in the

    A. cuticle layer
    B. epidermis layer
    C. dermis layer
    D. cutis layer

2. The uppermost layer of skin that protects the body is the

    A. epidermis
    B. dermis
    C. corium
    D. cutis

3. Dry, or oily skin is related to activity of the

    A. renal glands
    B. lymph glands
    C. sudoriferous glands
    D. sebaceous glands

4. During which hours should you AVOID sitting out to sun bathe?

    A. 2:00 - 4:00 P.M.
    B. 3:00 - 5:00 P.M.
    C. 1:00 - 5:00 P.M.
    D. 10:00 A.M. - 2:00 P.M.

5. Continued friction on the skin may cause a

    A. stain
    B. pimple
    C. wart
    D. callus

6. Nevus flammeus is the technical name for a

    A. mole
    B. wart
    C. birthmark
    D. acne

7. The skin can be protected from the sun by applying

    A. baby oil
    B. lotion with PABA
    C. moisturizing lotion
    D. coconut oil

8. The silhouette, shape, or contour of the body is affected by bone structure, and amount of

    A. adipose tissue
    B. nerve tissue
    C. follicle tissue
    D. shaft tissue

____ 9. Body temperature (98.6) is regulated by the blood, and the

A. thyroid gland
B. adrenal glands
C. sebaceous glands
D. sweat glands

____ 10. Sweat and oil glands are alike in that they both move a fluid through a

A. tube
B. duct
C. vessel
D. canal

____ 11. Sebum goes through a duct from the oil gland, and empties into the hair

A. papilla
B. root
C. follicle
D. cuticle

____ 12. The outer layer of skin that contains 10% to 20% water is the

A. basal layer
B. granular layer
C. horny layer
D. lucid layer

____ 13. One way to penetrate unbroken skin is through the

A. adipose tissue
B. follicle
C. corium
D. subcutaneous tissue

____ 14. The temperature of the human body is

A. 97.3 degrees
B. 97.6 degrees
C. 98.4 degrees
D. 98.6 degrees

____ 15. Adipose tissue is also referred to as

A. cuticle
B. fatty
C. epidermis
D. dermis

____ 16. The microscopic study of the skin is called

A. dermatology
B. psychology
C. histology
D. trichology

____ 17. The outermost (top) layer of the skin is the

A. epidermis
B. corium
C. subcutaneous tissue
D. adipose tissue

____ 18. Another name for milaria rubra is

A. prickly heat
B. sweat retention
C. anhidrosis
D. a cold sweat

____ 19. Increased sweating caused by an overactivity of the thyroid gland is known as

A. hyperthalmus
B. hypohidrosis
C. hyperhidrosis
D. thyroidism

____ 20. The smaller sweat glands that are the heat regulators for the body are called

A. eccrine
B. apocrine
C. sudoriferous
D. cornified

____ 21. The name of the sweat gland that empties into the hair follicle is the

A. sudoriferous
B. apocrine
C. eccrine
D. papilla

____ 22. An esthetician is a person who is mainly concerned with the promoting and preserving of health and beauty of the

A. fingernails
B. toenails
C. eyebrows
D. skin

___ 23. A sun block lotion would have what number for a rating?

A. 5
B. 8
C. 12
D. 15

Poss.	Wrong	%	Right
23	0	100%	23
23	1	96%	22
23	2	91%	21
23	3	87%	20
23	4	83%	19
23	5	78%	18
23	6	74%	17
23	7	70%	16
23	8	65%	15
23	9	61%	14

24 DESCRIBING THE SKIN PRE-TEST 2

23 Questions

___ 1. What percentage does perspiration water-down an application of suntan lotions?

A. 20%
B. 50%
C. 70%
D. 80%

___ 2. As an infant grows older, the flow of sebum from the sebaceous glands

A. increases
B. decreases
C. remains the same
D. B and C

___ 3. Sebaceous glands are present all over the body except the

A. palms and soles
B. elbows and knees
C. lips and nose
D. forehead and ears

___ 4. When the skin lacks oil (sebum), the skin will lose

A. color
B. softness
C. moisture
D. suppleness

___ 5. One of the two ways to penetrate unbroken skin is through the

A. adipose tissue
B. papilla
C. corium
D. sebaceous duct

___ 6. The true skin is also known as the

A. epidermis
B. adipose tissue
C. tissue
D. dermis

___ 7. How does the skin benefit the human body?

A. protection
B. sensation
C. secretion
D. all of the above

___ 8. The middle layer of the skin is called

A. adipose tissue
B. epidermis
C. cuticle
D. dermis

___ 9. The largest and most efficient organ of the human body is the

A. heart
B. liver
C. pancreas
D. skin

___ 10. The thinnest layer of the skin is the

A. epidermis
B. corium
C. subcutaneous tissue
D. adipose tissue

11. The three main divisions of the skin are the epidermis, subcutaneous tissue, and the

    A. dermis
    B. cutis
    C. sebaceous
    D. basal

12. Skin gets its color from a pigment known as

    A. sebum
    B. apocrine
    C. keratin
    D. melanin

13. The skin is an example of

    A. hard keratin
    B. soft keratin
    C. hard melanin
    D. hard cutis

14. Oil glands are absent from the

    A. nose and forehead
    B. palms and soles
    C. arms and neck
    D. face and ears

15. What do the initials SPF mean?

    A. strong personal factors
    B. sun protection factor
    C. special pale face
    D. small protective feet

16. When a skin lesion has definite boundaries, it is said to be

    A. elevated
    B. circumscribed
    C. surrounded
    D. subcutaneous

17. A medical doctor that specializes in the treatment of skin diseases is called a

    A. trichologist
    B. toxicologist
    C. dermatologist
    D. skin expert

18. Pathology is a science that studies a disease in terms of its

    A. origin
    B. cause
    C. nature
    D. all of the above

19. A simple word for the medical term verruca would be

    A. freckle
    B. mole
    C. callus
    D. wart

20. When a person has white hair and pink eyes from birth, this condition is called

    A. albinism
    B. canities
    C. keratoma
    D. dermatitis

21. If you over-expose your skin to the sun, what will happen?

    A. thickening of the skin
    B. wrinkling of the skin
    C. herpes simplex
    D. all of the above

22. Hyperkeratosis is a technical name for a

    A. callus
    B. pimple
    C. mole
    D. cut

23. Sensory nerves of the skin react to

    A. warts
    B. boils
    C. touch
    D. tone

74

Poss.	Wrong	%	Right		23	4	83%	19
23	0	100%	23		23	5	78%	18
23	1	96%	22		23	6	74%	17
23	2	91%	21		23	7	70%	16
23	3	87%	20		23	8	65%	15
					23	9	61%	14

25 FACIAL TREATMENTS PRE-TEST 1

31 Questions

___ 1. Emollient cream is used in facial massage as a(n)

A. astringent
B. lubricant
C. cleanser
D. toner

___ 2. Cold cream is used on the face as a

A. foundation
B. base
C. emollient
D. cleanser

___ 3. The effleurage massage movement is done lightly and slowly, so it is

A. stimulating
B. soothing
C. exciting
D. irritating

___ 4. The massage movement that uses a kneading technique is called

A. petrissage
B. effleurage
C. friction
D. vibration

___ 5. When the petrissage massage movement is used, it has a(n)

A. soothing effect
B. relaxing effect
C. invigorating effect
D. mellowing effect

___ 6. Tapotement is a massage movement that uses a

A. kneading technique
B. pinching technique
C. stroking technique
D. tapping technique

___ 7. The main purpose of a massage is to stimulate and strengthen

A. nerve branches
B. fatty tissue
C. muscle tone
D. cartilage

___ 8. In the presence of severe acne, the cosmetologist should

A. avoid facial massage
B. use tapotement massage
C. use kneading massage
D. avoid use of emollient cream

___ 9. Of all the light from the sun, infrared rays make up about

A. 20% of it
B. 40% of it
C. 60% of it
D. 80% of it

___ 10. Ultra-violet rays are also called

A. red rays
B. gold rays
C. actinic rays
D. deep penetrating rays

___ 11. Of all the light from the sun, ultra-violet rays make up about

A. 8% of it
B. 12% of it
C. 24% of it
D. 36% of it

___ 12. A clay pack is recommended for skin that is

A. dusty
B. oily
C. dry
D. flakey

75

___ 13. After a blackhead has been removed, the cosmetologist should apply a(n)

A. hot towel
B. antiseptic
C. fumigant
D. deodorant

___ 14. The word used to describe a kneading or rolling facial movement is

A. effleurage
B. petrissage
C. friction
D. tapotement

___ 15. What percentage of the sunlight is represented by infrared rays?

A. 40%
B. 60%
C. 80%
D. 90%

___ 16. A facial mask should be used on which of the following skin types?

A. normal skin
B. oily skin
C. dry skin
D. moist skin

___ 17. What effect does alcohol have on the skin?

A. moisturizing
B. drying
C. lusterizing
D. beautifying

___ 18. When should you advise the client against having a facial treatment?

A. the face is bruised
B. the face has diseased skin
C. the face has broken open sores
D. all of the above

___ 19. What direction are most facial movements used to most benefit the sagging and wrinkling of the client's skin?

A. downward movements
B. upward movements
C. circular movements to the side
D. strong stretching movement about the eyes

___ 20. Where on the face is it very important to be very careful when using pointed facial implements?

A. eye area
B. nose area
C. ear area
D. lower cheek area

___ 21. Which of the following facial implements should be recapped immediately after use during a facial?

A. bottles
B. jars of facial creams
C. facial preparations
D. all of the above

___ 22. Of the choices below, select the preparation or product that should be used when giving a facial to normal, or oily skin.

A. mask
B. pack
C. oil-based emollient cream
D. cotton

___ 23. What is the effect of sponging the skin during a facial treatment?

A. remove impurities and excess oil
B. obtain deeper penetration of the oil
C. soften the skin
D. allow the fingertips to slide more easily across the skin

___ 24. What purpose does the application of witch hazel to the skin serve in the facial process?

A. softens the skin
B. moisturizes the skin
C. soothes and cleanses the skin
D. makes skin hard and leathery

___ 25. How is a facial pack usually removed from the face?

A. alcohol scrub
B. witch hazel rub
C. cutting from edges
D. peeling from the edges

26. Before giving clients a pack or mask treatment, it is important to

    A. give an allergy test
    B. ask them why they want one
    C. heat the pack or mask on the stove
    D. all of the above

27. Why is the Wood's Light used mainly in the analysis of the skin?

    A. to see it better magnified for fine details
    B. to detect inflamed, or overactive oil glands
    C. to pick up subtle skin tone not seen otherwise
    D. to select the correct makeup

28. For what skin condition is a mildly abrasive skin cleanser recommended?

    A. normal skin
    B. oily skin
    C. dry skin
    D. all of the above

29. When using a clay mask, what areas of the face should you be careful to avoid?

    A. mouth
    B. nose
    C. eyes
    D. all of the above

30. To prevent the spread of disease, what should be done as part of the facial procedure?

    A. sponge the face with an antiseptic
    B. wash the face with soap and water
    C. vacuum the face with a facial machine
    D. massage the face with alcohol

31. With respect to makeup, what does it have a tendency to do to the pores of the skin?

    A. clog them
    B. cleanse them
    C. close them
    D. open them

Poss.	Wrong	%	Right
31	0	100%	31
31	1	97%	30
31	2	94%	29
31	3	90%	28
31	4	87%	27
31	5	84%	26
31	6	81%	25
31	7	77%	24
31	8	74%	23
31	9	71%	22
31	10	68%	21
31	11	65%	20

25 FACIAL TREATMENTS PRE-TEST 2

20 Questions

1. Ultra-violet rays are also called

    A. red
    B. sunlight
    C. white
    D. actinic

2. An ultra-violet lamp should be placed

    A. 36″ from the client
    B. 72″ from the client
    C. 84″ from the client
    D. 96″ from the client

3. When the skin is exposed to ultra-violet rays, there is an increase in Vitamin

    A. D
    B. C
    C. E
    D. K

4. What type of lamp is used for dry skin when an emollient is used?

    A. ultra-violet
    B. infrared
    C. quartz
    D. actinic

___ 5. Facial massage is not given on skin that is

A. diseased
B. broken
C. abraded
D. all of the above

___ 6. A facial massage movement that uses a light stroking movement is called

A. friction
B. effleurage
C. tapotement
D. petrissage

___ 7. What is the rubbing facial movement that is done with the flat of the hand or fingertips?

A. effleurage
B. petrissage
C. tapotement
D. friction

___ 8. During a treatment using infrared or ultra-violet light, cotton pads saturated with water are used to cover the client's

A. hands
B. eyes
C. forehead
D. ears

___ 9. Deep penetrating light rays used in light therapy are

A. blue
B. red
C. green
D. yellow

___ 10. If a client's eyes and skin are over-exposed to ultra-violet rays, the injury will appear as a

A. deep cut
B. large scab
C. severe burn
D. large abrasion

___ 11. To prevent sagging facial muscles and wrinkling of the skin, what direction should all facial movements be given to the client?

A. downward toward the chin
B. across, from ear to ear
C. upward, toward the front hairline
D. all of the above

___ 12. The high frequency facial treatment is advised for skin that has

A. freckles
B. moles
C. acne
D. warts

___ 13. Fast massage movements given with moderate pressure will cause body tissue to be

A. stimulated
B. relaxed
C. cooled
D. fatigued

___ 14. Massage that uses deep rubbing movements requires a

A. friction technique
B. tapping technique
C. stroking technique
D. vibrating technique

___ 15. A vibration massage technique affects the skin by

A. soothing it
B. cooling it
C. relaxing it
D. stimulating it

___ 16. A facial mask should be used on which of the following skin types?

A. normal skin
B. oily skin
C. dry skin
D. moist skin

___ 17. What effect does alcohol have on the skin?

A. moisturizing
B. drying
C. lusterizing
D. beautifying

___ 18. When should you advise the client against having a facial treatment?

A. the face is bruised
B. the face has diseased skin
C. the face has broken open sores
D. all of the above

78

____ 19. What direction are most facial movements used to most benefit the sagging and wrinkling of the client's skin?

A. downward movements
B. upward movements
C. circular movements to the side
D. strong stretching movements about the eyes

Poss.	Wrong	%	Right
20	0	100%	20
20	1	95%	19
20	2	90%	18
20	3	85%	17
20	4	80%	16
20	5	75%	15
20	6	70%	14

____ 20. Where on the face is it important to be very careful when using pointed facial implements?

A. eye area
B. nose area
C. ear area
D. lower cheek area

---

26 APPLYING MAKEUP PRE-TEST 1

23 Questions

____ 1. To tweeze the eyebrows correctly, this should be done in the direction

A. toward the forehead
B. toward the chin
C. of their natural growth
D. opposite their natural growth

____ 2. To maintain sanitation, color applied to the lips should be done with a sanitized

A. pledget
B. brush
C. crayon
D. cotton ball

____ 3. If base makeup is applied correctly, the cosmetologist should be able to conceal

A. eye lids
B. blemishes
C. wrinkles
D. facial hair

____ 4. Knowledge of facial structure is important for the application of makeup to achieve the most attractive facial shape which is

A. round
B. square
C. diamond
D. oval

____ 5. Removal of unsightly matter on the facial area can be best achieved with a(n)

A. cleanser
B. astringent
C. freshener
D. emollient creme

____ 6. Foundation makeup is applied to the facial area to enhance the client's skin tone and

A. smooth it
B. dampen it
C. protect it
D. cleanse it

____ 7. Which of the following should be applied to remove cleansing creme from oily skin?

A. soap
B. astringent
C. toner
D. alcohol

____ 8. Lash and brow tint is applied with, then against, the natural direction of the hair's

A. insertion
B. growth
C. follicle
D. strand

___ 9. When applying corrective or contour makeup, the rule is "lights in the valley, shadows on the hills". This means that indentations should be filled, and protrusions should be

A. shadowed
B. lightened
C. toned up
D. highlighted

___ 10. When tinting lashes and brows, petroleum jelly is used to protect the skin from

A. injury
B. abrasion
C. stain
D. scratches

___ 11. What should be applied down the center of the nose to create an illusion that will make the nose appear longer?

A. corrective stick
B. rouge line
C. shadow
D. highlighter

___ 12. When tweezing the eyebrows, this should be done in which direction?

A. against the growth direction
B. with the growth direction
C. in an upward direction
D. downward toward the nose

___ 13. The application of semipermanent lashes is also referred to as

A. temporary lashes
B. permanent lashes
C. strip lashes
D. eye tabbing

___ 14. If strip eyelashes are to fit correctly, what must be done before the lashes are put on the client?

A. measuring
B. weighing
C. cleansing
D. arching

___ 15. In terms of the client's natural eyelashes, where are the strip lashes placed?

A. below
B. above
C. even with
D. on

___ 16. When the foundation base makeup protrudes from the surface of the skin, what should this tell you about the alkalinity of the skin?

A. high
B. low
C. neutral
D. zero

___ 17. Small eyes can be made to appear larger. What type of makeup is applied to create this illusion?

A. contour
B. foundation
C. lip
D. white

___ 18. To blend in facial scars and blemishes, what kind of makeup stick should be used?

A. contour
B. rouge
C. corrective
D. powder

___ 19. Powder is applied over foundation makeup to

A. black it out
B. set it
C. cover it
D. blend it

___ 20. What type of movement should be used when tweezing the eyebrows?

A. slow, sliding movement
B. quick movement
C. circular movement
D. zig-zag movement

21. After strip lashes are correctly positioned, the outside and inside ends are held in place for

A. one minute
B. two minutes
C. three minutes
D. four minutes

22. What effect does the freshener have on the pores?

A. medicates
B. cleanses
C. opens
D. sanitizes

23. When applying semipermanent lashes, dip the end of the lash in adhesive, stroke the client's lash, then

A. remove it
B. attach it
C. slip it over
D. slide it onto the lid

Poss.	Wrong	%	Right
23	0	100%	23
23	1	96%	22
23	2	91%	21
23	3	87%	20
23	4	83%	19
23	5	78%	18
23	6	74%	17
23	7	70%	16
23	8	65%	15
23	9	61%	14

27 NAIL ANATOMY, DISORDERS, AND DISEASES PRE-TEST 1

17 Questions

1. The symptoms of athlete's foot are white patches between the toes, and

A. flat, oval patches
B. red, inflamed open sores
C. clear, water-filled blisters
D. round, white patches all over the foot

2. The eponychium is the

A. skin that surrounds the entire nail
B. outside point where the skin overlaps the nail
C. inside point where the nail enters the skin
D. deep fold of skin where the nail root is imbedded

3. Tinea(onychomycosis) is a disturbance of nail growth due to a vegetable fungi that is

A. very common
B. contagious
C. noncontagious
D. beneficial

4. Nail growth can be decreased or slowed down because of

A. illness
B. old age
C. poor nutrition
D. all of the above

5. When a fungus is growing beneath the nail plate, what color would be seen under the nail?

A. green
B. blue
C. yellow
D. red

6. The average daily growth rate of the nail is

A. .7 mm
B. .5 mm
C. .3 mm
D. .1 mm

7. The inner part of the nail that affects the nail's shape, size, regeneration, and growth is

A. nail wall
B. matrix
C. lunula
D. nail root

___ 8. The nail root is located

    A. at each side of the nail wall
    B. beneath the skin at the base of the nail
    C. beyond the end of the fingertip
    D. near the skin directly beneath the nail's free edge

___ 9. That portion of the skin directly beneath the nail's free edge is the

    A. mantle
    B. eponychium
    C. hyponychium
    D. nail groove

___ 10. Onychogryposis is the technical name for

    A. ingrown nail
    B. ringworm
    C. claw nail
    D. felon

___ 11. Overgrowth or thickening of the nail is known as

    A. hypertrophy
    B. hypotrophy
    C. tinea
    D. agnails

___ 12. When the skin around the nail is very sore, inflamed, swollen, and infectious, this disease is known as

    A. onycholysis
    B. onychophagy
    C. paronychia
    D. bosphorus

___ 13. The inner part of the nail that affects its shape, size, and growth is known as the

    A. plate
    B. matrix
    C. lunula
    D. cuticle

___ 14. When the cuticle sticks to the base of the nail as it grows out, this condition is known as

    A. agnails
    B. tinea
    C. blue nails
    D. pterygium

___ 15. Trimming or filing nails too deeply into corners can cause

    A. hangnails
    B. ingrown nails
    C. nail thickening
    D. brittle nails

___ 16. If hangnails are neglected, they may become

    A. brittle
    B. fragile
    C. infected
    D. loose

___ 17. Once a nail becomes infected, it should be treated by a

    A. barber
    B. cosmetologist
    C. manicurist
    D. physician

Poss.	Wrong	%	Right
17	0	100%	17
17	1	94%	16
17	2	88%	15
17	3	82%	14
17	4	76%	13
17	5	71%	12
17	6	65%	11

27 Questions

___ 1. The free edge of the nail is shaped using a(n)
A. orangewood stick
B. nail pusher
C. nail nipper
D. emery board

___ 2. Implements to be used for manicuring should be
A. rinsed in water
B. wiped off with a towel
C. cleaned and sanitized
D. cleaned with a sponge

___ 3. Brittle fingernails, or dry cuticles should be given a(n)
A. oil manicure
B. regular manicure
C. pedicure
D. foam manicure

___ 4. Manicure implements should be sanitized
A. once a week
B. twice a week
C. twice a month
D. after every use

___ 5. Should a small cut occur during the manicure, the cosmetologist should apply a(n)
A. piece of cotton
B. paper towel
C. antiseptic
D. bandage

___ 6. A glass container that has cotton and alcohol at the bottom of it, is used to keep
A. manicure implements sanitized
B. cold waving combs sanitized
C. hair color bottles sanitized
D. styling combs sanitized

___ 7. The application of cuticle cream during the manicure prevents
A. enamel from sticking
B. free edge from splitting
C. dry skin around nails
D. chapping of hands

___ 8. Fingernail shaping with an emery board should be done from
A. center to corner
B. corner to corner
C. corner to center
D. curved across

___ 9. If a minor cut should occur during a manicure, apply powdered styptic, or a(n)
A. shampoo
B. antiseptic
C. creme rinse
D. disinfectant

___ 10. The fingerbowl used in manicuring usually contains liquid soap and
A. alcohol
B. hydrogen peroxide
C. warm water
D. sodium bromate

___ 11. Filing nails and applying polish are alike because both should be done with
A. quick and smooth strokes
B. choppy and heavy strokes
C. jerky and light strokes
D. circular and oval strokes

___ 12. The best time to apply nail enamel is
A. after the base coat has dried
B. before the base coat is applied
C. before the cuticle cream is applied
D. right after the nails have been filed

___ 13. The art of caring for the toenails, feet, and legs is known as
A. manicuring
B. dermatology
C. pedicuring
D. nail wrapping

___ 14. The product used to remove oil or stains from the nails is
A. stain remover
B. polish remover
C. nail bleach
D. cuticle remover

_____ 15. A substitute for nail bleach would be

   A. hydrogen peroxide
   B. cleanser
   C. styptic
   D. alum

_____ 16. The product that softens the cuticle and the dead skin beneath the free edge is the

   A. polish remover
   B. nail base coat
   C. nail peeler
   D. cuticle remover

_____ 17. The product that prevents the polish from chipping is the sealer, or

   A. solvent coat
   B. base coat
   C. top coat
   D. cuticle coat

_____ 18. One way to prevent nails from splitting is to apply a strengthener, which is called a nail

   A. builder
   B. lever
   C. coat
   D. cover

_____ 19. When manicuring, the cuticle will be softened in the

   A. polishing step
   B. finger bowl step
   C. polish removal step
   D. base coat step

_____ 20. Before applying artificial nails, it is necessary to

   A. remove all polish
   B. remove all polish and thoroughly dry the nails
   C. buff all nails
   D. buff all nails then apply artificial nails to moist fingernails

_____ 21. An oil pedicure is recommended for the client with which of the following skin types?

   A. oily, fragile skin
   B. normal skin
   C. dry, callused skin
   D. red, inflamed skin

_____ 22. One way to fix a torn fingernail would be to apply

   A. alum
   B. an artificial nail
   C. high-frequency current
   D. cuticle cream

_____ 23. What is the most important thing that a salon should have when artificial nails are offered as a service?

   A. comfortable chairs
   B. good ventilation
   C. an adequate supply of cold water
   D. proper supervision

_____ 24. After an emery board has been used to file the client's nails, it should be

   A. boiled for 10 minutes
   B. thrown in the refuse
   C. dipped in alcohol
   D. washed with soap and water

_____ 25. Why is the nail wrapping service offered in the salon?

   A. to shorten and widen the nail
   B. to lengthen and lusterize the natural nail
   C. to strengthen and protect the nails
   D. to soften and moisturize the nails

_____ 26. To prevent burning the client's fingers when giving a hot oil (cream) manicure, you should

   A. remove the cream with a towel
   B. put a towel over the cream
   C. stir the cream with an orangewood stick
   D. check the temperature first

_____ 27. If injured, which part of the finger could cause the nail to grow in a distorted shape?

   A. nail matrix
   B. nail body
   C. free edge
   D. nail groove

Poss.	Wrong	%	Right
27	0	100%	27
27	1	96%	26
27	2	93%	25
27	3	89%	24
27	4	85%	23

27	5	81%	22
27	6	78%	21
27	7	74%	20
27	8	70%	19
27	9	67%	18
27	10	63%	17
27	11	59%	16

28 MANICURING AND PEDICURING PRE-TEST 2

26 Questions

___ 1. The product that softens the cuticle and the dead skin beneath the free edge is the

A. polish remover
B. nail base coat
C. nail peeler
D. cuticle remover

___ 2. Filing nails and applying polish are alike because both should be done with

A. quick and smooth strokes
B. choppy and heavy strokes
C. jerky and light stokes
D. circular and oval strokes

___ 3. The product that prevents the polish from chipping is the sealer, or

A. solvent coat
B. base coat
C. top coat
D. cuticle coat

___ 4. The best time to apply nail enamel is

A. after the coat has dried
B. before the base coat is applied
C. before the cuticle cream is applied
D. right after the nails have been filed

___ 5. A substitute for nail bleach would be

A. hydrogen peroxide
B. cleanser
C. styptic
D. alum

___ 6. The product used to remove oil or stains from the nails is

A. stain remover
B. polish remover
C. nail bleach
D. cuticle remover

___ 7. The fingerbowl used in manicuring usually contains liquid soap and

A. alcohol
B. hydrogen peroxide
C. warm water
D. sodium bromate

___ 8. The art of caring for the toenails, feet, and legs is known as

A. manicuring
B. dermatology
C. pedicuring
D. nail wrapping

___ 9. Manicure implements should be sanitized

A. once a week
B. twice a week
C. twice a month
D. after every use

___ 10. If a minor cut should occur during a manicure, apply powdered styptic, or a(n)

A. shampoo
B. antiseptic
C. creme rinse
D. disinfectant

___ 11. Should a small cut occur during the manicure, the cosmetologist should apply a(n)

A. piece of cotton
B. paper towel
C. antiseptic
D. bandage

___ 12. Fingernail shaping with an emery board should be done from

A. center to corner
B. corner to corner
C. corner to center
D. curved across

___ 13. One way to fix a torn fingernail would be to apply

A. alum
B. an artificial nail
C. high-frequency current
D. cuticle cream

___ 14. The application of cuticle cream during the manicure prevents

A. enamel from sticking
B. free edge from splitting
C. dry skin around nails
D. chapping of hands

___ 15. Implements to be used for manicuring should be

A. rinsed in water
B. wiped off with a towel
C. cleaned and sanitized
D. cleaned with a sponge

___ 16. A glass container that has cotton and alcohol at the bottom of it, is used to keep

A. manicure implements sanitized
B. cold waving combs sanitized
C. hair-color bottles sanitized
D. styling combs sanitized

___ 17. Brittle fingernails, or dry cuticles should be given a(n)

A. oil manicure
B. regular manicure
C. pedicure
D. foam manicure

___ 18. An oil pedicure is recommended for the client with which of the following skin types?

A. oily, fragile skin
B. normal skin
C. dry, calloused skin
D. traumatized skin

___ 19. Before applying artificial nails, it is necessary to

A. remove all polish
B. remove all polish and thoroughly dry the nails
C. buff all nails
D. buff all nails and apply artificial nails to moist fingernails

___ 20. The free edge of the nail is shaped using a(n)

A. orangewood stick
B. nail pusher
C. nail buffer
D. emery board

___ 21. One way to prevent nails from splitting is to apply a strengthener, which is called a nail

A. builder
B. lever
C. coat
D. cover

___ 22. When manicuring, the cuticle will be softened in the

A. polishing step
B. fingerbowl step
C. polish-removal step
D. base coat step

___ 23. What is the most important thing that a salon should have when artificial nails are offered as a service?

A. comfortable chairs
B. good ventilation
C. an adequate supply of cold water
D. proper supervision

___ 24. Which of the following manicuring chemicals is very flammable when exposed to fire, such as a match or a cigarette?

A. 1% hydrogen peroxide
B. ammonium thio
C. permanent hair color
D. polish remover

___ 25. Before giving your client a manicure, you discover that the client has what you think is a contagious nail disease. You should

A. use a nail antiseptic, and give the service
B. suggest a nail wrap, and give the service
C. stop the service, and recommend that the client see a doctor
D. rinse nails with alcohol, and proceed with the service

___ 26. If nail decorations are used, when should they be applied?

A. before the nails are filed
B. after the application of the polish
C. before the cuticles have been pushed
D. after the base coat, but before the polish

Poss.	Wrong	%	Right
26	0	100%	26
26	1	96%	25
26	2	92%	24
26	3	88%	23
26	4	85%	22
26	5	81%	21
26	6	77%	20
26	7	73%	19
26	8	69%	18
26	9	65%	17
26	10	62%	16
26	11	58%	15

29 WIGS AND HAIRPIECES PRE-TEST 1

10 Questions

___ 1. A hairpiece that covers 80 to 100 percent of a client's head is called a

A. wiglet
B. cascade
C. wig
D. toupee

___ 2. The most expensive type of hair from which hairgoods are made is

A. synthetic hair
B. yak hair
C. angora hair
D. human hair

___ 3. Hand-tied hairpieces are quite expensive because the hair in them is

A. synthetic
B. constructed in an area where labor costs are high
C. in great demand
D. individually attached to the netting by hand

___ 4. To secure a wig on a canvas block, use

A. bobby pins
B. hair pins
C. common pins
D. T-pins

___ 5. Small, circular-based hairpieces usually made from angora and yak hair are termed

A. postiches
B. switches
C. falls
D. chignons

___ 6. The most expensive type of human hair is classified as

A. Oriental
B. Asiatic
C. European
D. West Indian

___ 7. When selecting a hairpiece for a client, you will be able to match the color more easily by using a

A. pH color chart
B. color triangle
C. JL color ring
D. color comparison chart

___ 8. To prevent a canvas block from molding and giving an odor, it is advisable to cover it with

A. a nylon cap
B. synthetic fiber
C. a plastic bag
D. a rubber sheet

___ 9. The size of the canvas block should correspond with the

A. length of the hair the wig contains
B. client's head size
C. texture of hair the wig contains
D. amount of hair the wig contains

___ 10. If a wig is made of human hair, it should be cleaned with a

A. liquid shampoo
B. mild detergent
C. dry cleaning fluid
D. wet cleaning fluid

Poss.	Wrong	%	Right
10	0	100%	10
10	1	90%	9
10	2	80%	8
10	3	70%	7
10	4	60%	6

30 SHAVING PRE-TEST 1

10 Questions

___ 1. What is the name for the stone used to sharpen a straight razor?

A. hone
B. whetstone
C. strop
D. crop

___ 2. When shaving, what purpose does the application of lather serve?

A. softens the skin
B. smoothes the beard
C. softens the beard
D. feels soothing

___ 3. If you should accidently draw blood when giving the client a shave, what should you do first?

A. apply pressure to stop the bleeding
B. put on rubber gloves
C. apply antiseptic
D. put styptic on wound

___ 4. Which of the following should be used to put a finishing edge on your straight razor?

A. towel
B. strop
C. hone
D. comb

___ 5. What should be used to sanitize a straight razor?

A. wet sanitizer
B. soap and water
C. 70% alcohol
D. towel

___ 6. What type of motion should be used when applying lather to the face before shaving?

A. circular
B. back and forth
C. zig zag
D. up and down

___ 7. How should an ingrown hair be removed from the skin?

A. dig it out with a needle
B. scrape it to the surface
C. apply a drying lotion
D. use a tweezers

___ 8. In which area of the neck should you be extra careful?

A. Adam's apple
B. base of the chin
C. jaw line
D. base of the neck

___9. If the client's skin is mildly inflamed, which step of the shaving procedure should you skip?

A. lathering the beard
B. shaving
C. feathering the razor's edge
D. the steamer towel

___10. If you use a straight razor, how do you protect yourself and your client from accidental cuts during the shaving service?

A. use of a guard
B. protective spray
C. use an upward motion
D. being very careful

Poss.	Wrong	%	Right
10	0	100%	10
10	1	90%	9
10	2	80%	8
10	3	70%	7
10	4	60%	6

31 PLANNING A SALON PRE-TEST 1

23 Questions

___1. The highest fixed-cost percentage associated with planning a beauty salon is the cost for

A. supplies
B. advertising
C. laundry
D. rent

___2. If a planned beauty salon intends to employ several operators, it must be zoned

A. commercial
B. residential
C. industrial
D. accessible

___3. The lessor should state in writing that the beauty salon will be kept at

A. 68-72 degrees
B. 73-76 degrees
C. 77-80 degrees
D. 81-84 degrees

___4. If all other sale terms are acceptable, the buyer of an existing salon should have how many years remaining on the lease?

A. 1 to 2
B. 3 to 4
C. 4 to 6
D. 7 or more

___5. For a beauty salon, the lessor should provide a space that has good plumbing, lighting, and

A. neighbors
B. hair dryers
C. parking
D. styling chairs

___6. Restrictions on size, shape, and location of beauty salons' signs is controlled by local

A. statutes
B. rules
C. ordinances
D. notices

___7. The type of business ownership that limits, or protects a person from individual losses is called a

A. partnership
B. corporation
C. proprietorship
D. sole ownership

___8. In the absence of a written agreement, each person in a partnership has

A. limited liability
B. specific assets
C. limited assets
D. unlimited liability

___ 9. For most written legal agreements, there is need for a(n)

A. lawyer
B. doctor
C. banker
D. accountant

___ 10. If the lessor verbally agrees to make certain building changes, these changes should be in the

A. agreement
B. lease
C. contract
D. arrangement

___ 11. When selecting a name for a beauty salon, avoid the name of the

A. lessor
B. owner
C. landlord
D. assignor

___ 12. The written legal agreement between the owner of a building and a tenant is called a

A. lease
B. lessee
C. lessor
D. mortgage

___ 13. When retailing in the salon, it is important to keep the merchandise

A. clean and neat
B. priced with a sticker
C. attractively labeled and displayed
D. all of the above

___ 14. When purchasing an existing salon, the buyer should receive information and advice from an

A. accountant
B. advisor
C. existing occupant
D. all of the above

___ 15. The salon operator is protected from dollar losses resulting from service lawsuits by

A. mortgage insurance
B. liability insurance
C. malpractice insurance
D. major-medical insurance

___ 16. If the planning stage for installation of a beauty salon indicates a low population density for the area, it means that

A. no one lives in the area
B. only a few people live in the area
C. the area has many other salons
D. a lot of people live in the area

___ 17. Before purchasing an existing beauty salon, one should consider the

A. cost of supplies
B. available parking
C. attitude of the landlord
D. all of the above

___ 18. When one person owns a business, this legal form of ownership is called a

A. corporation
B. partnership
C. sole proprietorship
D. company

___ 19. A partnership operates best when there is a written partnership

A. lease
B. agreement
C. declaration
D. contract

___ 20. The person who grants someone the use of a building is called the

A. assignee
B. assignor
C. lessee
D. lessor

___ 21. Before signing a lease, advice should be obtained from a licensed

A. physician
B. chiropractor
C. attorney
D. cosmetologist

___ 22. If a client slips and falls to the floor and files a lawsuit for the injury, the salon owner is protected from dollar loss by

A. income insurance
B. liability insurance
C. malpractice insurance
D. major-medical insurance

23. What is the name for the person that answers the phone and schedules appointments in the salon?

A. clerk
B. receptionist
C. sales person
D. appointment clerk

Poss.	Wrong	%	Right
23	0	100%	23
23	1	96%	22
23	2	91%	21
23	3	87%	20
23	4	83%	19
23	5	78%	18
23	6	74%	17
23	7	70%	16
23	8	65%	15
23	9	61%	14

32 SALON OPERATIONS PRE-TEST 1

17 Questions

1. As the number of services given in a beauty salon increases, variable costs tend to

A. increase
B. remain constant
C. decrease
D. become fixed

2. The usual effect on the salon that accepts credit cards is

A. decrease in sales
B. theft by employees
C. losses from stolen credit cards
D. increase in overall sales

3. The largest single expense in operating a beauty salon is

A. advertising/telephone
B. salaries/commissions
C. supplies/depreciation
D. dues/travel

4. Besides rent and salaries, the next largest expense is

A. advertising
B. supplies
C. education
D. towels

5. After all expenses have been deducted, the remaining money from the business is called

A. lien
B. liability
C. asset
D. profit

6. Tax laws mandate that each business keep proper and accurate

A. advertising
B. records
C. supply bills
D. telephone bills

7. If a salon can afford to pay 8% of their gross income for supplies, and the supply bill last year was $3,200, their gross income was

A. $20,000
B. $25,000
C. $35,000
D. $40,000

8. The basic accounting equation is Assets equals

A. Liabilities + Proprietorship
B. Expenses - Costs
C. Proprietorship + Liabilities
D. Liabilities - Expenses

9. In addition to other taxes, salon owners are responsible for payment of employee

A. social security taxes
B. stamp taxes
C. coupon taxes
D. ticket taxes

91

___ 10. Depending on which services are given in the salon, time will determine the difference between

A. services accepted
B. employees fired
C. supplies used
D. profit or loss

___ 11. When salon equipment, such as dryers and chairs, have been purchased on time payments, what would happen if you made a monthly payment late?

A. the equipment would be repossessed
B. you would be sued
C. there would be a service charge
D. the business would be bankrupt

___ 12. What is the communications link between the salon and the manufacturer of supplies used in the salon?

A. salesperson
B. magazines
C. newsletters
D. telephone calls

___ 13. Your supply costs can be larger than they need to be if you are not careful in terms of

A. using one application of a product for two clients
B. product duplication
C. ordering enough supplies for three months
D. ordering from 2 or 3 suppliers

___ 14. Who pays for FUTA?

A. the employer
B. the employee
C. both employee and employer
D. all of the above

___ 15. Who pays for FICA?

A. the employer
B. the employee
C. both employee and employer
D. none of the above

___ 16. Who pays for Workman's Compensation Insurance?

A. the employer
B. the employee
C. both employer and employee
D. all of the above

___ 17. A written set of items that specifies what an employer expects from an employee is call the salon's

A. want list
B. requirement list
C. operating policies
D. reading policy

Poss.	Wrong	%	Right
17	0	100%	17
17	1	94%	16
17	2	88%	15
17	3	82%	14
17	4	76%	13
17	5	71%	12
17	6	68%	11

32 SALON OPERATIONS PRE-TEST 2

15 Questions

___ 1. An asset means something a business

A. owes
B. owns
C. delivers
D. supplies

___ 2. The cost of purchasing new equipment will increase depending on the

A. color of the equipment
B. fabric of the equipment
C. style of the equipment
D. all of the above

3. The best place to borrow money is from a
   A. credit fund
   B. neighbor
   C. union fund
   D. commercial bank

4. After making an appointment for a job interview, the applicant should
   A. be on time
   B. wear neat and clean clothes
   C. have his/her hair styled
   D. all of the above

5. In terms of the dollars taken into a beauty salon, usable supplies should represent
   A. 2%
   B. 4%
   C. 6%
   D. 8%

6. The main disadvantage of ordering supplies C.O.D. is
   A. handling
   B. time
   C. bookkeeping
   D. cost

7. Fixed costs tend to
   A. increase
   B. remain constant
   C. decrease
   D. become variable

8. The average cost per operator for opening a new salon ranges from
   A. $1,200 to $1,500
   B. $1,600 to $1,800
   C. $1,900 to $2,100
   D. $2,000 to $2,500

9. If cash is paid for equipment, the purchaser can usually expect
   A. better equipment
   B. a friendly dealer
   C. a discount
   D. a rebate

10. An employer is likely to ask a prospective employee
    A. for the name of the cosmetology school that he/she graduated from
    B. names of others who have employed the student or operator
    C. his/her place of residence
    D. all of the above

11. The beauty salon owner should decide the amount to be paid the supply house from
    A. the statement
    B. packing slips
    C. bills of lading
    D. invoices

12. The general concept of how many people would be willing to pay for the salon services offered in a particular area is known as
    A. supply
    B. density
    C. demand
    D. socio-economic

13. FUTA is an abbreviation for
    A. Federal Unitary Travel Area
    B. Forced Unit Tax Act
    C. Future Tax Act
    D. Federal Unemployment Tax Act

14. For tax purposes, you must report all tips received and pay income tax if those tips exceed
    A. $10.00 per month
    B. $20.00 per month
    C. $30.00 per month
    D. $40.00 per month

15. What is one disadvantage for the salon that accepts credit cards for services?
    A. time for writing a sales slip
    B. the fee charged by the card company
    C. collecting uncollectible accounts
    D. employee errors in making a sale

Poss.	Wrong	%	Right
15	0	100%	15
15	1	93%	14
15	2	86%	13

15	3	80%	12
15	4	73%	11
15	5	66%	10
15	6	60%	9

33 PSYCH. OF INTERP. SKILLS & RETAILING PRE-TEST 1

20 Questions

___ 1. What is at least one factor that society uses to determine the success or failure of a person's career?

   A. how tall they are
   B. how much money they make
   C. what kind of car they drive
   D. how they dress

___ 2. What is the common goal set between you and your clients before you have done anything to their hair, nails, or face?

   A. improve their appearance
   B. make money
   C. buy a new car
   D. make their hair shinier

___ 3. How does the cosmetologist obtain personal satisfaction and financial gain from working in the salon?

   A. scheduling a lot of appointments
   B. answering the phone frequently
   C. helping others
   D. taking risks

___ 4. When the stylist and the client have developed a common set of thoughts, what is the term used to describe this relationship?

   A. rapport
   B. charisma
   C. charm
   D. poise

___ 5. Given two students with identical training, what factors determine why one student will graduate from school and earn a lot more money than his or her classmate?

   A. the greater money earner gives many free services
   B. the one making more money treats clients better
   C. the student earning less money can't technically do the desired work
   D. the student earning less money didn't attend school regularly

___ 6. What can be done to make the client want to come into the salon?

   A. make them feel good about their salon experience
   B. sell them products they don't need
   C. always call them by their first names
   D. all of the above

___ 7. Today, salon stylists should think of themselves as

   A. salespersons
   B. helpers
   C. educators
   D. all of the above

___ 8. What is the greatest fear faced by people in sales-related jobs?

   A. which clothes to wear
   B. what to do with the client's hair
   C. what to do with the client's face
   D. how to overcome rejection

___ 9. What is the first step in becoming a successful cosmetologist?

   A. styling the hair well
   B. answering the phone well
   C. realizing you are a salesperson
   D. knowing that you can help all clients

10. What is the name for the establishment of a positive emotional relationship between you and your client?

    A. caring
    B. bonding
    C. rapport
    D. support

11. When you are asking the clients questions about their needs, what strategy are you using to provide services or products to them?

    A. grilling
    B. discovery
    C. anticipation
    D. all of the above

12. Talking with your clients about the possible solutions to some of their appearance problems is known as a

    A. meeting
    B. consultation
    C. conversation
    D. revelation

13. When a cosmetologist has so many appointments that it is difficult to fit in new clients, what is this called?

    A. booked solid
    B. full book
    C. booked-up
    D. booked to the hilt

14. If a client is booked for a permanent wave, which of the following would be classified as an extra service?

    A. haircut
    B. frosting
    C. protein conditioner
    D. all of the above

15. How is a stylist usually paid for the sale of retail products in the salon to their clients?

    A. $2.00 per item
    B. $3.00 per item
    C. $5.00 per item
    D. a commission

16. What is the term used to describe new clients visiting you for a service as the result of another client sending them to you?

    A. word of mouth
    B. a referral
    C. lucky to have good friends
    D. a random chance

17. How do stylists provide additional money for themselves in addition to the money earned for providing services?

    A. retail sales
    B. rebooking clients before they leave the salon
    C. stealing clients from co-workers
    D. hogging phoned-in appointments

18. If you are at a social event, such as a party, what would be an effective way to let fellow party goers know what kind of work you do, and where you can be contacted for cosmetology services?

    A. write your phone number on a napkin
    B. ask them to look you up in the book
    C. pass out business cards
    D. ask your friends to write your number down on a scrap of paper and pass it along to others

19. What percentage of your business should come from friends recommending your services to friends?

    A. 1-2%
    B. 2-3%
    C. 4-6%
    D. all of the above

20. What is the term used for describing the relationship between you and your client that keeps them coming back into the salon

    A. client retention
    B. bonding
    C. referral
    D. client rapport

34 PRINCIPLES OF ELECTRICITY PRE-TEST 1

15 Questions

___ 1. What is the electrical device that reduces 120 volts of electricity down so that it can be used for facial treatments?

A. wall plate
B. resistor
C. transformer
D. reformer

___ 2. When a current and heat are used together to remove unwanted hair, this method is known as

A. the blend
B. waxing
C. epilating
D. zipping

___ 3. What is the name for the electrical process that forces chemicals through the unbroken skin?

A. osmosis
B. phoresis
C. photosynthesis
D. static

___ 4. Faradic electro-therapy is used on the skin to

A. maintain muscle tone
B. reduce circulation
C. reduce production of sebum
D. maintain skin color

___ 5. Which current is used in a high-frequency treatment?

A. faradic
B. galvanic
C. tesla
D. sinusoidal

___ 6. If a high-frequency treatment is given indirectly, the metal electrode is held by the

A. cosmetologist
B. receptionist
C. client
D. operator

___ 7. High-frequency scalp treatments are only used on hair that is

A. dry
B. wet
C. damp
D. towel dry

___ 8. The device that stops the flow of electricity when wires are overloaded is called a fuse or

A. live wire
B. circuit breaker
C. electric breaker
D. electric stopper

___ 9. A continuous flow of electricity that only flows in one direction is known as

A. mm
B. c c
C. d c
D. a c

___ 10. An ohm is a measure of electrical

A. potential
B. strength
C. resistance
D. pressure

___ 11. A measure of electrical potential or pressure is called a(n)

A. ampere
B. volt
C. current
D. ohm

12. The device that regulates the flow of electricity is called a(n)

A. regulator
B. conductor
C. insulator
D. rheostat

13. Something that allows electricity to travel along easily is called a(n)

A. electron
B. conductor
C. insulator
D. inductor

14. Traveling units of electricity are called

A. protons
B. electrons
C. electrolytes
D. leukocytes

15. Which of the following is not a benefit of using a high-frequency unit on the scalp?

A. normalizing
B. stimulating
C. germicidal
D. relaxing

Poss.	Wrong	%	Right
15	0	100%	15
15	1	93%	14
15	2	87%	13
15	3	80%	12
15	4	73%	11
15	5	67%	10

---

35 CHEMISTRY OF COSMETOLOGY PRE-TEST 1

32 Questions

1. The science that deals with the makeup of matter and its changes is called

A. etiology
B. chemistry
C. bacteriology
D. cosmetology

2. Inorganic chemistry deals mainly with things made from

A. salt
B. minerals
C. compounds
D. carbon

3. An example of gas used in a beauty salon is

A. ammonium
B. ultra-violet
C. high-frequency
D. formaldehyde

4. The chemical properties of a substance are changed during

A. air waving
B. permanent coloring
C. bleaching
D. B and C

5. A liquid used to dissolve one substance into another one is called a(n)

A. solvent
B. organic
C. substitute
D. suspension

6. Elements joined together but which keep their individual identities are called

A. atoms
B. solutes
C. mixtures
D. solvents

7. When something has a definite form, such as wood, glass, or ice, it is an example of a

A. liquid
B. solid
C. gas
D. gel

97

___ 8. A solution containing more hydroxyl than hydrogen ions is a

A. sugar
B. salt
C. base
D. crystal

___ 9. Kitchen salt is an example of a

A. base
B. compound
C. gas
D. liquid

___ 10. Hydrogen peroxide would have a pH value in the range of

A. 3.5 to 4
B. 4.5 to 5.5
C. 6.5 to 7.5
D. 8 to 8.5

___ 11. Chemical relaxers would have a pH value in the range of

A. 4.5 to 5.5
B. 6 to 7.5
C. 8 to 8.5
D. 11.5 to 14

___ 12. What is the smallest structural unit of a substance?

A. atom
B. molecule
C. micron
D. element

___ 13. Compounds are a combination of two or more

A. elements
B. atoms
C. molecules
D. substances

___ 14. Suspensions generally have an appearance that is

A. clear
B. cloudy
C. translucent
D. opaque

___ 15. The pH range of a cold waving solution would be

A. 3.5 to 4.5
B. 5.0 to 6.0
C. 6.0 to 7.5
D. 8.5 to 9.5

___ 16. The pH value of distilled water would be

A. 3
B. 5
C. 7
D. 9

___ 17. A solution that has more hydrogen ions is said to be

A. acid
B. alkali
C. a base
D. neutral

___ 18. A neutral pH is

A. 4
B. 5
C. 6
D. 7

___ 19. Organic chemistry is mainly interested in things that used to be

A. dead
B. materials
C. alive
D. chemicals

___ 20. Anything that occupies space and has weight is called

A. a molecule
B. an atom
C. matter
D. velocity

___ 21. Chemical energy is released during which of the following services?

A. temporary color
B. lightening
C. air waving
D. shaping

___ 22. The smallest unit of a substance that still has all the properties of that substance is a(n)

    A. mixture
    B. atom
    C. compound
    D. carbon

___ 23. When a new product is made by joining two or more substances, this would be called a

    A. compound
    B. base
    C. atom
    D. element

___ 24. An atom is the smallest part of a(n)

    A. element
    B. neutron
    C. mixture
    D. eon

___ 25. Particles dissolved by a solvent are called

    A. acids
    B. solutes
    C. bases
    D. compounds

___ 26. When a solid is mixed with a liquid, the new substance is called a(n)

    A. alkaline
    B. acid
    C. base
    D. suspension

___ 27. Mixtures differ from compounds in that they are not mixed

    A. in a liquid form
    B. physically
    C. chemically
    D. in a gaseous form

___ 28. The main function of an emulsifying agent is to

    A. suspend one liquid in another
    B. break up and dispense dirt
    C. break up oil into separate droplets
    D. suspend a mixture in a colloid substance

___ 29. A solution containing an equal number of hydrogen and hydroxyl ions is said to be

    A. acid
    B. alkaline
    C. neutral
    D. none of the above

___ 30. Hydrogen ions are electrically charged particles of

    A. hydrogen
    B. oxygen
    C. sulfur
    D. hydroxis

___ 31. The expression "acid-balanced" refers to a product that has a pH in the range of

    A. 2.5 to 3.5
    B. 3.5 to 4.5
    C. 4.5 to 5.5
    D. 5.5 to 6.5

___ 32. The basic unit for a substance is a(n)

    A. element
    B. compound
    C. carbon
    D. reduction

Poss.	Wrong	%	Right
32	0	100%	32
32	1	97%	31
32	2	94%	30
32	3	91%	29
32	4	88%	28
32	5	84%	27
32	6	81%	26
32	7	78%	25
32	8	75%	24
32	9	72%	23
32	10	69%	22
32	11	66%	21

36 ANATOMY – BONES & MUSCLES PRE-TEST 1

    29 Questions

1. The muscle used to pucker is the
   A. obicularis oculi
   B. orbicularis oris
   C. levator labii superioris
   D. levator anguli oris

2. The depressor labii inferioris is the muscle that
   A. lowers the forearm
   B. forms the orbits
   C. raises the upper lip
   D. lowers the lower lip

3. The buccinator muscle is located in the area of the
   A. mouth
   B. nose
   C. ear
   D. nape

4. When smiling, the muscle that pulls the corners of the mouth up is the
   A. temporalis
   B. platysma
   C. masseter
   D. risorius

5. The muscle that draws the head back and from side to side is the
   A. latissimus dorsi
   B. orbicularis oculi
   C. trapezius
   D. sternocleidomastoideus

6. The study of the nervous system is called
   A. neurology
   B. myology
   C. osteology
   D. angiology

7. All communication in the body is controlled by the
   A. vascular system
   B. skeletal system
   C. endocrine system
   D. nervous system

8. What types of neurons carry impulses away from the brain?
   A. afferent
   B. efferent
   C. sensory
   D. dendrite

9. The brain and the spine (cerebrospinal) are also known as the
   A. central nervous system
   B. autonomic nervous system
   C. parasympathetic nervous system
   D. sympathetic nervous system

10. Voluntary muscles are controlled by which system?
   A. peripheral
   B. skeletal
   C. autonomic
   D. sympathetic

11. The part of the brain encased by the occipital bone is the
   A. cerebellum
   B. cerebrum
   C. pons
   D. medulla oblongata

12. During a facial that includes the forehead, eyebrows, and nose, which nerves are affected?
   A. supratrochlear
   B. maxillary
   C. mandibular
   D. auriculotemporal

13. Mental nerves are facial nerves that are located in the area of the
   A. eyelids and forehead
   B. nose and eyelids
   C. upper lip and cheeks
   D. lower lip and jaw

14. Which facial nerve is the main motor nerve of the face?
   A. third
   B. fifth
   C. seventh
   D. eleventh

15. The forehead is formed by the

    A. ethmoid bone
    B. frontal bone
    C. phenoid bone
    D. mandible bone

16. The nerve that goes to the thumb side of the forearm and hand is the

    A. clavicle
    B. digital
    C. radial
    D. medial

17. Nerves in the fingers are called

    A. finger nerves
    B. phalangy nerves
    C. digital nerves
    D. hand nerves

18. Study of the structure of the human body is called

    A. anatomy
    B. psychology
    C. myology
    D. angiology

19. The smallest functional unit in the human body is the

    A. pore
    B. molecule
    C. atom
    D. cell

20. The name given to the brain of each cell is the

    A. cytoplasm
    B. nucleus
    C. center
    D. mitotic

21. The ability of the body to move is provided by which system?

    A. vascular
    B. nervous
    C. muscular
    D. skeletal

22. A group of organs that work together to keep the body alive is called a

    A. network
    B. tissue
    C. gland
    D. system

23. Osteology is the scientific study of

    A. muscles
    B. nerves
    C. blood
    D. bones

24. Bones serve the body by

    A. supplying blood to nourish it
    B. covering and protecting it
    C. supporting it and protecting it
    D. keeping tissue together and protecting it

25. Compact bone tissue is found mainly in the

    A. sockets of short bones
    B. shaft of long bones
    C. outside ligaments
    D. skull

26. A fibrous sheath that covers each bone is known as the

    A. periosteum
    B. ventricle
    C. matrix
    D. lunula

27. The smooth, elastic tissue that acts as a shock absorber between bones is called

    A. marrow
    B. cartilage
    C. ligament
    D. epithelial

28. The point at which two or more bones are joined is referred to as a

    A. junction
    B. union
    C. joint
    D. intersection

___ 29. The eight bones that encase the brain are known as the

A. epicranius
B. cranium
C. cerebrum
D. skull

Poss.	Wrong	%	Right
29	0	100%	29
29	1	97%	28
29	2	93%	27
29	3	90%	26
29	4	86%	25
29	5	83%	24
29	6	79%	23
29	7	76%	22
29	8	72%	21
29	9	69%	20
29	10	66%	19
29	11	62%	18

37 ANATOMY – VASCULAR & ENDOCRINE PRE-TEST 1

32 Questions

___ 1. Angiology is related to the study of

A. bones
B. muscles
C. blood
D. nerves

___ 2. The circulatory system functions to bring food materials and what else to the cells of the body?

A. oxygen
B. melanin
C. hydrogen
D. calcium

___ 3. The two upper chambers of the heart that receive the blood are also known as the

A. auricles
B. ventricles
C. bicuspids
D. tricuspids

___ 4. Vessels that carry blood from the heart to the body tissue are called

A. veins
B. arteries
C. capillaries
D. lymphatics

___ 5. Very small blood vessels that are composed of only one layer of tissue are

A. veins
B. arteries
C. ventricles
D. capillaries

___ 6. Which item below rids the body of carbon dioxide?

A. kidneys
B. heart
C. lungs
D. liver

___ 7. Generally, the temperature of the body and blood is

A. 96.6 degrees
B. 97.6 degrees
C. 98.6 degrees
D. 99.6 degrees

___ 8. The substance that gives blood its characteristic red color is

A. thrombocytes
B. leukocytes
C. hemoglobin
D. plasma

___ 9. Which blood cells are the main infection fighters of the body?

   A. leukocytes
   B. erythrocytes
   C. hemoglobin
   D. red blood cells

___ 10. Blood platelets cause the blood to

   A. oxygenate
   B. clot
   C. flow
   D. hydrogenate

___ 11. Blood cells that fight infection in the body are called

   A. white
   B. red
   C. erythrocytes
   D. thrombocytes

___ 12. A colorless liquid that comes from plasma is

   A. lacteals
   B. lymph
   C. platelets
   D. vena cava

___ 13. The large lymphatic vessels empty into the

   A. chest
   B. stomach
   C. heart
   D. pancreas

___ 14. The main artery branch of the aorta that supplies blood to the head, face, and neck is the

   A. posterior auricular
   B. anterior auricular
   C. common carotid
   D. common fumer

___ 15. The posterior auricular artery supplies blood to the scalp behind and above the

   A. neck
   B. occipital
   C. forehead
   D. ear

___ 16. The endocrine system contains only

   A. ducted glands
   B. ductless glands
   C. compact bones
   D. cancellous bones

___ 17. The body's ability to withstand stress is determined by the chemical known as

   A. iron
   B. potassium
   C. thiamine
   D. adrenaline

___ 18. The gland found at the base of the brain is the

   A. pituitary
   B. renal
   C. hypothalamus
   D. adrenal

___ 19. If the pancreas is not functioning the way it should, what condition develops?

   A. hair loss
   B. diabetes
   C. hyperthyroidism
   D. hardening of the arteries

___ 20. The thyroid gland is located in the

   A. stomach
   B. head
   C. neck
   D. chest

___ 21. The yellow, watery fluid part of blood is

   A. red blood cells
   B. thrombocytes
   C. plasma
   D. erythrocytes

___ 22. Leukocytes are also called

   A. red blood cells
   B. white blood cells
   C. blue blood cells
   D. none of the above

___ 23. The colorless cells that cause blood to clot are

A. erythrocytes
B. leukocytes
C. thrombocytes
D. melanocytes

___ 24. The vascular system is divided into two systems, the circulatory system and the

A. endocrine system
B. lymphatic system
C. nervous system
D. respiratory system

___ 25. The special cells made by lymph nodes are called

A. erythrocytes
B. platelets
C. lacteals
D. lymphocytes

___ 26. A special set of vessels that carry chyle in the lymph system is called

A. lacteals
B. platelets
C. lymphocytes
D. lymph nodes

___ 27. The largest artery in the body is the

A. aorta
B. internal carotid
C. external carotid
D. pulmonary

___ 28. The facial artery that supplies blood to the lower part of the face, mouth, and nose is the

A. external maxillary
B. superficial temporal
C. transverse facial
D. ophthalmic

___ 29. The brachial artery divides in the arm to become the radial and

A. fumer arteries
B. ulnar arteries
C. humerus arteries
D. tibi arteries

___ 30. The endocrine system releases special chemicals in the blood called

A. serums
B. steroids
C. hormones
D. platelets

___ 31. The endocrine system controls

A. reproduction
B. general health
C. growth
D. all of the above

___ 32. The gland that has the special job of regulating the water balance in the body is called the

A. pituitary
B. thyroid
C. hypothalamus
D. adrenal

Poss.	Wrong	%	Right
32	0	100%	32
32	1	97%	31
32	2	94%	30
32	3	91%	29
32	4	88%	28
32	5	84%	27
32	6	81%	26
32	7	78%	25
32	8	75%	24
32	9	72%	23
32	10	69%	22
32	11	66%	21

24 Questions

___ 1. Hairstyling contests may include

A. daytime hairstyling
B. men's hairstyling
C. fantasy hairstyling
D. all of the above

___ 2. A manager-operator should be a cosmetologist who

A. is at least thirty years old
B. has been a working cosmetologist for two or three years
C. has experience in managing beauty schools
D. owns his/her own beauty salon

___ 3. The advantage(s) of being a manager-operator may include the opportunity to learn about

A. overhead expenses
B. accounts payable
C. inventory
D. all of the above

___ 4. A salon owner's income may vary according to the

A. number of salons owned
B. size of the salon
C. location of the salon
D. all of the above

___ 5. Cosmetology instructors must have

A. a license issued by the State Board of Cosmetology
B. a five year college degree in psychology
C. five years of experience in a salon
D. three years of experience as a field technician

___ 6. The successful instructor must have

A. above average patience
B. an interest in students' learning
C. an interest in the profession
D. all of the above

___ 7. Personal grooming relates to one's

A. daily appearance
B. daily cleanliness
C. hairstyle and voice
D. A and B

___ 8. Which term below fits the job description for a person that specializes in preserving the beauty of the client's face and neck in the beauty salon?

A. facial expert
B. esthetician
C. electrologist
D. dermatologist

___ 9. Personal hygiene relates to

A. promoting one's own health
B. preservation of one's health
C. oral care
D. A and B

___ 10. To communicate, a thought or attitude is conveyed

A. verbally
B. nonverbally
C. person to person
D. all of the above

___ 11. Verbal communication refers to

A. what is said
B. the way something is said
C. tone of voice
D. all of the above

___ 12. A good telephone voice expresses

A. distinct communication
B. pleasant attitude
C. enthusiasm
D. all of the above

___ 13. A cosmetologist cannot legally work while having

A. a headache
B. a contagious disease
C. problems outside the salon
D. oral surgery done

14. A licensed cosmetologist may also be referred to as a(n)

    A. operator
    B. coiffeur
    C. hairdresser
    D. all of the above

15. The cosmetologist is paid 50 percent commission after she/he has

    A. equaled the minimum wage law
    B. tripled the minimum wage law
    C. doubled the minimum wage law
    D. worked in the salon for six years

16. The main job of an electrologist is

    A. removal of unwanted facial hair
    B. shaping the eyebrows and eye lashes
    C. shaping the toenails and fingernails
    D. removal of curl from over-curly hair

17. A field technician demonstrates the use of products in

    A. various cities
    B. the salon
    C. the schools
    D. all of the above

18. After bathing, a common sense practice to prevent body odor might be to apply

    A. a dry towel
    B. a deodorant
    C. perfume
    D. alcohol

19. Dental care for preserving healthy teeth starts with a daily mouthwash and

    A. rinsing and flushing
    B. rubbing and scratching
    C. rinsing and rubbing
    D. brushing and flossing

20. Halitosis is another name for

    A. scalp odor
    B. body odor
    C. oily skin
    D. bad breath

21. An antiseptic mouthwash will minimize or treat

    A. halitosis
    B. osmosis
    C. hygiene
    D. sanitation

22. The cosmetologist practicing correct posture will find it reduces

    A. skin discoloration
    B. acne
    C. canities
    D. back strain

23. For good standing posture, the abdomen should be flat, chin level with the floor, and

    A. knees together
    B. shoulders relaxed
    C. legs crossed
    D. arms folded

24. The prevention of fatigue is one of the benefits of good

    A. posture
    B. hygiene
    C. sanitation
    D. personality

Poss.	Wrong	%	Right
24	0	100%	24
24	1	96%	23
24	2	92%	22
24	3	88%	21
24	4	83%	20
24	5	79%	19
24	6	75%	18
24	7	71%	17
24	8	67%	16
24	9	63%	15

16 Questions

___ 1. The governing body in most states that is supposed to discipline members who violate professional ethics is the

A. bureau of ethics
B. state legislature
C. state association
D. state board

___ 2. Responsibility means your own reliability and

A. integrity
B. honesty
C. discipline
D. punctuality

___ 3. Your professional responsibility to your co-workers should include not

A. recruiting employees from other salons
B. saying that another's work is inferior
C. learning new techniques
D. attending educational classes

___ 4. Ethics is a system that measures human behavior that is

A. voluntary
B. involuntary
C. imposed by local police
D. imposed by the federal government

___ 5. A professional attitude is

A. natural
B. given when you are licensed
C. acquired in enrollment
D. learned

___ 6. An employer has to assume responsibility for

A. services given by employees
B. giving advanced training classes
C. setting fair and equal prices
D. all of the above

___ 7. Competence means mastering information and

A. art
B. skill
C. science
D. craft

___ 8. You are conducting yourself in an ethical way toward your employer if you

A. promote a good reputation for the salon
B. provide only quality service
C. keep private information given to you in confidence
D. all of the above

___ 9. Professional ethics are expressed in

A. rules
B. regulations
C. codes
D. traditions

___ 10. Proper behavior toward other people, such as clients, employer, and co-workers, is known as professional

A. attitude
B. ethics
C. sincerity
D. diligence

___ 11. The responsible cosmetologist will

A. overcharge according to what the traffic will bear
B. falsely advertise products and services
C. talk about one client to another
D. provide only needed services

___ 12. A professional code of ethics

A. is always enforced by the state board
B. is not always necessary for cosmetology
C. is always covered by rules and regulations
D. goes beyond laws and regulations

13. It is very unethical to

    A. condition hair
    B. gossip
    C. give cold waves
    D. shape hair

14. The cosmetologist who is dependable will earn

    A. the honor and praise of others
    B. the respect and loyalty of others
    C. the advice and counsel of others
    D. fame and fortune

15. Ethical codes are set for the beauty industry especially to earn the respect and confidence of the

    A. other members
    B. barbers
    C. public
    D. state board

16. It is your responsibility to

    A. give as much service as needed by the client
    B. learn new methods of hairstyling
    C. give services based on quality and price
    D. all of the above

Poss.	Wrong	%	Right
16	0	100%	16
16	1	94%	15
16	2	88%	14
16	3	81%	13
16	4	75%	12
16	5	69%	11

3 SANITATION AND STERILIZATION POST-TEST 1

30 Questions

1. Once sanitized, combs and brushes may be kept that way by ultraviolet rays, or

    A. boiling water
    B. autoclave
    C. a fumigant
    D. borax

2. Sterilizing chemicals are

    A. allergenic
    B. harmless
    C. nontoxic
    D. poisonous

3. A fumigant is made for a dry sanitizer when a tablespoon of borax is combined with a tablespoon of

    A. peroxide
    B. formaldehyde
    C. distilled water
    D. acid shampoo

4. A method of sterilizing that uses moist heat or steam is called

    A. germicidal
    B. physical
    C. chemical
    D. animal

5. An effective chemical used in a wet sanitizer is

    A. soap
    B. quats
    C. alcohol
    D. alum

6. A chemical solution used to halt the growth of bacteria is a (n)

    A. fumigant
    B. bactericide
    C. antiseptic
    D. disinfectant

___ 7. A wet sanitizer contains

   A. germicides
   B. bactericides
   C. fungicides
   D. all of the above

___ 8. In order to work in a beauty salon, the cosmetologist must be free from

   A. acute rheumatism
   B. contagious diseases
   C. chronic arthritis
   D. dandruff

___ 9. Bacteriology is the scientific study of

   A. parasites
   B. bacteria
   C. nonpathogenic bacteria
   D. staphylococci

___ 10. Antiseptics are used in the beauty school or salon to

   A. activate chemicals for sterilization
   B. prevent the growth of bacteria
   C. accelerate the growth of bacteria
   D. destroy bacteria

___ 11. If diseases are identified in the beauty salon, they should always be treated by a

   A. chiropractor
   B. dentist
   C. cosmetologist
   D. medical doctor

___ 12. Viewed with a microscope, cocci bacteria would appear as what shape?

   A. spiral
   B. square
   C. round
   D. rod

___ 13. Clean towels should be stored

   A. in a closed container
   B. on top of the styling station
   C. on the floor near the shampoo area
   D. in an open laundry basket

___ 14. A pimple is an infection which is classified as

   A. communicable
   B. general
   C. local
   D. chronic

___ 15. Metal electrodes should be sanitized with

   A. 2% quats
   B. 80% ammonium
   C. 20% peroxide
   D. 70% alcohol

___ 16. Sharp metallic implements, such as scissors, should be sanitized with

   A. 40% alcohol
   B. 50% alcohol
   C. 60% alcohol
   D. 70% alcohol

___ 17. When not in use, a sanitized comb should be kept in a (n)

   A. wet sanitizer
   B. uniform pocket
   C. ordinary drawer
   D. dry sanitizer

___ 18. Moist heat sanitizing is done by

   A. cooking in an oven
   B. boiling
   C. fumes in a cup
   D. frying in a pan

___ 19. Sterilization is a process in which

   A. foul odors are destroyed
   B. bacteria remains alive
   C. only beneficial bacteria are destroyed
   D. both types of bacteria are destroyed

___ 20. A clean, laundered towel should be used

   A. when the one in use becomes stained
   B. when the one in use looks soiled
   C. for every person
   D. every third person

21. All products poured from their original containers and used in the beauty salon should be

    A. tightly capped with a lid
    B. clearly labeled
    C. poured into clear bottles
    D. poured into glass bottles only

22. A client trips in the shampoo area and falls down. You think the leg is broken. What should you do?

    A. pack leg with ice compresses
    B. set the leg with splints
    C. call for medical assistance
    D. lift client to facial chair

23. By law, which of the following must each beauty salon have available?

    A. a fire blanket
    B. a hot water dispenser
    C. an emergency eye wash station
    D. a fire extinguisher

24. Wet sanitizers should contain a solution that is

    A. 1/2% formalin
    B. 1/2% hydrogen peroxide
    C. 1/2% alcohol
    D. a disinfectant

25. To be effective, quats is used in a strength range of

    A. 1:200 solution
    B. 1:250 solution
    C. 1:500 solution
    D. 1:1000 solution

26. To be an effective antiseptic, hydrogen peroxide is used in a strength of

    A. 3% solution
    B. 4% solution
    C. 5-6% solution
    D. 7-10% solution

27. How is the AIDS disease transmitted from one person to another?

    A. blood
    B. semen
    C. vaginal secretions
    D. all of the above

28. What route of transmission does the disease follow?

    A. injection
    B. blood transfusion
    C. maternal
    D. all of the above

29. How is the AIDS virus destroyed outside the body?

    A. exposure to air and heat
    B. cold water
    C. rubbing with a towel
    D. wiping with a sponge

30. In order for a quats solution to effectively sanitize combs and brushes, what is needed?

    A. short immersion time
    B. long immersion time
    C. infrared light rays
    D. heat

Poss.	Wrong	%	Right
30	0	100%	30
30	1	97%	29
30	2	93%	28
30	3	90%	27
30	4	87%	26
30	5	83%	25
30	6	80%	24
30	7	77%	23
30	8	73%	22
30	9	70%	21
30	10	67%	20
30	11	63%	19

30 Questions

___ 1. To equal the strength of 70% ethyl alcohol, you would have to use

   A. 20% isopropyl alcohol
   B. 39% isopropyl alcohol
   C. 85% isopropyl alcohol
   D. 99% isopropyl alcohol

___ 2. If cosmetology implements are aseptic, then they are

   A. free from bacteria
   B. unsanitary
   C. soiled
   D. covered

___ 3. A person immune to a disease, but who can infect others is known as a(n)

   A. clinical
   B. medical
   C. agent
   D. carrier

___ 4. Things that may be considered a health hazard are

   A. forced air furnaces
   B. impure air
   C. clean body and clothes
   D. hygienic salon practices

___ 5. The germicidal light used in some dry sanitizers is known as

   A. fluorescent light
   B. ultra-violet light
   C. infrared light
   D. incandescent light

___ 6. Uncleanliness can produce germs that cause

   A. good health
   B. local canities
   C. disease
   D. malnutrition

___ 7. Another name for public hygiene is

   A. grooming
   B. hair care
   C. sanitation
   D. community

___ 8. Disease is caused mainly from the lack of

   A. cleanliness
   B. deodorizers
   C. cold water
   D. hairspray

___ 9. The electrical device that removes stale air from the salon is called a(n)

   A. humidifier
   B. ceiling fan
   C. dehumidifier
   D. exhaust fan

___ 10. Practices in the beauty salon that help preserve the health of the public are called

   A. fumigation/deodorization
   B. salon grooming
   C. cleaning/washing
   D. sanitation/sterilization

___ 11. To be effective, a solution of quaternary ammonium compound solution requires

   A. mixing with alcohol
   B. lengthy contact time
   C. mixing with peroxide
   D. short contact time

___ 12. An article that would melt if exposed to heat may be sanitized using

   A. a soapy water solution
   B. a hydrogen peroxide solution
   C. a disinfectant solution
   D. infrared rays

___ 13. A dry sanitizer is only effective when it contains

   A. formaldehyde fumes
   B. 10% alcohol
   C. hydrogen peroxide
   D. disinfectant solutions

___ 14. If the eye has been chemically burned, what should be done?

   A. flush eye with cool water
   B. flush eye with boric acid
   C. apply alcohol
   D. apply quats

15. When removing implements from a wet sanitizer you should wear

    A. an operator apron
    B. a hair net
    C. rubber gloves
    D. a neutralizing bib

16. An example of the chemical method of sanitization is

    A. boiling
    B. quats
    C. infrared rays
    D. steaming

17. To be effective for sanitation, the strength of the quats to be used should be at least

    A. 1:1000
    B. 1:1300
    C. 1:1400
    D. 1:2000

18. What do electronic air precipitators remove from the air?

    A. viruses
    B. bacteria
    C. disinfectants
    D. all of the above

19. Formaldehyde discs are used in a

    A. towel sanitizer
    B. opened container
    C. dry sanitizer
    D. wet sanitizer

20. Generally, bacteria are classified into how many types?

    A. three
    B. five
    C. seven
    D. nine

21. Quaternary ammonium compound is used mainly in the school or salon as a(n)

    A. soapy solution
    B. astringent
    C. disinfectant
    D. wave set

22. Hair cutting implements are sanitized with

    A. 70% alcohol
    B. 40% alcohol
    C. 30% formalin solution
    D. 30% alcohol

23. Disinfectants and germicides affect the growth of bacteria by

    A. destroying growth
    B. decreasing growth
    C. increasing growth
    D. halting growth

24. A carrier is a person who has a disease that is

    A. acute
    B. occupational
    C. common
    D. contagious

25. Nonpathogenic bacteria is defined by the cosmetologist as being

    A. beneficial
    B. harmless
    C. disease producing
    D. A and B

26. Blow combs should be sanitized by immersion in a solution that is

    A. 10% formalin
    B. soapy
    C. 5% formalin
    D. none of the above

27. While giving a manicure, implements such as orangewood sticks should be kept

    A. in your pocket
    B. in a drawer
    C. in disinfectant solution
    D. sitting on the work station

28. Before and after using the shampoo bowl to shampoo a client, you should

    A. sanitize it with a disinfectant
    B. wipe it with a towel
    C. spray it with some water
    D. wash it with a lemon rinse

29. Because headrest covers are in the same category as towels used on the client, how often should they be changed?

   A. once a week
   B. after each use
   C. twice a day
   D. every other week

30. A chemical vapor used in the sanitation of cosmetology implements is known as

   A. an antiseptic
   B. a fumigant
   C. a disinfectant
   D. an autoclave

Poss.	Wrong	%	Right
30	0	100%	30
30	1	97%	29
30	2	93%	28
30	3	90%	27
30	4	87%	26
30	5	83%	25
30	6	80%	24
30	7	77%	23
30	8	73%	22
30	9	70%	21
30	10	67%	20
30	11	63%	19

3 SANITATION AND STERILIZATION POST-TEST 3

25 Questions

1. The basic procedure for sanitizing soiled implements, such as brushes, is to

   A. remove hair
   B. wash in soapy water
   C. place in wet sanitizer
   D. all of the above

2. Most sanitizing chemicals

   A. are quite harmless
   B. may be taken internally
   C. are very poisonous if swallowed
   D. are safe for all uses

3. The plumbing device that protects the fresh-water supply from the back-up contaminated water is called a

   A. vacuum breaker
   B. horizontal elbow
   C. union joint
   D. safety connector

4. A 70 percent alcohol solution would be used to sanitize which of the following items?

   A. styling chair
   B. dry sanitizer
   C. scissors and razor
   D. wet sanitizer

5. After implements are removed from the ultraviolet sanitizer, they should be placed in a(n)

   A. wet sanitizer
   B. opened sanitizer
   C. dry sanitizer
   D. cold sanitizer

6. Which of the items below is used to sanitize and dry combs and brushes?

   A. cleanser
   B. ultraviolet sanitizer
   C. wet sanitizer
   D. alcohol

7. Which of the following products is flammable?

   A. alcohol
   B. nail polish remover
   C. hair spray
   D. all of the above

8. Soiled towels should be stored in a covered

   A. linen basket
   B. closed container
   C. plastic container
   D. laundry basket

9. With flammable salon chemicals, what should be your most important consideration?

   A. light
   B. heat
   C. moisture
   D. air

10. If a salon has a fire extinguisher, how often must it be serviced and inspected?

    A. monthly
    B. bi-monthly
    C. semi-annually
    D. annually

11. After combs and brushes are removed from a formalin solution, they should be placed in a(n)

    A. opened drawer
    B. ultraviolet sanitizer
    C. roller tray
    D. all of the above

12. An ammonium solution or Lysol is used mainly to sanitize a

    A. pressing comb
    B. cosmetologist's shoe
    C. manicuring chair
    D. shampoo bowl

13. To be effectively sanitized, combs and brushes should be immersed in a solution that is

    A. a disinfectant
    B. a cleanser
    C. caustic
    D. a deodorant

14. Waste materials, such as hair removed from combs and brushes, should be put

    A. in a closed container
    B. in a corner
    C. alongside a waste basket
    D. in a neat pile

15. Quats is used in the beauty salon as a (n)

    A. astringent
    B. deodorant
    C. disinfectant
    D. fumigant

16. To be effective, a dry sanitizer should contain

    A. a fumigant
    B. alcohol
    C. violet-ray sanitizer
    D. wet sanitizer

17. Bacteria are also referred to as one-celled

    A. viruses
    B. inorganics
    C. microorganisms
    D. matter

18. A common skin antiseptic would be

    A. 3% hydrogen peroxide
    B. 6%hydrogen peroxide
    C. 9%hydrogen peroxide
    D. 12% hydrogen peroxide

19. Formaldehyde, if taken internally, is

    A. harmless
    B. toxic
    C. sometimes harmful
    D. nontoxic

20. A soapy solution is used to remove foreign particles from

    A. brushes
    B. thinning shears
    C. a razor
    D. an ultraviolet sanitizer

21. Rollers, combs, and brushes should be immersed in a 10 percent formalin solution for

    A. 5 minutes
    B. 10 minutes
    C. 15 minutes
    D. 20 minutes

22. Ultraviolet rays are important sanitizers because they

    A. are the most effective physical method of sanitation
    B. have a germicidal effect
    C. kill most bacteria and some viruses
    D. all of the above

23. The sanitizing method most often used in a beauty salon is that of

A. chemical disinfectants
B. boiling
C. baking in stoves
D. washing in soap and water

24. When a disinfectant solution is put in a receptacle with a cover, it is called a

A. closed sanitizer
B. dry sanitizer
C. violet-ray sanitizer
D. wet sanitizer

25. The basic procedure for sanitizing soiled implements, such as brushes, is to

A. remove hair
B. wash in soapy water
C. rinse, dry, and place in dry sanitizer
D. all of the above

Poss.	Wrong	%	Right
25	0	100%	25
25	1	96%	24
25	2	92%	23
25	3	88%	22
25	4	84%	21
25	5	80%	20
25	6	76%	19
25	7	72%	18
25	8	68%	17
25	9	64%	16
25	10	60%	15

4 DESCRIBE THE HAIR POST-TEST 1

21 Questions

1. Before using a hot wax depilatory, the cosmetologist should

A. apply gauze to the work area
B. give the client instructions
C. check to be sure client is comfortable
D. check the temperature of the wax

2. A baby born with gray hair would have a condition described by the cosmetologist as

A. acquired canities
B. pediatric canities
C. congenital canities
D. premature canities

3. When viewed under a microscope, cross-sections of wavy hair will usually appear

A. flat
B. semi-flat
C. semi-oval
D. round

4. Generally, the rate of hair growth on different parts of the body will be

A. the same everywhere
B. faster above the waist
C. faster below the waist
D. different from area to area

5. The technical term applied to the cyclical period when the hair begins to grow is the

A. anagen stage
B. terminal stage
C. telogen stage
D. origin stage

6. A client with natural red hair color will have about

A. 90,000 scalp hairs
B. 91,000 scalp hairs
C. 93,000 scalp hairs
D. 95,000 scalp hairs

7. If a client with natural red, black, brown, and blond hair colors, respectively, entered the school or salon, which color would normally have the greatest number of scalp hairs?

A. red
B. brown
C. black
D. blond

115

8. Hair usually grows faster in a climate that is
   A. warm
   B. cold
   C. moderate
   D. humid

9. The condition of the hair is determined by its
   A. texture
   B. porosity
   C. elasticity
   D. all of the above

10. When describing the amount of moisture the hair will absorb, we are referring to its
    A. appearance
    B. texture
    C. elasticity
    D. porosity

11. Shaving is one way to remove hair from the
    A. palms
    B. armpits
    C. soles
    D. eyebrows

12. When wet hair is stretched 50 percent longer than its original length, we are referring to the hair's
    A. flexibility
    B. longevity
    C. elasticity
    D. durability

13. What general prefix is used to describe most hair diseases?
    A. tricho
    B. tricko
    C. trio
    D. trigo

14. Hypertrichosis is a condition that is also called
    A. supercilia hair
    B. superfluous hair
    C. ringed hair
    D. twisted hair

15. When alopecia appears on the head, it looks like
    A. red, circular bald patches
    B. scaly, rectangular bald patches
    C. non-inflamed, oval bald patches
    D. oily scales and oval bald patches

16. Alopecia areata is nonscarring, and the hair loss is usually
    A. temporary
    B. permanent
    C. semipermanent
    D. universal

17. Tinea of the scalp is characterized by
    A. oily yellow scales
    B. silver and gray scales
    C. dry yellow scales
    D. brown and yellow scales

18. Trichorrhexis nodosa is the technical name for
    A. tied hair
    B. twisted hair
    C. stretched hair
    D. knotted hair

19. Pili annulati is a technical term for hair that is
    A. beaded
    B. knotted
    C. notched
    D. ringed

20. A permanent method for removing hair is
    A. analysis
    B. electrolysis
    C. encephalitis
    D. hydrolysis

21. If a short-wave machine is used for electroloysis, hair growth is stopped because of damage to the
    A. cortex
    B. medulla
    C. papilla
    D. cuticle

Poss.	Wrong	%	Right
21	0	100%	21
21	1	95%	20
21	2	90%	19
21	3	86%	18

21	4	81%	17
21	5	76%	16
21	6	71%	15
21	7	67%	14
21	8	62%	13
21	9	57%	12

4 DESCRIBING THE HAIR POST-TEST 2

21 Questions

___ 1. The common term for canities is

A. red hair
B. grey hair
C. brown hair
D. black hair

___ 2. The common term for trichoptilosis is

A. twisted hair
B. beaded hair
C. split ends
D. waxed ends

___ 3. Using a short-wave electrical machine to stop the growth of a hair is called

A. electrolysis
B. trichosis
C. cometose
D. osmosis

___ 4. The hair is mainly made made up of a hard protein called

A. hydrogen
B. keratin
C. sodium
D. melanin

___ 5. The hair follicle gives the hair its size, direction, and

A. tone
B. shine
C. length
D. shape

___ 6. A cross-section picture of curly hair would be seen as a shape that is

A. round and circular
B. oval and semi-oval
C. square and rectangular
D. double angles

___ 7. The part of the hair that projects above the skin is known as the hair

A. root
B. follicle
C. bulb
D. shaft

___ 8. The hair follicle contains that part of the hair known as the hair

A. root
B. cuticle
C. shaft
D. appendage

___ 9. The tubelike pocket that encases the hair down into the skin is the

A. cortex
B. shaft
C. follicle
D. medulla

___ 10. The small cone-shaped projection at the base of follicle that makes hair grow is the

A. root
B. shaft
C. bulb
D. papilla

___ 11. The center layer of the hair contains the

A. cuticle
B. root
C. medulla
D. cortex

___ 12. Hair grows because it is nourished by the papilla, which contains

A. blood vessels
B. keratin cells
C. melanin cells
D. nerve cells

___ 13. The cuticle of the hair is the

   A. outer layer
   B. center layer
   C. middle layer
   D. innermost layer

___ 14. Dry hair in normal condition should stretch about

   A. 1/5 of its length
   B. 2/5 of its length
   C. 3/5 of its length
   D. 4/5 of its length

___ 15. Goose bumps are caused by the shortening of the

   A. tricep muscle
   B. bicep muscle
   C. arrector muscle
   D. facial muscle

___ 16. Hair is usually removed from the chin, or eyebrows by

   A. waxing
   B. clipping
   C. streaking
   D. tweezing

___ 17. Hair is absent from the

   A. arms
   B. chin
   C. legs
   D. lips

___ 18. The life span of an average hair is

   A. 2-4 months
   B. 5-11 months
   C. 12-18 months
   D. more than 2 years

___ 19. Excessive growth of body hair is known as

   A. hypertrichosis
   B. hypertension
   C. hypotrichosis
   D. hypotension

___ 20. The sebaceous glands secrete sebum, which keeps the hair

   A. dry
   B. soft
   C. flaky
   D. scaly

___ 21. During one month, the average hair will grow

   A. 1/4˝
   B. 1/2˝
   C. 3/4˝
   D. 1˝

Poss.	Wrong	%	Right
21	0	100%	21
21	1	95%	20
21	2	90%	19
21	3	86%	18
21	4	81%	17
21	5	76%	16
21	6	71%	15
21	7	67%	14
21	8	62%	13
21	9	57%	12

21 Questions

___ 1. When referring to fine or coarse hair, the cosmetologist is describing hair

  A. porosity
  B. elasticity
  C. texture
  D. condition

___ 2. Hair elasticity refers to how far the hair can be stretched, and return to its original shape before

  A. curling
  B. breaking
  C. shrinking
  D. contracting

___ 3. The name for hair-coloring pigment is

  A. toxin
  B. keratin
  C. melanin
  D. protein

___ 4. The name for the natural oil that keeps the hair and scalp soft and supple is

  A. grease
  B. cream
  C. sebum
  D. ointment

___ 5. When wet, a normal hair can be stretched

  A. 5-10% of its length
  B. 20-25% of its length
  C. 30-35% of its length
  D. 40-50% of its length

___ 6. Trichology is defined as the study of the

  A. hair
  B. nails
  C. skin
  D. arms

___ 7. A condition seen as oval bald patches on the head is known as alopecia

  A. totalis
  B. universalis
  C. areata
  D. axillary

___ 8. When hair loss begins well before middle age, it is called alopecia

  A. totalis
  B. prematura
  C. senilis
  D. universalis

___ 9. Hair loss resulting from old age is known as alopecia

  A. totalis
  B. prematura
  C. senilis
  D. diffuse

___ 10. The common name for tinea of the scalp is

  A. alopecia
  B. ring worm
  C. baldness
  D. diffuse

___ 11. The center layer of the hair is the

  A. cuticle
  B. cortex
  C. medulla
  D. focal

___ 12. The second, and largest layer of the hair is the

  A. cuticle
  B. cortex
  C. medulla
  D. bulb

___ 13. Natural hair-coloring pigment is located in the

  A. cuticle layer
  B. cortex layer
  C. medulla layer
  D. shaft layer

___ 14. When the hair bulb stops making melanin, the hair turns gray because the pigment is

  A. red
  B. gone
  C. blue
  D. yellow

15. The arrector pili muscle is connected to the hair

    A. shaft
    B. cortex
    C. follicle
    D. medulla

16. The part of the hair located beneath the skin is the hair

    A. shaft
    B. cuticle
    C. root
    D. cortex

17. The nerve and blood supply for a hair is the

    A. shaft
    B. papilla
    C. cortex
    D. cuticle

18. The papilla is the nipplelike projection located at the lower part of the hair

    A. cuticle
    B. melanin
    C. shaft
    D. bulb

19. Hair histology means study of the hair from a view that is

    A. cosmic
    B. microscopic
    C. atomic
    D. macro

20. Hair growth begins at its blood and nerve supply, which is the

    A. papilla
    B. shaft
    C. cuticle
    D. root

21. A liquid used to remove hair temporarily is called a

    A. remover
    B. dissolver
    C. depilatory
    D. short wave

Poss.	Wrong	%	Right
21	0	100%	21
21	1	95%	20
21	2	90%	19
21	3	86%	18
21	4	81%	17
21	5	76%	16
21	6	71%	15
21	7	67%	14
21	8	62%	13
21	9	57%	12

5 SHAMPOOING POST-TEST 1

17 Questions

1. The common term for miliaria rubra is

   A. herpes simplex
   B. milia
   C. acne
   D. prickly heat

2. If chemical services will not follow the shampoo, the service begins with which of the following procedures?

   A. examination of the scalp
   B. removal of jewelry
   C. removal of hairpins and ornaments
   D. all of the above

3. What two actions are involved in shampooing?

   A. electrical and chemical
   B. chemical and clinical
   C. physical and chemical
   D. clinical and biological

4. If a shampoo has a neutral pH, then its number value on the pH scale would be

   A. 4
   B. 5
   C. 6
   D. 7

5. To prevent water from dripping onto the floor from the shampoo bowl, what position should you leave the shampoo hose in?

   A. drain position
   B. handle position
   C. vacuum breaker position
   D. none of the above

6. If a shampoo has pH below seven (7), it is said to be

   A. acid
   B. alkaline
   C. neutral
   D. a base

7. An acid-balanced shampoo would be listed on the pH scale in the range of

   A. 3.5–4.5
   B. 4.5–5.5
   C. 5.5–6.5
   D. 6.5–7.5

8. Which of the following is not a natural acid?

   A. apple-cider vinegar
   B. lemon juice
   C. creme rinse
   D. white vinegar

9. Shampoos used to control certain scalp diseases or disorders are called

   A. herbal
   B. medicated
   C. special
   D. conditioning

10. Liquid-dry shampoos are dangerous because they are very

   A. high in pH
   B. low in pH
   C. flammable
   D. combustible

11. How should you protect the client's clothing before shampooing the hair?

   A. drape the cape over the back of the chair
   B. cover all clothing with towels
   C. place in plastic clothing protectors
   D. place plastic towels across client's shoulder

12. A disease that exists at birth is known as

   A. chronic
   B. congenital
   C. acute
   D. acquired

13. A long-term disease, such as emphysema, is called

   A. chronic
   B. congenital
   C. acute
   D. acquired

14. The medical term for dandruff is

   A. psoriasis
   B. steatoides
   C. pityriasis
   D. pediculosis

15. An excessive number of oily or waxy yellow scales that remain close to the scalp is called

   A. pityriasis capitis simplex
   B. pityriasis steatoides
   C. pediculosis
   D. herpes simplex

16. A disease caused by an animal parasite that cannot be treated in the school or salon is

   A. psoriasis
   B. herpes simplex
   C. pityriasis capitis simplex
   D. pediculosis

17. Which type of shampoo would the cosmetologist recommend for bleached (lightened) hair?

   A. medicated shampoo
   B. liquid-dry shampoo
   C. nonstripping shampoo
   D. egg shampoo

Poss.	Wrong	%	Right
17	0	100%	17
17	1	94%	16
17	2	88%	15
17	3	82%	14
17	4	76%	13
17	5	71%	12
17	6	65%	11

121

6 CONDITIONING POST-TEST 1

10 Questions

___ 1. The extent that hair can be stretched without breaking is known as

A. pressure
B. tone
C. elasticity
D. texture

___ 2. Hair texture refers to how the hair feels, and its

A. tone
B. elasticity
C. diameter
D. perimeter

___ 3. The basic protein found in the hair shaft is

A. cuticle
B. medulla
C. sebum
D. keratin

___ 4. Very small bits of protein applied to the hair are called

A. macro-proteins
B. micro-proteins
C. poultry proteins
D. substantive proteins

___ 5. A basic name for the best combination of proteins for the hair is known as

A. neutron filler
B. nucleic acid
C. vegetable protein
D. mineral protein

___ 6. Collagen is an animal protein used to

A. straighten the hair
B. wave the hair
C. condition the hair
D. curl the hair

___ 7. If damaged hair is going to be given a service that uses strong chemicals, the cosmetologist should recommend

A. preconditioning
B. prelightening
C. prefilling
D. preneutralizing

___ 8. When the hair is conditioned using strong chemicals, this is known as

A. pretreating
B. preconditioning
C. duration conditioning
D. in-process conditioning

___ 9. A more professional term used to describe hair conditioning is hair

A. repairing
B. revitalizing
C. reconstructing
D. revolutionizing

___ 10. Hair can be damaged chemically by

A. improper bleaching
B. wave setting
C. shampooing
D. hair cutting

Poss.	Wrong	%	Right
10	0	100%	10
10	1	90%	9
10	2	80%	8
10	3	70%	7
10	4	60%	6

7 SCALP TREATMENTS POST-TEST 1

5 Questions

1. You must not promise that scalp manipulations will

   A. stimulate the scalp nerves
   B. make the scalp look healthier
   C. make the hair grow
   D. increase blood circulation

2. Scalp manipulations should not be given if the hair is going to be

   A. cold waved
   B. permanently colored
   C. chemically lightened
   D. all of the above

3. Scalp conditioners are made for hair that is either oily or

   A. long
   B. dry
   C. short
   D. thin

4. If overly tight, the scalp may be made more loose and pliable from a

   A. scalp treatment
   B. cold wave
   C. shampoo
   D. hair conditioner

5. The usual benefit of a scalp treatment is that it helps normalize the

   A. hair shaft
   B. sebaceous glands
   C. thyroid gland
   D. pineal gland

Poss.	Wrong	%	Right
5	0	100%	5
5	1	80%	4
5	2	60%	3
5	3	40%	2
5	4	20%	1

8 FINGER WAVING POST-TEST 1

11 Questions

1. In order to give a good finger wave, you must first locate the

   A. new hair growth
   B. receding hairline
   C. natural wave line
   D. discolored streaks

2. Hair is much easier to finger wave with the use of a thick or heavy

   A. permanent tint
   B. cold waving lotion
   C. setting lotion
   D. acid neutralizer

3. The part of the finger-wave shaping between two ridges is the wave

   A. pattern
   B. trough
   C. arch
   D. crown

4. After the hair has been finger waved, it should only be combed out when

   A. thoroughly pressed
   B. air waved
   C. sprayed with lacquer
   D. thoroughly dried

5. The terms used to describe how a strand or section of hair is combed are

   A. hair shaping
   B. hair direction
   C. shoulder ridge
   D. ridge molding

6. In finger waving, an important aid is

   A. hair lacquer
   B. ammonia water
   C. cold wave lotion
   D. setting lotion

123

___ 7. A curved line between two points on a curved surface is called a(n)

A. arc
B. angle
C. shaping
D. ridge

___ 8. When shifting the hair to form a wave ridge, the comb is parallel to the

A. ring finger
B. forefinger
C. index finger
D. thumb

___ 9. When combing the hair before finger waving, the general direction should be

A. circular
B. triangular
C. straight
D. diagonal

___ 10. A lasting finger wave must be shaped and molded

A. against the growth direction
B. with the growth direction
C. with the parting
D. away from the parting

___ 11. When finger waving, the hair is held against the head to make troughs and ridges with the

A. thumb and little finger
B. index and little finger
C. index and middle finger
D. middle finger and thumb

Poss.	Wrong	%	Right
11	0	100%	11
11	1	91%	10
11	2	82%	9
11	3	73%	8
11	4	64%	7

9 SCULPTURE CURLS POST-TEST 1

20 Questions

___ 1. A line running across the page from the left side to the right side would be what kind of a line?

A. diagonal
B. vertical
C. horizontal
D. octagonal

___ 2. There are only two circular directions; they are

A. horizontal and vertical
B. parallel and perpendicular
C. clockwise and counterclockwise
D. half stem and no stem

___ 3. A loose curl (one with the least strength) is produced by a

A. quarter-stem curl
B. half-stem curl
C. long-stem curl
D. no-stem curl

___ 4. The kind of curl stem used to produce a curl of medium strength would be a

A. quarter-stem curl
B. half-stem curl
C. long-stem curl
D. no-stem curl

___ 5. Hair may be stiff and gummy during the comb-out if too much

A. setting lotion was used during setting
B. water was used during setting
C. hair spray was used during setting
D. balsam conditioning was used during setting

___ 6. After the setting lotion has been applied, should the hair dry out during setting, spray more

A. filler on it
B. conditioner on it
C. water on it
D. setting lotion on it

___ 7. To control difficult hair ends when making sculpture curls, or winding rollers, use

A. end papers
B. wax
C. roller clips
D. hair pins

___ 8. The section on the top of the head that goes from the front hairline back is the

A. nape
B. top
C. crown
D. right side

___ 9. The section of the head above the right ear is called

A. the left side
B. the right side
C. the crown
D. the nape

___ 10. Which of the following is not a part of a sculpture curl?

A. end circle
B. base
C. stem
D. body

___ 11. To get the strongest sculpture curls, you should use

A. no-stem curls
B. half-stem curls
C. long-stem curls
D. quarter-stem curls

___ 12. The implement used to sculpture curls is a

A. pin-tail comb
B. styling comb
C. teasing comb
D. rake comb

___ 13. A right angle is a

A. 90° angle
B. 45° angle
C. 75° angle
D. A and B

___ 14. A line that is straight up and down is

A. diagonal
B. octagonal
C. horizontal
D. vertical

___ 15. What angle is formed where perpendicular lines meet?

A. 75°
B. 180°
C. 90°
D. 360°

___ 16. When large strands of hair are used to make stand-up curls, they are called cascade curls, or

A. wheel curls
B. roller curls
C. barrel curls
D. sculpture curls

___ 17. Set sculpture curls within a shaping should

A. be separate
B. overlap
C. swing down
D. swing over

___ 18. Stand-up curls may be made with bases that are square, rectangular, or

A. vertical
B. diagonal
C. triangular
D. horizontal

___ 19. To avoid splits around the hairline and strength to the comb out, the cosmetologist should use which type of curls?

A. triangular bases and no-stem curls
B. square bases and half-stem curls
C. rectangular bases and full-stem curls
D. octangular bases and full-stem curls

___ 20. Very fine, limp hair may require the use of mostly

A. full-stem curls
B. no-stem curls
C. half-stem curls
D. long-stem curls

Poss.	Wrong	%	Right
20	0	100%	20
20	1	95%	19
20	2	90%	18
20	3	85%	17
20	4	80%	16
20	5	75%	15
20	6	70%	14

9 SCULPTURE CURLS POST-TEST 2

20 Questions

___ 1. All the client's hair has been set in pin curls and dried, but the cosmetologist has not yet begun to comb it out. What should be done if wet curls are discovered?

    A. air dry the curls with a fan
    B. let friction from the brush dry the curls
    C. reset curls and dry under hair dryer
    D. dry curls with heat from hand

___ 2. Alternating rows of sculpture curls and unset shapings are used to form waves known as

    A. semiwaving
    B. skip waving
    C. triangle waving
    D. finger waving

___ 3. A large stand-up curl could also be called a barrel curl or

    A. skip curl
    B. clockwise curl
    C. closed-end curl
    D. cascade curl

___ 4. One good way to obtain vertical or diagonal waves on the side of the head is to use a

    A. stand-up wave
    B. flair wave
    C. skip wave
    D. barrel wave

___ 5. When securing the sculpture curl with a clip, avoid messing up the base of the

    A. shaft
    B. shaping
    C. root
    D. stem

___ 6. The pick-up point in the sculpture shaping is the place where the comb slices or

    A. shortens the curl
    B. turns the curl
    C. carves out the curl
    D. clips the curl

___ 7. The part of the sculpture curl located between the base and the circle end is the

    A. spiral
    B. stem
    C. root
    D. strand

___ 8. The half-stem curl allows the circle end to

    A. curl behind the base
    B. spiral onto the stem
    C. move onto the base
    D. move away from the base

___ 9. The amount of tightness, mobility, and direction of the sculpture curl is determined by its

    A. circle end
    B. spiral
    C. curve
    D. stem

___ 10. When setting sculpture curls where in the shaping should you begin?

    A. top
    B. open end
    C. center
    D. closed end

___ 11. The width and strength of a sculpture wave depends on the

    A. size of the comb
    B. size of the curl
    C. setting lotion
    D. drying method

12. When setting sculpture curls, comb in the shaping, then begin setting from the

    A. top
    B. open end
    C. closed end
    D. center

13. Another name for a sculpture curl is

    A. bob curl
    B. base curl
    C. pin curl
    D. end curl

14. The more fixed part of the hair forming a sculpture curl that grows from the scalp is the

    A. stem
    B. base
    C. circle
    D. strand

15. Two lines alongside of each other with an equal amount of space between them are called

    A. diagonal
    B. perpendicular
    C. parallel
    D. arcs

16. The three parts of a sculpture curl are the circle, the stem, and the

    A. curve
    B. section
    C. base
    D. strand

17. The section of the head that is closest to the neck is the

    A. left side section
    B. right side section
    C. crown section
    D. nape section

18. If hair is hard to set because of texture, shortness, or lack of curl, you should use

    A. a sanek strip
    B. cotton
    C. wave crepe
    D. end papers

19. For the least amount of tightness when setting sculpture curls, you should use a

    A. long-stem curl
    B. half-stem curl
    C. no-stem curl
    D. quarter-stem curl

20. Removal of tangles from a mannequin begins in the

    A. crown section
    B. right side section
    C. nape section
    D. top section

Poss.	Wrong	%	Right
20	0	100%	20
20	1	95%	19
20	2	90%	18
20	3	85%	17
20	4	80%	16
20	5	75%	15
20	6	70%	14

16 Questions

___ 1. The strength of the curl produced by a roller is determined by

A. the type of stem used in placing the roller
B. the size of the strand of hair
C. the length of the roller
D. A and B

___ 2. The width of the hair subsection used for roller setting should be equal to the

A. diameter of the roller
B. circumference of the roller
C. length of the hair
D. length of the roller

___ 3. Setting the hair with rollers is usually done with a rat-tail comb, or a

A. teasing comb
B. styling comb
C. blow comb
D. rake comb

___ 4. Another name for height in a hairstyle would be

A. highness
B. inside movement
C. volume
D. tension

___ 5. To be a proficient hairstylist, the cosmetologist must master the skills of hair cutting, cold waving, and

A. eyebrow arching
B. lash and brow tinting
C. hair painting and frosting
D. sculpture curl and roller placement

___ 6. The length of the hair strand being set with a roller should be

A. 1/2˝ longer than the roller
B. slightly shorter than the roller length
C. half the length of the roller
D. equal to the length of the roller

___ 7. Rollers may be secured with

A. double-prong clips
B. roller pins
C. single-prong clips
D. all of the above

___ 8. To support the base of the hair strand in a comb out, the cosmetologist should use

A. brush rollers
B. back-brushing
C. back-combing
D. B or C

___ 9. To get a curly hairstyle, as the hair becomes shorter, the diameter of the roller should

A. decrease
B. increase
C. remain the same
D. not be of importance

___ 10. A hairstyle that appears the same on both sides is called

A. three-dimensional
B. symmetrical
C. asymmetrical
D. cylindrical

___ 11. When using rollers, and maximum height or volume is desired, use

A. no-stem rollers
B. half-stem rollers
C. full-stem rollers
D. long-stem rollers

___ 12. No-stem rollers are set directly

A. off their base
B. half on their base
C. on their base
D. below their pick-up line

___ 13. The shape of the hair section used for roller placement is usually

A. round
B. rectangular
C. square
D. oval

128

___ 14. If the hair is improperly set, the final hairstyle will most likely be

A. successful
B. uneven
C. too flat
D. a failure

___ 15. To obtain more bulk and blend roller splits during a comb out, the cosmetologist should

A. smooth the hair
B. back- comb the hair
C. feather the hair
D. strip the hair

___ 16. The technique of combing short hairs in the strand toward the scalp is called

A. silking
B. back-combing
C. effilating
D. pressing

Poss.	Wrong	%	Right
16	0	100%	16
16	1	94%	15
16	2	88%	14
16	3	81%	13
16	4	75%	12
16	5	69%	11

11 SELECTING HAIRSTYLES POST-TEST 1

17 Questions

___ 1. When deciding on a hairstyle for the client, a side part or bangs will be determined by the

A. eye shape
B. ear size
C. hair length
D. facial shape

___ 2. The percentage of married women who work outside the home is at least

A. 20 percent
B. 30 percent
C. 40 percent
D. 50+percent

___ 3. To design a hairstyle that is suitable for the client, the cosmetologist should consider

A. shortening long hair
B. lightening the hair to a pastel color
C. the client's features, personality, and occupation
D. setting the hair with sculpture curls

___ 4. The problem with a diamond-shaped face is that it is narrow at the chin and

A. eyebrows
B. cheekbones
C. jaw
D. forehead

___ 5. To keep up the ever-changing hair fashion trends, it is important for the cosmetologist to

A. improve hair porosity and elasticity
B. know basic hairstyling techniques
C. change hair colors often
D. change hair-shaping techniques often

___ 6. The profile is the view of the head from the

A. front
B. back
C. side
D. face

___ 7. One-third of the standard face would extend from the chin to the bottom of the

A. lower lip
B. eyebrows
C. eyelashes
D. nose

___ 8. What other factor(s) is considered in determining a hairstyle?

A. hair cut
B. hair color
C. hair texture
D. all of the above

___ 9. Round or square facial shapes are given a front parting to create the illusion of

A. volume
B. height
C. width
D. fullness

___ 10. The oval-shaped face is best characterized by a profile that is

A. straight
B. concave
C. convex
D. wavy

___ 11. The problem with a heart-shaped face is that the chin is too narrow, and the width is at the

A. eyebrows
B. cheekbones
C. jaw
D. forehead

___ 12. The use of bangs will reduce the forehead area, which is desirable for the person with a

A. heart-shaped face
B. oval-shaped face
C. triangular-shaped face
D. diamond-shaped face

___ 13. An example of a physical imperfection would be

A. a hangnail
B. blue eyes
C. brown eyes
D. a scar

___ 14. The standard or ideal facial shape is

A. oblong
B. round
C. oval
D. square

___ 15. The text recommends a certain style for a heart-shaped face. The style is a

A. bubble
B. pageboy
C. French twist
D. shag

___ 16. The silhouette is the view of the head from

A. the back
B. the side
C. the front
D. any position

___ 17. To correct a diamond-shaped face, fullness is needed everywhere, EXCEPT at the

A. cheekbones
B. eyebrows
C. forehead
D. jaw

Poss.	Wrong	%	Right
17	0	100%	17
17	1	94%	16
17	2	88%	15
17	3	82%	14
17	4	76%	13
17	5	71%	12
17	6	65%	11

12 HAIR SHAPING POST-TEST 1

25 Questions

___ 1. For a basic hair cut, the cosmetologist would begin cutting the hair in the

A. top
B. side
C. crown
D. nape

___ 2. If too much bulk is removed from coarse hair, it tends to

A. look smooth and natural
B. stick out from the head
C. be super-curly
D. set more easily

3. It is better to cut very fine guideline hairs with a

   A. razor
   B. thinning scissors
   C. regular scissors
   D. double-edge razor

4. When shaping the hair, avoid thinning it within

   A. 1-1/2–2″ from the scalp
   B. 2-1/2–3″ from the scalp
   C. 3-1/2–4″ from the scalp
   D. 4-1/2–5″ from the scalp

5. What draping supply is recommended for the client that is about to have a hair shaping only?

   A. towel
   B. shampoo cape
   C. comb-out cape
   D. chair cloth

6. Double-notch hair cutting scissors are used on the hair to remove

   A. color
   B. taper
   C. soil
   D. bulk

7. A low-elevation hair shaping means the hair is held and cut at an angle from the nape that does NOT exceed how many degrees from the head?

   A. 45 degrees
   B. 65 degrees
   C. 85 degrees
   D. none of the above

8. When thinning coarse hair, avoid cutting too close to the

   A. wave
   B. scalp
   C. strand
   D. root

9. If an area of hair that has been cut is stepped, then the hair is said to be

   A. marked
   B. struck
   C. dropped
   D. chunked

10. Super-curly hair is be cut wet with a

    A. clipper
    B. scissors
    C. razor
    D. thinning shears

11. When razor cutting, strokes that the cosmetologist should use are

    A. firm and long
    B. smooth and long
    C. smooth and short
    D. jerky and short

12. Blunt cutting is called

    A. hair designing
    B. razor cutting
    C. club cutting
    D. angle cutting

13. To prevent the electric clipper blades from pulling the hair, what should you do?

    A. apply oil to them
    B. soak them in alcohol
    C. apply ammonia to them
    D. dip them in peroxide

14. When hair in the top and side sections is cut to a length of 3-1/2 - 4-1/2 inches and styled away from the face, this is called

    A. edging
    B. feathering
    C. elevating
    D. contouring

15. When a man's hair is cut very short in the nape of the neck in a graduated way and seems to disappear into the neck, this is known as

    A. stepping
    B. feathering
    C. feather edge
    D. layering

16. For a hair shaping, the hair is sectioned off because the finished results tend to be more

    A. uniform
    B. uneven
    C. choppy
    D. individual

17. Double-notched scissors are used mainly to

    A. shorten the hair
    B. thin the hair
    C. elevate the hair
    D. all of the above

18. A razor used to cut the hair is called a

    A. shaper
    B. cutter
    C. clipper
    D. nipper

19. Proper storage of cutting implements is important to prevent

    A. over-use of implements
    B. injury to small children
    C. rust from forming
    D. the edges from becoming dull

20. The technique of holding the hair upward toward the crown or top of the head during a hair shaping is called

    A. low-elevation
    B. high-elevation
    C. feather edging
    D. stepping

21. What is the name given to one or more subsections of hair cut in the hairline or crown of the head that serve as a yardstick for cutting the rest of the hair?

    A. trendline
    B. radial line
    C. bias line
    D. guideline

22. You should NOT use an electric clipper if

    A. the client wants a trim
    B. the set screw has been adjusted
    C. it is noisy
    D. any teeth are broken

23. When cutting the hair with a shaper, it is important to

    A. cut using the guard
    B. thin toward the scalp
    C. use long, sliding strokes
    D. blunt all hair

24. What will happen if you submerge your electric clipper in a wet sanitizer while it is plugged into an outlet?

    A. the blades will slide
    B. the clipper won't cut correctly
    C. you will get an electric shock
    D. your clipper will vibrate

25. When the hair is cut straight across without any thinning, this is called

    A. slither cutting
    B. feathering
    C. blunt cutting
    D. effilating

Poss.	Wrong	%	Right
25	0	100%	25
25	1	96%	24
25	2	92%	23
25	3	88%	22
25	4	84%	21
25	5	80%	20
25	6	76%	19
25	7	72%	18
25	8	68%	17
25	9	64%	16
25	10	60%	15

28 Questions

___ 1. Definite lines of demarcation that appear on the hair after a hair shaping are known as

A. shingles
B. elevations
C. slices
D. steps (marks)

___ 2. When hair is cut very short in the nape area of the head, this is known as

A. feathering
B. tailoring the neckline
C. sculpturing
D. effilating

___ 3. When the hair is combed downward, what is the name for bottom lengths of hair on the hairstyle?

A. sign line
B. hanging length
C. angle cut
D. elevation line

___ 4. The slithering movement of the scissors used to shorten hair is also called

A. elevating
B. effilating
C. thinning
D. tapering

___ 5. Hair may be thinned with a razor, thinning shears, or

A. finger tang
B. regular scissors
C. electric clipper
D. hand clipper

___ 6. The hair can be shaped after a

A. cold (chemical) wave
B. permanent hair color
C. frosting
D. all of the above

___ 7. When using the electric clipper, it is important NOT to

A. clip the hair on the neck
B. nick a mole
C. cut the hair too fast
D. notch the hair

___ 8. After each hair-shaping service, sanitize your scissors with

A. 1% lemon rinse
B. 2% hydrogen peroxide
C. 50% ethyl alcohol
D. 70% isopropyl alcohol

___ 9. Storing your scissors in your uniform pocket may result in

A. a severe cut
B. tarnishing of finish on the scissors
C. dulling of blades of the scissors
D. rust forming on the scissors

___ 10. If a razor is used to cut the hair, the hair should be

A. completely dry
B. slightly damp
C. completely wet
D. slightly moist

___ 11. During a razor cut, as the razor is cutting the hair, the comb is placed in the

A. pocket
B. drawer
C. other hand
D. other section

___ 12. It is ALWAYS better to cut the hair with a

A. razor
B. scissors
C. thinning shears
D. razor or scissors

13. The hanging length cut around the hairline from which the rest of the hair is shaped is called the

   A. highsign
   B. cutting length
   C. guideline
   D. form

14. The foundation for a good hairstyle is a correct hair

   A. setting lotion
   B. shaping
   C. styling comb
   D. brush

15. To thin hair during a shaping means to

   A. shorten it
   B. add to its length
   C. increase its bulk
   D. decrease its bulk

16. The amount of bulk removed from the hair during a razor shaping is determined by the

   A. pressure of the razor
   B. weight of the razor
   C. type of blade used
   D. position of the razor guard

17. Coarse hair should be thinned

   A. closest to the scalp
   B. nearest the scalp
   C. farthest from the scalp
   D. on the scalp

18. The texture of hair that sticks out the most when thinned too much is

   A. wavy hair
   B. coarse hair
   C. fine hair
   D. medium hair

19. Slither cutting is a method of shortening and

   A. layering the hair
   B. thinning the hair
   C. elevating the hair
   D. feathering the hair

20. When giving a basic hair shaping, the hair is sectioned into

   A. two sections
   B. three sections
   C. four sections
   D. five sections

21. When hair is shortened for a graduated effect, this is called

   A. chopping
   B. thinning
   C. bulking
   D. tapering

22. When combing through the hair during a hair shaping, the scissors should be

   A. open with fingers in scissors
   B. closed with fingers in scissors
   C. placed on your station
   D. closed and resting in the palm of your hand

23. The technique of cutting the upper sections of the hair shorter while the lower sections of the hair are left longer is known as

   A. low-elevation cutting
   B. layering the hair
   C. high-elevation effilating
   D. under cutting

24. When not in use, scissors should be stored

   A. on top of your station
   B. in your uniform pocket
   C. in a dry sanitizer
   D. on top of the cash register

25. What should you do to prevent an electric clipper from "pulling" the hair?

   A. soak it for 10 minutes in alcohol
   B. apply heavy oil to the blades
   C. apply light oil to the blades
   D. soak blades in acid-balanced shampoo for 5 minutes

26. If one of the teeth are missing from your electric clipper, what should you do?

   A. tighten adjustment screw
   B. replace the blade
   C. use a light clipper oil
   D. it is okay to use without the tooth

27. When giving a scissors haircut, how should the hair strand be held to provide maximum protection for the client?

    A. your fingers should be between the client and the end of the hair strand
    B. your scissors should be between the client and where the hair is held
    C. your thumb is between the client and the scissors
    D. your comb is between the client and the scissors

Poss.	Wrong	%	Right
28	0	100%	28
28	1	96%	27
28	2	93%	26
28	3	89%	25
28	4	86%	24
28	5	82%	23
28	6	79%	22
28	7	75%	21
28	8	71%	20
28	9	68%	19
28	10	64%	18

28. When razor cutting the client's hair, an important safety consideration is to

    A. spray the hair frequently with water
    B. spray the hair often with conditioner
    C. use a razor guard
    D. thoroughly dry the hair

---

13 AIR-WAVING AND BLOW-DRYING POST-TEST 1

16 Questions

1. Quick-service hairstyling in the salon saves time for the

    A. receptionist
    B. client
    C. supplier
    D. A and B

2. To ensure safety, all air wavers and blow dryers must be

    A. set at low temperature settings
    B. used on damp to dry hair
    C. Underwriters Laboratories approved
    D. inspected at time of purchase

3. Hotter air settings on the air waver are generally used on hair that is

    A. very fine
    B. coarse
    C. bleached
    D. tinted

4. Wave set may be used in quick-service styling if it is

    A. paste
    B. liquid
    C. gel
    D. cream

5. By rotating an air comb on the hair, the cosmetologist may achieve

    A. elasticity
    B. closeness
    C. height
    D. texture

6. The heat from the air waver should be directed

    A. away from the scalp
    B. toward the scalp
    C. at the ends
    D. toward the hair root

7. Appliances for air waving may differ in their

    A. electrical power
    B. heating elements
    C. air velocity
    D. all of the above

8. For quick-service hairstyling, use a(n)

    A. air clipper
    B. blow waver
    C. roller
    D. clamper

135

___ 9. Another term for air waving is

A. iron waving
B. press waving
C. thermal waving
D. blow waving

___ 10. Heat is concentrated during blow waving
through the use of attachments that are
plastic or

A. metal
B. mineral
C. organic
D. vinyl

___ 11. Cooler air settings on an air waver are
generally used on hair that is

A. coarse
B. bleached
C. medium
D. normal

___ 12. When air waving the hair, the head should
be subdivided into strands that are the same
size as those used for

A. cold waving
B. tint applications
C. roller setting
D. hair shaping

___ 13. On an electrical appliance, the abbreviation
U.L. stands for the words

A. Under Load
B. Under Level
C. Union Label
D. Underwriters Laboratories

___ 14. When air waving, the cosmetologist should
never place the blow comb on the

A. ends
B. scalp
C. sides
D. bangs

___ 15. By turning the brush of the blow comb into
the strand near the scalp, this will help
achieve

A. fullness
B. tone
C. elasticity
D. texture

___ 16. Extra care must be taken when blow waving
long hair because it

A. could become hard to manage and curl
B. may dry too quickly and become oily
C. may be drawn into the air intake of the
dryer
D. could stick to the brush and become
straight

Poss.	Wrong	%	Right
16	0	100%	16
16	1	94%	15
16	2	88%	14
16	3	81%	13
16	4	75%	12
16	5	69%	11

13 BLOW-DRYING POST-TEST 2

16 Questions

___ 1. Quick-service hairstyling in the salon saves
time for the

A. receptionist
B. client
C. supplier
D. A and B

___ 2. To ensure safety, all air wavers and blow
dryers must be

A. set at low temperature settings
B. used on damp to dry hair
C. Underwriters Laboratories approved
D. inspected at time of purchase

3. Hotter air settings on the air waver are generally used on hair that is

A. baby-fine
B. coarse
C. bleached
D. tinted

4. Wave set may be used in quick-service styling if it is

A. paste
B. liquid
C. gel
D. cream

5. By rotating an air comb on the hair, the cosmetologist may achieve

A. elasticity
B. closeness
C. height
D. texture

6. The heat from the air waver should be directed

A. away from the scalp
B. toward the scalp
C. at the ends
D. toward the hair root

7. Appliances for air waving may differ in their

A. electrical power
B. heating elements
C. air velocity
D. all of the above

8. For quick-service hairstyling, use a(n)

A. air clipper
B. blow waver
C. roller
D. clamper

9. Another term for air waving is

A. iron waving
B. press waving
C. thermal waving
D. blow waving

10. Heat is concentrated during blow waving through the use of attachments that are plastic or

A. metal
B. mineral
C. organic
D. vinyl

11. Cooler air settings on an air waver are generally used on hair that is

A. coarse
B. bleached
C. medium
D. normal

12. When air waving the hair, the head should be subdivided into strands that are the same size as those used for

A. cold waving
B. tint applications
C. roller setting
D. hair shaping

13. On an electrical appliance, the abbreviation U.L. stands for the words

A. Under Load
B. Under Level
C. Union Label
D. Underwriters Laboratories

14. When air waving, the cosmetologist should never place the blow comb on the

A. ends
B. scalp
C. sides
D. bangs

15. By turning the brush of the blow comb into the strand near the scalp, this will help achieve

A. fullness
B. tone
C. elasticity
D. texture

16. Extra care must be taken when blow waving long hair because it

A. could become hard to manage and curl
B. may dry too quickly and become oily
C. may be drawn into the air intake of the dryer
D. could stick to the brush and become straight

Poss.	Wrong	%	Right
16	0	100%	16
16	1	94%	15
16	2	88%	14
16	3	81%	13
16	4	75%	12
16	5	69%	11

---

14 IRON CURLS POST-TEST 1

20 Questions

1. Poker curls are made in a spiral fashion from the

A. ends to the scalp
B. mid-strand to the ends
C. ends to the mid-strand
D. scalp to the ends

2. Croquignole curling involves winding the hair strand from the

A. ends to the scalp
B. mid-strand to ends
C. ends to mid-strand
D. scalp to ends

3. In order to heat evenly, thermal irons should be made of high quality

A. brass
B. steel
C. aluminum
D. B and C only

4. As the iron is rolled toward the scalp, what does the cosmetologist use to protect the client's scalp?

A. cotton
B. towel
C. comb
D. an end paper

5. Which of the following would be an example of a standard hairstyling implement for forming spiral curls in the hair?

A. crimping iron
B. marcel-style curling iron
C. spring clamp-style curling iron
D. B and C only

6. Which of the following curling irons should be used to form a rippling effect in longer hair lengths?

A. marcel-style curling iron
B. clamp-style curling iron
C. crimping iron
D. pressing comb

7. What is the name for the smallest diameter curling iron used for curling the hair?

A. mini or midget curling iron
B. C-size curling iron
C. D-size curling iron
D. quarter-size curling iron

8. Which term describes the non-moveable hot part of the curling iron?

A. barrel
B. shell handle
C. swivel base
D. B and D only

9. Which part of the curling iron safety feature allows the cord to remain untangled as the iron is rotated so you could avoid the possibility of an electrical shock?

A. shell handle
B. rod
C. swivel base
D. shell clamp

10. What safety feature should be present on your curling iron that will allow you to regulate the temperature?

A. circuit breaker
B. thermostat
C. rotating handle
D. support clip

___ 11. When iron curling, which of the following stem formations gives the hair the maximum amount of volume?

A. no-stem curls
B. half-stem curls
C. full-stem curls
D. none of the above

___ 12. Which of the following is a safety feature that allows you to rest your curling iron on the top of the styling station?

A. support clip
B. rotating handle
C. thermostat
D. A and C only

___ 13. During iron curling, what is the name for the curling method that curls the hair from the scalp to the ends?

A. spiral curl
B. poker curl
C. croquignole curl
D. candlestick curl

___ 14. When thermal curling the light hair, what condition will cause the hair to be scorched?

A. over conditioning
B. coloring the hair too dark
C. rinsing with too much water
D. curling wet hair

___ 15. If your curling iron doesn't have a thermostat, and you determine that the temperature of your curling iron is too hot for the hair texture and condition of the strand you are going to curl, what should you do?

A. blow on the iron
B. wave the iron in the air
C. towel cool the iron
D. place barrel in a glass of water

___ 16. The term "clicking" used in connection with thermal curling methods refers to

A. the sound of the iron as it heats up
B. the opening/closing of the clamp as the iron is rotated
C. the sound of the iron as it turns in the strand
D. the opening/closing of the conditioner bottle during the curling process

___ 17. When the hair is iron curled, what holds the hair against the barrel of the iron while the hair strand is being curled?

A. shell clamp
B. non-moveable handle
C. rod
D. the moveable handle

___ 18. To achieve a curly hairstyle, which hair length will require the maximum rotations of the curling iron?

A. short hair
B. medium-length hair
C. long hair
D. A and B only

___ 19. If using your curling iron close to the client's scalp, what should be placed between the iron and the scalp to protect the client?

A. aluminum foil
B. an end wrap
C. a comb
D. a duck-bill clip

___ 20. What are the names for the chemicals used for sanitizing and cleaning your curling iron?

A. shampoo
B. alcohol
C. alcohol and ammonia
D. thio and ammonia

Poss.	Wrong	%	Right
20	0	100%	20
20	1	95%	19
20	2	90%	18
20	3	85%	17
20	4	80%	16
20	5	75%	15
20	6	70%	14

26 Questions

___ 1. To test the strength of hydrogen peroxide, you would use which instrument?

A. barometer
B. hydrometer
C. odometer
D. chronometer

___ 2. One disadvantage of permanent hair color is

A. a more youthful appearance
B. the natural color is restored
C. a retouch is required
D. facial features are enhanced

___ 3. A soap cap may be applied to the hair to achieve a brightening or

A. highlighting effect
B. oxidizing effect
C. waving effect
D. neutralizing effect

___ 4. When applying a tint retouch, tint applied beyond the new growth of hair will cause a line of

A. bleach
B. broken hairs
C. demarcation
D. metallic salts

___ 5. Toners are used with

A. temporary hair colors
B. semipermanent hair colors
C. double-application tints
D. single-application tints

___ 6. The best time to mix the hair lightener is

A. immediately before application
B. one day before application
C. two days before application
D. two weeks before application

___ 7. If the hair has been tinted with a metallic dye, it is

A. safe to cold wave
B. unfit for conditioning
C. rendered unfit for cold waving
D. safe for acid waving

___ 8. Compound henna colors the hair by

A. penetrating it
B. dissolving it
C. coating it
D. curling it

___ 9. When hydrogen peroxide is added to a permanent color, the chemical process that occurs is called

A. oxidation
B. oxygenation
C. liquidation
D. fluoridation

___ 10. If shampoo was added to the bleach mixture, the bleaching action would be

A. stopped
B. hastened
C. slowed down
D. speeded up

___ 11. The instrument that determines the strength of peroxide is a

A. barometer
B. hydrometer
C. odometer
D. thermometer

___ 12. The two basic types of fillers used to equalize hair porosity are conditioning fillers, and

A. lotion fillers
B. H_2O_2 fillers
C. creme fillers
D. color fillers

___ 13. When tint is applied to a very small section of hair to predetermine the overall color formula and timing, this is called

A. predisposition test
B. strand test
C. patch test
D. scratch test

14. Egyptian henna colors the hair by coating the

A. cortex
B. cuticle
C. medulla
D. follicle

15. Temporary hair colorings are also known as

A. aniline tints
B. color rinses
C. toners
D. bleaches

16. Before the application of a toner, the hair is required to be

A. prelightened
B. prewaved
C. pretinted
D. prerinsed

17. Another name for an allergy test would be a

A. tint test
B. predisposition test
C. strand test
D. test curl

18. Aniline derivative tints are also known as

A. metallic tints
B. partly-coating tints
C. penetrating tints
D. coating tints

19. A temporary rinse is applied

A. before shampooing the hair
B. to shampooed and towel-dried hair
C. after application of the setting solution
D. before brushing the hair

20. Chromatic colors are formulated from three primary colors. They are

A. blue-green-violet
B. orange-violet-yellow
C. red-yellow-blue
D. blue-violet-yellow

21. Color rinses are also called

A. permanent colors
B. temporary colors
C. semipermanent colors
D. coating dyes

22. In professional tinting, peroxide is sometimes referred to as a(n)

A. activator
B. energizer
C. developer
D. catalyst

23. To protect oneself from the chemical found in hair tint, the hairdresser must wear

A. rubber gloves
B. eye goggles
C. comfortable shoes
D. a clean uniform

24. An example of a primary color is

A. violet
B. red
C. green
D. orange

25. To protect the client, a predisposition test is required by the

A. Department of Agriculture
B. Federal Board of Health
C. Department of Transportation
D. Federal Food and Drug Administration

26. A chemical abbreviation for hydrogen peroxide is

A. H_2O
B. H_2O_2
C. H_2O_3
D. H_2O_4

Poss.	Wrong	%	Right
26	0	100%	26
26	1	96%	25
26	2	92%	24
26	3	88%	23
26	4	85%	22

26	5	81%	21
26	6	77%	20
26	7	73%	19
26	8	69%	18
26	9	65%	17
26	10	62%	16
26	11	58%	15

15, 16, 17 HAIR COLOR POST-TEST 2

22 Questions

___ 1. Aniline derivative tint is applied to hair that is

A. towel-dried
B. dryer-dried
C. completely dried
D. slightly moist

___ 2. Sometimes during a tint retouch, the tint is lathered up, and brought through the hair ends to blend the color and make it

A. discolored
B. rinse
C. even
D. darker

___ 3. Hair that has never had chemicals applied to it, such as cold-waving solution or bleach, is referred to as

A. virgin hair
B. baby hair
C. new hair
D. common hair

___ 4. In order to tint damaged and over-porous hair evenly, it may be necessary to apply a color

A. builder
B. blender
C. filler
D. primer

___ 5. Using hair color theory, what is the term used to describe differences in a particular hair color?

A. stars
B. levels
C. variances
D. reflections

___ 6. Hair is NOT fit for permanent waving if it has been previously tinted with a(n)

A. vegetable dye
B. aniline derivative tint
C. metallic dye
D. penetrating tint

___ 7. Egyptian henna colors the hair by coating the

A. body of the hair
B. cortex of the hair
C. medulla of the hair
D. cuticle of the hair

___ 8. Which hair rinse contains a certified color?

A. acetic acid rinse
B. henna rinse
C. peroxide rinse
D. temporary color rinse

___ 9. To neutralize a green cast in a client's hair, add

A. blue
B. red
C. violet
D. yellow

___ 10. When testing the hair for metallic salts, the action of the peroxide can be hastened (made faster) by adding

A. 14% ammonia water
B. 28% ammonia water
C. 32% ammonia water
D. 36% ammonia water

11. Semipermanent hair colors are gradually shampooed from the hair in

    A. 1–2 weeks
    B. 2–3 weeks
    C. 3–4 weeks
    D. 4–6 weeks

12. Hair colors that only remain in the hair 4-6 weeks are classified as

    A. semipermanent rinses
    B. temporary rinses
    C. toners
    D. certified rinses

13. No patch test is required for a

    A. penetrating dye
    B. tint
    C. toner
    D. temporary rinse

14. If the hair is gray and the client wishes a lighter color, the cosmetologist should select a color that is

    A. lighter than the client's selection
    B. the same as the client's selection
    C. one shade darker than the selection
    D. two shades darker than the selection

15. To equalize hair porosity, and achieve an even color on tinted hair, it should be treated with a

    A. color blender
    B. color filler
    C. creme tint
    D. creme rinse

16. Professional salon services, such as a cold wave, can be given to hair colored with a(n)

    A. silver dye
    B. compound dye
    C. metallic salt
    D. aniline derivative tint

17. Coloring lightened hair to its natural color is known as a

    A. tint back
    B. soap cap
    C. filler
    D. toner

18. Progressive hair dyes, such as those containing lead and silver, would also include dye made with

    A. temporary rinses
    B. certified rinses
    C. aniline derivatives
    D. metallic salts

19. After applying a temporary color to the hair,

    A. rinse it thoroughly with water
    B. dry the hair under the dryer
    C. towel-blot excess color and proceed to set
    D. proceed to cut the hair

20. Color fillers are recommended for damaged hair, or hair that is

    A. overly porous
    B. very fine
    C. very coarse
    D. resistant

21. One of the advantages of permanent hair color is it

    A. shampoos out easily
    B. completely covers gray hair
    C. requires a patch test
    D. costs more than other tints

22. A compound dye is a combination of a metallic salt and a

    A. temporary color spray
    B. powder rinse
    C. animal tint
    D. vegetable tint

Poss.	Wrong	%	Right
22	0	100%	22
22	1	95%	21
22	2	91%	20
22	3	86%	19
22	4	82%	18
22	5	77%	17
22	6	73%	16
22	7	68%	15
22	8	64%	14
22	9	59%	13
22	10	55%	12

22 Questions

___ 1. The medical term for the positive reaction to a skin test is

    A. nodosa
    B. senilis
    C. venenata
    D. corona

___ 2. Over-porous hair ends can be prevented from absorbing too much tint by applying a

    A. cold wave solution
    B. temporary rinse
    C. color filler
    D. acid shampoo

___ 3. When explaining the advantages of the use of a temporary hair color, the hairdresser would inform the client that the color will

    A. highlight the natural color
    B. be removed with a shampoo
    C. not change the condition of the hair
    D. all of the above

___ 4. Since there are metallic salts in compound dyes, hair colored with them is unfit for

    A. cold waving
    B. shampooing
    C. rinsing
    D. cutting

___ 5. Rinses made to last from 4–6 weeks are known as

    A. semipermanent hair colors
    B. temporary hair colors
    C. toners
    D. fillers

___ 6. An advantage for the cosmetologist in giving a permanent hair color is that it

    A. can be shampooed
    B. guarantees the return of the client
    C. requires a patch test
    D. requires more time

___ 7. To lighten the hair, how far away from the scalp is a virgin color applied?

    A. 1/2″ to 1″
    B. 1″
    C. 1-1/2″ to 2″
    D. 2″

___ 8. When giving a tint retouch, the tint is applied first to the

    A. hair ends
    B. hair roots
    C. new growth
    D. hairline

___ 9. The tint service record should be completed

    A. for each tint that is given
    B. only for the first patch test
    C. only when damage occurs
    D. only if the hair was given a cold wave

___ 10. During tinting, the part of the hair that absorbs the tint the fastest is the

    A. hair most difficult to tint
    B. middle of the hair shafts
    C. hair next to the scalp
    D. hair ends

___ 11. The hydrogen peroxide used for tinting is made of water, and

    A. 2% hydrogen peroxide
    B. 4% hydrogen peroxide
    C. 6% hydrogen peroxide
    D. 8% hydrogen peroxide

___ 12. If a client has a yellowish hue in her hair, what tertiary color base in a weekly rinse would neutralize the yellow?

    A. blue-violet
    B. red-orange
    C. yellow-green
    D. red-violet

___ 13. Temporary color rinses contain

    A. distilled color
    B. certified color
    C. aniline color
    D. coal-tar color

14. Temporary hair colors remain in the hair for
    A. one shampooing
    B. four weeks
    C. six weeks
    D. eight weeks

15. Bleach or tint mixed with peroxide must be discarded because of
    A. relaxation
    B. oxidation
    C. presoftening
    D. hardening

16. Two secondary colors that neutralize each other are
    A. violet-blue
    B. blue-green
    C. yellow-violet
    D. none of the above

17. Certified colors used in temporary rinses are regulated by which of the following agencies?
    A. The American Medical Association
    B. The Department of Hair Coloring
    C. The Federal Food and Drug Administration
    D. The National Pharmaceutical Board

18. Egyptian henna is an example of a(n)
    A. progressive dye
    B. metallic tint
    C. aniline derivative tint
    D. semipermanent color

19. A compound dye is a combination of a vegetable hair tint with
    A. an aniline derivative tint
    B. metallic salts
    C. a color rinse
    D. a shampoo tint

20. When peroxide and tint are mixed, they should be mixed only in a
    A. metal dish
    B. metal pan
    C. glass or plastic container
    D. iron bowl

21. If tinted hair is reconditioned, the conditioning will be directed to
    A. the entire hair length
    B. all hair follicles
    C. the hair bulb
    D. the entire papilla

22. Before using a dye remover on hair thought to have a metallic tint on it, the cosmetologist should test for
    A. sodium salts
    B. chlorinated water
    C. metallic salts
    D. hard water

Poss.	Wrong	%	Right
22	0	100%	22
22	1	95%	21
22	2	91%	20
22	3	86%	19
22	4	82%	18
22	5	77%	17
22	6	73%	16
22	7	68%	15
22	8	64%	14
22	9	59%	13
22	10	55%	12

22 Questions

___ 1. To test the strength of hydrogen peroxide, you would use which instrument?

   A. barometer
   B. hydrometer
   C. odometer
   D. chronometer

___ 2. Natural hair color is determined by its

   A. porosity
   B. pigment
   C. medulla
   D. cuticle

___ 3. If a strand of hair was tested and found to have a metallic dye on it, the strand would look

   A. coarse
   B. discolored
   C. hardened
   D. stripped

___ 4. Semipermanent hair color partially penetrates the

   A. cuticle
   B. cortex
   C. medulla
   D. follicle

___ 5. After what number of shampoos will semi-permanent hair color wash out of the hair?

   A. 2 to 3
   B. 4 to 6
   C. 5 to 6
   D. 7 to 8

___ 6. The pH of a semipermanent color falls in the range of

   A. 4 to 6
   E. 5 to 6
   C. 7 to 9
   D. 9 to 10

___ 7. In choosing a semipermanent hair color for your client, the factor to be considered is the

   A. color rub off
   B. coating quality
   C. color penetration
   D. all of the above

___ 8. Hair colors that have no red or gold tones are classified as

   A. toners
   B. auburn
   C. highlighted
   D. drab

___ 9. Hair ends may turn darker when using an oxidizing tint if those ends are extremely

   A. straight
   B. over-porous
   C. resistant
   D. curly

___ 10. Before tinting, extremely porous hair ends should be treated with a

   A. cold wave
   B. color filler
   C. toner
   D. rinse

___ 11. As a safety measure when giving a permanent hair color, it is required by federal law that the cosmetologist give a predisposition test

   A. once very other year
   B. twice a year
   C. before each monthly application
   D. before each weekly application

___ 12. To prevent a line of demarcation during a tint retouch, it is important to avoid

   A. rotating a bottle
   B. overlapping the tint
   C. mixing tint
   D. rubbing the scalp

13. The oxidizing agent for an aniline derivative tint is
    A. hydrogen peroxide
    B. metallic salts
    C. sodium bromate
    D. sodium hydroxide

14. Since some toners are aniline derivative tints, they require a
    A. strand test
    B. patch test
    C. color test
    D. test curl

15. Terms such as cool, drab, and warm describe
    A. tones of a hair color
    B. shades of a hair color
    C. brightness of a hair color
    D. depth of a hair color

16. To achieve a permanent hair color, the color molecules must penetrate into the
    A. cuticle
    B. cortex
    C. medulla
    D. follicle

17. If the site of the patch test is positive, for example burning, swollen, and inflamed, this condition is known as
    A. dermatitis acne
    B. dermatitis freckles
    C. dermatitis venenata
    D. dermatitis pimple

18. Semipermanent rinses seldom, if ever, are mixed with
    A. hydrogen peroxide
    B. bleach
    C. aniline tints
    D. aniline toners

19. Temporary hair colors contain
    A. aniline tint
    B. bleach
    C. certified color
    D. peroxide

20. Temporary hair colors are removed by
    A. bleaching
    B. stripping
    C. shampooing
    D. rinsing

21. An example of a secondary color is
    A. blue
    B. red
    C. violet
    D. yellow

22. By law, a predisposition test must be given before each
    A. oxidation tint
    B. bleach
    C. temporary rinse
    D. conditioning treatment

Poss.	Wrong	%	Right
22	0	100%	22
22	1	95%	21
22	2	91%	20
22	3	86%	19
22	4	82%	18
22	5	77%	17
22	6	73%	16
22	7	68%	15
22	8	64%	14
22	9	59%	13
22	10	55%	12

23 Questions

___ 1. How many stages does black hair go through to become pale blonde?

A. four
B. five
C. six
D. seven

___ 2. Powder bleaches should not be applied to the

A. lashes
B. scalp
C. nape
D. crown

___ 3. A toner with a yellow base would be described by the manufacturer as having

A. lemon tones
B. maize tones
C. orange tones
D. gold tones

___ 4. Which of the following is the best definition of a permanent toner?

A. an aniline derivative tint in pastel colors
B. an aniline tint having a gold base
C. para-phenylene-diamine dyes
D. color that cannot be removed

___ 5. If you overlap bleach when doing a bleach retouch, it will result in

A. more elasticity
B. less elasticity
C. breakage
D. hair yellowing

___ 6. When a cap is used, and strands of hair all over the head are lightened, this is known as

A. tinting
B. frosting
C. streaking
D. painting

___ 7. The three basic bleach classifications are oil, cream, and

A. moist
B. powder
C. liquid
D. dry

___ 8. The lightest toner can only be applied to hair bleached to the

A. brown stage
B. red-gold stage
C. pale yellow stage
D. red stage

___ 9. A hair lightener should never be applied to a scalp that has

A. scratches and abrasions
B. a small lump
C. a bump
D. an old scar

___ 10. The process of lightening and toning the hair is also known as a double

A. timer
B. service
C. process
D. stripping

___ 11. Lightening the hair begins with the application of a

A. stripping agent
B. toning agent
C. moisturizing agent
D. bleaching agent

___ 12. Decolorization takes place in which layer of the hair?

A. cuticle
B. cortex
C. medulla
D. all of the above

148

13. Which lightener should you use for a lightener retouch and toner?

   A. cream lightener
   B. powder lightener
   C. oil lightener
   D. frosting bleach

14. The lightest stage that hair can be bleached is

   A. gold
   B. pale yellow
   C. pale red-gold
   D. pale orange

15. Lightening small strands of hair toward the front of the head is known as

   A. retouching
   B. tipping
   C. a soap cap
   D. a filler

16. Lightening larger strands of hair toward the front of the head is called

   A. tipping
   B. streaking
   C. frosting
   D. toning

17. Sulfonated oil bleaches are activated using

   A. ammonium thioglycolate
   B. sodium hydroxide
   C. sodium bromate
   D. hydrogen peroxide

18. The length of time the hair lightener remains on the hair varies with hair porosity, condition, and

   A. desired toner shade
   B. time scheduled
   C. amount of bleach used
   D. amount of peroxide used

19. Hydrogen peroxide (20 volume) added to the bleaching agent acts as a

   A. booster
   B. stripper
   C. catalyst
   D. protinator

20. Bleaching decolorizes pigments that are brown, red, and

   A. blue
   B. gray
   C. green
   D. yellow

21. Before giving a lightener retouch, what should you do?

   A. a predisposition test
   B. brush the hair vigorously
   C. examine scalp for cuts and abrasions
   D. give the client a strand test

22. During lightening, the condition of the hair becomes more

   A. elastic
   B. spongy
   C. stringy
   D. porous

23. When lightening and toning the hair, you should wear

   A. protective shoes
   B. a hair net
   C. an operator apron
   D. protective gloves

Poss.	Wrong	%	Right
23	0	100%	23
23	1	96%	22
23	2	91%	21
23	3	87%	20
23	4	83%	19
23	5	78%	18
23	6	74%	17
23	7	70%	16
23	8	65%	15
23	9	61%	14

24 Questions

___ 1. When an aniline toner is used, what test must be given first?

    A. shampoo
    B. strand
    C. patch
    D. elasticity

___ 2. The chemical process of bleach on the hair is (known as)

    A. stimulation
    B. neutralization
    C. evaporation
    D. oxidation

___ 3. Full-strength bleach on the scalp MAY cause

    A. stinging
    B. irritation
    C. blistering
    D. all of the above

___ 4. Before applying a toner to gray or white hair, it is necessary to prelighten the hair in order to make the hair

    A. resistant enough
    B. porous enough
    C. lower in pH
    D. lower in alkaline

___ 5. A creme bleach continues to lighten because it remains

    A. moist
    B. thick
    C. thin
    D. dry

___ 6. When giving a lightener retouch, what would be the results if the mixture is overlapped?

    A. nothing
    B. a gold band
    C. incomplete bleaching
    D. breakage

___ 7. A drastic color change from dark to very light hair color requires

    A. pretoning
    B. prelightening
    C. pretipping
    D. prefrosting

___ 8. Applying bleach to selected strands of hair is known as

    A. weaving
    B. streaking
    C. tipping
    D. painting

___ 9. Containers used for mixing bleach should be made of

    A. ceramic
    B. wood
    C. metal
    D. glass

___ 10. When the proper stage of streaking is reached, which shampoo is BEST to remove bleach?

    A. mild
    B. medicated
    C. non-stripping (acid)
    D. alkaline

___ 11. The process of lightening the hair around the hairline is called

    A. retouching
    B. framing
    C. overlapping
    D. shelling

___ 12. To keep all sections separated and to assure that all bleached areas process evenly, apply

    A. a neutralizing cape
    B. a plastic cap
    C. duck bill clips
    D. aluminum foil

___ 13. During the frosting service, avoid pulling strands of hair through the cap from the

  A. crown
  B. hairline
  C. ears
  D. nape

___ 14. When lightening and toning the hair, you should wear

  A. protective shoes
  B. a hair net
  C. an operator apron
  D. protective gloves

___ 15. When giving a virgin bleach to medium brown hair, the cosmetologist should begin applying the lightener

  A. 1/2˝ from scalp up to ends
  B. from scalp to ends
  C. from ends to scalp
  D. from center of hair shaft to ends

___ 16. Applying tint or lightener to small, unevenly colored strands of hair missed during the first application of a tint or bleach is called spot bleaching, or spot

  A. smoothing
  B. tinting
  C. blending
  D. lathering

___ 17. Prebleaching (lightening) is required before the application of a

  A. semipermanent rinse
  B. one-process tint
  C. toner
  D. temporary rinse

___ 18. The removal of a penetrating tint from the hair is called

  A. relaxing
  B. a soap cap
  C. stripping
  D. tinting

___ 19. To equalize the porosity of the hair, use a

  A. steamer
  B. stripper
  C. filler
  D. equalizer

___ 20. Hair coloring formulas and their results are recorded on a

  A. comparison chart
  B. salon appointment book
  C. client record card
  D. color mixing chart

___ 21. A lightening and toning service is also called a

  A. double play
  B. two-bottle color
  C. double lightener
  D. double-application service

___ 22. Lightening the hair means the same as

  A. rinsing it
  B. toning it
  C. decolorizing it
  D. dying it

___ 23. Bleach SHOULD BE applied to hair that is

  A. wet
  B. dry
  C. shampooed
  D. dark

___ 24. If you overlap bleach when doing a bleach retouch, it will result in

  A. more elasticity
  B. less elasticity
  C. breakage
  D. hair yellowing

Poss.	Wrong	%	Right
24	0	100%	24
24	1	96%	23
24	2	92%	22
24	3	88%	21
24	4	83%	20
24	5	79%	19
24	6	75%	18
24	7	71%	17
24	8	67%	16
24	9	63%	15

24 Questions

___ 1. Dry, brittle, fragile hair may result from excessive use of hydrogen peroxide and a

   A. lightener
   B. rinse
   C. semipermanent rinse
   D. henna rinse

___ 2. The process of applying bleach through selected strands of hair is known as

   A. bleaching
   B. framing
   C. streaking
   D. stranding

___ 3. Applying a normalizing lotion to bleached hair will lower the hair's

   A. alkalinity
   B. affinity
   C. chemistry
   D. acidity

___ 4. Removing artificial color from the hair requires the use of a

   A. stripper
   B. steamer
   C. dye solvent
   D. bleach

___ 5. A retouch hair lightener is applied to the

   A. new growth of hair
   B. entire hair shaft
   C. ends only
   D. cold shaft only

___ 6. The use of foil on bleach strands accelerates

   A. breaking
   B. swelling
   C. stretching
   D. decolorizing

___ 7. When hair is pulled through a rubber or plastic cap, which bleach is recommended?

   A. paste
   B. oil
   C. creme
   D. powder

___ 8. Before giving a lightener retouch, what should you do?

   A. a predisposition test
   B. brush the hair vigorously
   C. examine the scalp for cuts and abrasions
   D. give the client a strand test

___ 9. The client has just received a frosting and complains that there are too many frosted strands of hair. How could the cosmetologist reduce the amount of frosted hair?

   A. apply tint all over the head
   B. give client a tintback
   C. apply a filler
   D. give client a reverse frosting

___ 10. Bleach can be kept moist during frostings by using

   A. an over-cap
   B. warm water
   C. a hot towel
   D. a dry towel

___ 11. If bleach drips onto the skin, the bleach should be removed using

   A. cold-cool water
   B. tepid-hot water
   C. hot water only
   D. very hot water

___ 12. When hydrogen peroxide is mixed with sulfonated oil (sodium persulfates) the result is an oil

   A. lightener
   B. rinse
   C. relaxer
   D. neutralizer

___ 13. When changing the color of the hair to a much lighter color, it is required that the hair be

   A. preneutralized
   B. prelightened
   C. prehardened
   D. preshaded

___ 14. Which bleach is recommended for frosting
and streaking?

    A. creme
    B. paste
    C. oil
    D. powder

___ 15. The alkalinity of bleach is neutralized by
applying a

    A. rinse
    B. normalizer
    C. conditioner
    D. neutralizer

___ 16. An effect achieved by placing a plastic or
rubber cap on the client's hair and pulling
strands through the cap is known as

    A. painting
    B. streaking
    C. frosting
    D. tipping

___ 17. Which lightener should you use for a
lightener retouch and toner?

    A. cream lightener
    B. powder lightener
    C. oil lightener
    D. frosting bleach

___ 18. The cosmetologist accidently drops his/her
only frosting hook on the floor when pulling
strands through the cap. What should the
cosmetologist do?

    A. sanitize the hook
    B. pick it up and continue working
    C. wipe it with a towel
    D. put it in his/her pocket

___ 19. When bleaching the hair, a hair lightening
catalyst would be

    A. ammonium thioglycolate
    B. peroxide
    C. sodium bromate
    D. sodium hydroxide

___ 20. During the application of a virgin hair
lightener, the bleach is applied away from
the scalp at a distance of about

    A. 1/2″ to 1″
    B. 1-1/2″ to 2″
    C. 2-1/4″ to 2-3/4″
    D. 3″ to 3-1/4″

___ 21. When applying a virgin bleach, how far
from the scalp is the bleach applied?

    A. 1/2″
    B. 1-1/2″
    C. 2″
    D. 3-1/2″

___ 22. To correctly lighten the hair, all bleaches
must be

    A. dry before removing
    B. dripping to properly process
    C. moist to be active
    D. warmed to body temperatures

___ 23. When bleaching hair that is very porous, it
may be necessary to use a

    A. filler
    B. conditioner
    C. softener
    D. restorer

___ 24. What volume hydrogen peroxide is the
oxidizing catalyst in bleach?

    A. 5 volume
    B. 10 volume
    C. 15 volume
    D. 20 volume

Poss.	Wrong	%	Right
24	0	100%	24
24	1	96%	23
24	2	92%	22
24	3	88%	21
24	4	83%	20
24	5	79%	19
24	6	75%	18
24	7	71%	17
24	8	67%	16
24	9	63%	15

22 Questions

___ 1. Before cold waving the entire head, the degree to which the hair will curl can be determined by using

A. concave curls
B. convex curls
C. test curls
D. pin curls

___ 2. The pH value of a regular cold-wave solution would be

A. oxygen
B. alkaline
C. neutral
D. acid

___ 3. The pH value of cold-wave neutralizers would be

A. oxide
B. alkaline
C. neutral
D. acid

___ 4. Cotton is placed around the hairline before applying the cold-waving solution; it should be

A. removed after it is applied
B. allowed to remain until the neutralizer is applied
C. removed following the neutralizer
D. removed when the rods are taken out

___ 5. The elastic strap of a cold-wave rod is normally fastened

A. along the very bottom of the section
B. next to the top parting of the section
C. along the vertical parting of the curl
D. across the top of the curl

___ 6. If the cosmetologist is NOT careful when drying the hair after a curly permanent wave, the hair can be burned with the

A. setting lotion
B. infra-red lamp
C. tint mixture
D. hydrogen

___ 7. In which of the following conditions should the cosmetologist REFUSE to give the client a cold wave?

A. a scar on the scalp
B. a cranial surgical wound
C. a scalp freckle
D. an ulna surgical wound

___ 8. During a wrapping procedure using waving solution, breakages can occur if too much tension is placed on the

A. hair
B. comb
C. end wrap
D. rod

___ 9. To remove dripping cold-waving solution, use a piece of cotton or the corner of a towel saturated with

A. cold water
B. warm water
C. tepid water
D. hot water

___ 10. If a couple of small areas of hair do not have enough curl one week after the wave process, the cosmetologist should give the client

A. a refund check
B. another cosmetologist
C. some pickup curls
D. another chemical wave

___ 11. When wrapping a ponytail cold wave, it is better to begin wrapping the

A. bottom section
B. top section
C. middle section
D. front section

___ 12. The action of cold-waving solution on the hair is one of

A. softening
B. hardening
C. shrinking
D. contracting

13. When processing the cold wave, the hair tends to swell, or

    A. expand
    B. contract
    C. harden
    D. shrink

14. Cold-waving resistant hair would usually require a

    A. longer processing time
    B. shorter processing time
    C. conditioner
    D. toner

15. If a plastic cap is used to cover the permanent waving rods during processing, what should you be careful NOT to do?

    A. allow too much heat to collect
    B. tighten the cap too much
    C. allow too much air to escape
    D. clip the cap in the front section

16. When relaxing a permanent wave that is too curly, where should you begin your application?

    A. the nape section
    B. the top section
    C. the side section
    D. the crown section

17. When sodium bromate fumes and ammonia fumes mix together in an open towel hamper, what could result?

    A. a fire
    B. a strong acid smell
    C. discoloration of towels
    D. stain in the hamper

18. One disadvantage of an acid wave is that it is

    A. difficult to time
    B. slow processing
    C. harder on the skin
    D. drying to the hair

19. If permanent waving solution drips along the client's forehead, what should you do?

    A. blot excess solution
    B. wipe off solution
    C. flush with alcohol
    D. flush with astringent

20. When relaxing naturally curly hair or an over-curly permanent wave, what should you do if the hair is processing slowly and you want to speed up the processing?

    A. reapply the relaxing mixture
    B. place cap over hair and seat client under a warm hair dryer
    C. rinse relaxer and dryer dry hair, then reapply mixture
    D. use ultra-violet lamp to speed up processing

21. After the hair has been wound and saturated with cold-waving lotion, test curls should be taken immediately, then every

    A. 1 minute
    B. 2 to 3 minutes
    C. 4 to 5 minutes
    D. 6 to 7 minutes

22. Before giving your client a permanent wave, you notice open sores on his/her scalp. What should you do?

    A. apply condition, and give service
    B. advise the client to reschedule after sores heal
    C. explain condition to client, use a medicated shampoo, and give permanent
    D. apply alcohol, then shampoo twice

Poss.	Wrong	%	Right
22	0	100%	22
22	1	95%	21
22	2	91%	20
22	3	86%	19
22	4	82%	18
22	5	77%	17
22	6	73%	16
22	7	68%	15
22	8	64%	14
22	9	59%	13
22	10	55%	12

21 Questions

___ 1. Before cold waving the entire head, the degree to which the hair will curl can be determined by using

 A. concave curls
 B. convex curls
 C. test curls
 D. pin curls

___ 2. The pH value of cold-wave neutralizers would be

 A. oxide
 B. alkaline
 C. neutral
 D. acid

___ 3. Cotton is placed around the hairline before applying the cold-waving solution; it should be

 A. removed after it is applied
 B. allowed to remain until the neutralizer is applied
 C. removed following the neutralizer
 D. removed when the rods are taken out

___ 4. The elastic strap of a cold-wave rod is normally fastened

 A. along the very bottom of the section
 B. next to the top parting of the section
 C. along the vertical parting of the curl
 D. across the top of the curl

___ 5. The pH value of a regular cold-wave solution would be

 A. oxygen
 B. alkaline
 C. neutral
 D. acid

___ 6. If the cosmetologist is NOT careful when drying the hair after a curly permanent wave, the hair can be burned with the

 A. setting lotion
 B. infra-red lamp
 C. tint mixture
 D. hydrogen

___ 7. In which of the following conditions should the cosmetologist REFUSE to give the client a cold wave?

 A. a scar on the scalp
 B. a cranial surgical wound
 C. a scalp freckle
 D. an ulna surgical wound

___ 8. During a wrapping procedure using waving solution, breakages can occur if too much tension is placed on the

 A. hair
 B. comb
 C. end wrap
 D. rod

___ 9. To remove dripping cold-waving solution, use a piece of cotton or the corner of a towel saturated with

 A. cold water
 B. warm water
 C. tepid water
 D. hot water

___ 10. If a couple of small areas of hair do not have enough curl one week after the wave process, the cosmetologist should give the client

 A. a refund check
 B. another cosmetologist
 C. some pickup curls
 D. another chemical wave

___ 11. When wrapping a ponytail cold wave, it is better to begin wrapping the the

 A. bottom section
 B. top section
 C. middle section
 D. front section

___ 12. The action of cold-waving solution on the hair is one of

 A. softening
 B. hardening
 C. shrinking
 D. contracting

___ 13. When processing the cold wave, the hair tends to swell, or

    A. expand
    B. contract
    C. harden
    D. shrink

___ 14. Cold waving resistant hair would usually require a

    A. longer processing time
    B. shorter processing time
    C. conditioner
    D. toner

___ 15. If a plastic cap is used to cover the permanent waving rods during processing, what should you be careful NOT to do?

    A. allow too much heat to collect
    B. tighten the cap too much
    C. allow too much air to escape
    D. clip the cap in the front section

___ 16. When relaxing a permanent wave that is too curly, where should you begin your application?

    A. the nape section
    B. the top section
    C. the side section
    D. the crown section

___ 17. When sodium bromate fumes and ammonia fumes mix together in an open towel hamper, what could result?

    A. a fire
    B. a strong acid smell
    C. discoloration of towels
    D. stain in the hamper

___ 18. One disadvantage of an acid wave is that it is

    A. difficult to time
    B. slow processing
    C. harder on the skin
    D. drying to the hair

___ 19. If permanent waving solution drips along the client's forehead, what should you do?

    A. blot excess solution
    B. wipe off solution
    C. flush with alcohol
    D. flush with astringent

___ 20. When relaxing naturally curly hair or an over-curly permanent wave, what should you do if the hair is processing slowly and you want to speed up the processing?

    A. reapply the relaxing mixture
    B. place cap over hair and seat client under a warm hair dryer
    C. rinse relaxer and dryer-dry the hair, then reapply mixture
    D. use ultra-violet lamp to speed up processing

___ 21. After the hair has been wound and saturated with cold-waving lotion, test curls should be taken immediately, then every

    A. 1 minute
    B. 2 to 3 minutes
    C. 4 to 5 minutes
    D. 6 to 7 minutes

Poss.	Wrong	%	Right
21	0	100%	21
21	1	95%	20
21	2	90%	19
21	3	86%	18
21	4	81%	17
21	5	76%	16
21	6	71%	15
21	7	67%	14
21	8	62%	13
21	9	57%	12

22 Questions

___ 1. The pH range for acid waves is

A. 2.5 to 4.5
B. 5.8 to 6.8
C. 7.9 to 8.8
D. 9.0 to 9.7

___ 2. When permanent waving the hair, how many turns must the hair be wound around the rod in order to achieve a curl pattern?

A. once
B. twice
C. four turns
D. five turns

___ 3. When appling the waving solution as part of the permanent waving process, the cosmetologist sees that there is a purple discoloration of the solution on the client's towel. What should the cosmetologist do?

A. stop and rinse the hair with water
B. apply neutralizer immediately
C. continue to give the permanent
D. apply a different waving solution

___ 4. If a neutralizing bib is used for neutralizing the permanent, where should you place a small piece of cotton?

A. by the ears
B. across the forehead
C. under the eye hook
D. around the nape

___ 5. Two basic chemicals used in a cold-waving solution are

A. ammonia and formalin
B. sulfuric acid and ammonia
C. carbolic acid and formalin
D. thioglycolic acid and ammonia

___ 6. Two basic chemicals used in neutralizing solutions are hydrogen peroxide and sodium

A. bicarbonate
B. hydroxide
C. crystaline
D. bromate

___ 7. During the winding process in cold waving, the physical bonds in the hair shaft that are broken are called

A. amino
B. cysteine
C. hydrogen
D. salt

___ 8. The main chemical in an acid permanent wave is

A. thio
B. ammonium thio
C. glyceryl monothioglycolate
D. ester

___ 9. Cold waving hair involves a physical action, and a

A. medical process
B. mineral process
C. chemical process
D. legal process

___ 10. The action of the cold-waving solution is stopped, and the curl is fixed with a

A. developer
B. curler
C. shaper
D. neutralizer

___ 11. The cold-waving solution is applied to the

A. rod, hair, and scalp
B. rod and hair
C. scalp and neutralizer
D. hair and scalp

___ 12. A self-timing permanent wave is one in which the manufacturer recommends that you

A. test curl every 3 minutes
B. towel blot each rod
C. process for a set period of time
D. place client under a dryer

13. The chemical (sulphur) bonds in the hair make it possible for the cosmetologist to

    A. cut the hair
    B. rinse the hair
    C. cold wave the hair
    D. comb the hair

14. During the cold-wave process, the waving solution breaks the cross bonds, and the neutralizer

    A. cracks them
    B. reforms them
    C. makes them triangular
    D. softens them

15. A neck towel saturated with waving solution, and left around a client's neck may cause a chemical

    A. burn
    B. reaction
    C. lesion
    D. sore

16. When applied, the neutralizer also has an effect on the hair called

    A. osmosis
    B. oxidation
    C. stimulation
    D. alteration

17. If cold waving hair that is bleached (lightened), it is best to select rods that are

    A. large
    B. small
    C. midget
    D. of any size

18. Cold waves can be successfully given to hair tinted with salon dyes that contain

    A. metallic salts
    B. aniline derivatives
    C. lead minerals
    D. copper minerals

19. When cold waving, the size of the curl or wave pattern will be controlled by the

    A. cold-wave solution
    B. type of neutralizer
    C. size of the rod
    D. size of the end papers

20. To achieve a good curl when permanent waving, how much tension should be applied to the hair as it is wound on the rods?

    A. very firm tension
    B. very little tension
    C. moderate-firm, even tension
    D. no tension

21. When permanent waving very sparse (thin) hair, what size rods and subsections will give the most curl?

    A. small rods, large subsections
    B. small rods, small subsections
    C. large rods, large subsections
    D. none of the above

22. If cotton is placed around the hairline during the application of the waving solution, what should be done to the cotton first as a safety precaution?

    A. twist it
    B. fold it
    C. spray mist water on it
    D. apply neutralizer on it

Poss.	Wrong	%	Right
22	0	100%	22
22	1	95%	21
22	2	91%	20
22	3	86%	19
22	4	82%	18
22	5	77%	17
22	6	73%	16
22	7	68%	15
22	8	64%	14
22	9	59%	13
22	10	55%	12

21 Questions

___ 1. In order for an acid permanent wave to curl the hair, what must be applied?

A. gel
B. heat
C. glaze
D. water

___ 2. When applying the waving lotion, what action will cause the solution to be readily absorbed by the hair?

A. capillary action
B. gravity
C. opposites attract
D. sponge action

___ 3. While giving a permanent wave using heated clamps, the client complains of a burning sensation in the left front side section. What should the cosmetologist do?

A. rinse that section immediately
B. place cotton under clamps in the section
C. spray section with water
D. unplug clamp heater

___ 4. If the neck towel becomes damp with waving solution during a permanent wave, what will happen?

A. mild irritation
B. chapping of the skin
C. a chemical burn
D. nothing will happen

___ 5. During the neutralizing process at the shampoo bowl, how may hair breakage occur?

A. applying too much water when rinsing
B. applying too much neutralizer when neutralizing
C. blotting rods with a dry towel, then damp towel
D. the weight of the client's head against rods and shampoo bowl

___ 6. Hair wound smoothly around the cold wave rod without stretching allows the hair to

A. expand during processing
B. contract during processing
C. harden during processing
D. shrink during processing

___ 7. Preconditioning of the hair before cold waving is done to equalize the

A. elasticity
B. longevity
C. porosity
D. resiliency

___ 8. If analysis of the hair before cold waving indicates it is porous, it should

A. be difficult to curl
B. be easy to curl
C. not curl at all
D. become frizzy

___ 9. Cold-waving solution should not be applied in the presence of

A. abrasions
B. cuts
C. redness
D. all of the above

___ 10. The degree to which the hair is curled during cold waving is determined by the

A. number of turns the hair goes around the rod
B. sizing of the partings used
C. hair's texture and condition
D. all of the above

___ 11. For the cold-waving application, most manufacturers advise wearing protective

A. aprons
B. eye glasses
C. gloves
D. hair nets

12. The cold-waving process includes all of the following items in the regular price except one. Which item is not usually included?

    A. conditioning
    B. wrapping
    C. processing
    D. neutralizing

13. When giving a permanent wave, the cosmetologist notices the waving solution turns purple after it is applied to the hair. What does this indicate?

    A. minerals are present in the hair
    B. the client has been tinting her hair at home
    C. a recent illness in the client's home
    D. no one knows why this happens

14. When giving a cold wave, the cosmetologist is about to neutralize the perm and discovers there is no neutralizer anywhere in the salon. What should the cosmetologist do to keep the most curl in the hair?

    A. rinse the hair and remove the rods
    B. blot the hair and apply 20 volume hydrogen peroxide
    C. blot rods with damp towel and air dry
    D. rinse rods and place client under dryer

15. Most cold waves have a pH range of

    A. 5.5 to 6.5
    B. 6.5 to 7.5
    C. 7.5 to 8.5
    D. 8.5 to 9.5

16. Neutralizers are also called

    A. relatives
    B. fixatives
    C. laxatives
    D. substantives

17. When sectioning to put in a cold wave rod, the section should be about the same length as the rod, or

    A. 1/2˝ longer
    B. 1/2˝ shorter
    C. 1˝ longer
    D. 1˝ shorter

18. If the hair is over-stretched and over-processed during cold waving, it will look too curly when wet, and

    A. straight when dry
    B. super-curly when dry
    C. wavy when dry
    D. kinky when dry

19. The cold-wave neutralizer affects the hair shaft by a

    A. rehardening, or shrinking process
    B. softening, or expanding process
    C. conditioning, or normalizing process
    D. damaging, or straightening process

20. The cold-waving solution breaks bonds in the hair that are made of

    A. salt
    B. protein
    C. amino
    D. sulfur

21. The general shape of cold-waving strand subsections would be

    A. triangular
    B. round
    C. oval
    D. rectangular

Poss.	Wrong	%	Right
21	0	100%	21
21	1	95%	20
21	2	90%	19
21	3	86%	18
21	4	81%	17
21	5	76%	16
21	6	71%	15
21	7	67%	14
21	8	62%	13
21	9	57%	12

27 Questions

___ 1. The process of chemically straightening super-curly hair is called chemical hair

    A. stabilizing
    B. crimping
    C. relaxing
    D. normalizing

___ 2. The actions of a chemical hair straightener causes the hair to

    A. soften and swell
    B. shape and curl
    C. shift and mold
    D. shrink and harden

___ 3. Before applying a chemical relaxer, analyze the hair for porosity, texture, and elasticity; then, examine the

    A. relaxing kit
    B. hairline
    C. scalp
    D. fingernails

___ 4. For chemically straightening the hair, use a chemical relaxer, and a

    A. setting lotion
    B. stabilizer
    C. pre-creme
    D. conditioner

___ 5. Before a chemical hair straightener, the cosmetologist would not

    A. read label directions
    B. examine the scalp
    C. analyze the hair
    D. brush the hair

___ 6. A thio relaxer affects the hair shaft by causing it to

    A. soften and swell
    B. soften and shrink
    C. harden and shrink
    D. harden and swell

___ 7. The best shampoo to use after a chemical relaxer is a shampoo that has a(n)

    A. neutral base
    B. alkaline pH
    C. acid pH
    D. oil base

___ 8. The most popular basic chemical used for relaxing kinky curly hair is sodium

    A. sulfur
    B. bicarbonate
    C. hydroxide
    D. bromate

___ 9. Chemical relaxers are also called

    A. presses
    B. perms
    C. thermal pressers
    D. curl straighteners

___ 10. The base in a no-base chemical relaxer is used to

    A. neutralize the relaxer
    B. protect the hair
    C. protect the scalp
    D. straighten the hair

___ 11. The straightening action is stopped during a chemical relaxer by using a

    A. stabilizing rinse
    B. neutralizing shampoo
    C. neutralizing creme
    D. stabilizing creme

___ 12. After chemically relaxing the hair for a client with super-curly hair, what service should NOT be given to the client?

    A. roller set
    B. regular electric curling iron set
    C. pressing comb/thermal iron set
    D. pick-out style after hair has been dried

___ 13. Hair should be conditioned after a sodium hydroxide relaxer to prevent

   A. breakage during combing and setting
   B. dry, scaly scalp
   C. red, irritated scalp
   D. breakage during thermal pressing

___ 14. The neutralizing shampoo used in the chemical relaxing service is also called a

   A. filler
   B. conditioner
   C. cleaner
   D. stabilizer

___ 15. After a chemical relaxer, a conditioner should be applied

   A. after the comb-out
   B. before the hair is styled with rollers
   C. just before the comb-out
   D. after the hair is set

___ 16. The stabilizer used in chemical hair relaxing is also called a(n)

   A. normalizer
   B. fixative
   C. acid
   D. controller

___ 17. The process of permanently changing the structural bonds of super-curly hair into a straight position is called

   A. bond straightening
   B. uncurling
   C. decurling
   D. chemical relaxing

___ 18. Hair is chemically straightened with thio, or

   A. formalin
   B. borax
   C. hydrogen peroxide
   D. sodium hydroxide

___ 19. Cosmetologists avoid giving a chemical relaxer when the scalp examination reveals the presence of

   A. loose, pliable scalp
   B. oily scalp and hair
   C. abrasions and scratches
   D. firm, tight scalp

___ 20. If the client has a little spot on the scalp that is burning during the processing of a chemical hair relaxer on super-curly hair, what should you do?

   A. rinse all relaxer from the hair immediately
   B. apply an astringent to the spot
   C. apply petrolatum to the spot
   D. spray spot with cool water

___ 21. Before applying a chemical relaxer, the hair and scalp must be

   A. tinted
   B. shampooed
   C. brushed
   D. examined

___ 22. To stop the action of the sodium hydroxide, and remove it from the hair, the cosmetologist

   A. air neutralizes the hair
   B. combs, then shampoos the hair
   C. conditions, then rinses the hair
   D. rinses and shampoos the hair

___ 23. If unsure which strength chemical relaxer should be used, the cosmetologist should take a(n)

   A. allergy test
   B. skin test
   C. strand test
   D. patch test

___ 24. When neutralizing a chemical relaxer, what is the minimum number times the hair should be shampooed?

   A. once
   B. twice
   C. three times
   D. four times

___ 25. During the processing and neutralizing of a chemical relaxer service, what can be done to minimize neck irritation?

   A. apply cotton coil
   B. change towel frequently
   C. keep the client's neck against the bowl
   D. apply neutralizing cream

26. What should you use to determine the correct processing and neutralizing time for a chemical relaxer?

    A. patch test
    B. pull test
    C. strand test
    D. hair texture

27. One of the most important things to remember about the processing of a chemical relaxer is

    A. apply it slowly and evenly
    B. never leave the client unattended
    C. never serve coffee during processing
    D. brush the hair before neutralizing

Poss.	Wrong	%	Right
27	0	100%	27
27	1	96%	26
27	2	93%	25
27	3	89%	24
27	4	85%	23
27	5	81%	22
27	6	78%	21
27	7	74%	20
27	8	70%	19
27	9	67%	18
27	10	63%	17
27	11	59%	16

---

21 CHEMICAL HAIR RELAXING POST-TEST 2

25 Questions

1. If you live in a very warm climate and your client arrives perspiring before having a chemical hair relaxer, what should you do?

    A. thoroughly shampoo the hair
    B. place client under cool dryer
    C. wait while client cools off
    D. blot moisture from scalp before starting

2. If super-curly hair has been thermal pressed, or is otherwise very damaged, the cosmetologist should

    A. refer the person to another salon
    B. refuse the chemical relaxer
    C. advise a tint to even the hair porosity
    D. use a mild-strength relaxer

3. As in cold waving, chemical relaxers work faster on hair that is

    A. wiry
    B. coarse
    C. non-porous
    D. porous

4. Before a chemical relaxer, the skin and scalp can be protected from chemical burns by applying a

    A. jelly
    B. base
    C. stabilizer
    D. neutralizer

5. Chemical relaxers are packaged in a

    A. kit
    B. unit
    C. carton
    D. set

6. A term often used in connection with sodium hydroxide is

    A. neutral
    B. alkaline
    C. caustic
    D. acid

7. The main chemical used to stop the relaxer is

    A. sodium hydroxide
    B. sodium bromate
    C. hydrogen peroxide
    D. ammonium thioglycolate

8. After a sodium hydroxide relaxer has processed, but before it is shampooed, the hair should be thoroughly

    A. brushed
    B. rinsed
    C. conditioned
    D. combed

___ 9. The application of a base or no-base relaxer would begin in the

A. crown section
B. right side section
C. left side section
D. nape section

___ 10. The difference between a base and no-base relaxer is that the no-base

A. is more dangerous to use, but requires more time
B. is safer to use, but requires more time
C. always requires the use of protective gloves
D. does not require application of the base

___ 11. Since all relaxers are basically the same, reading label directions is necessary

A. sometimes
B. always
C. seldom
D. never

___ 12. If you use all of a particular relaxer, but are in need of more to complete the service, it is best to

A. neutralize; continue when there is enough material to complete
B. add a relaxer made by another company
C. add water to what is left in the jar, then apply to hair
D. add water to what is on the hair

___ 13. The chemical relaxer begins to work when what is applied?

A. medium heat hair dryer
B. heat and friction
C. cold water and stabilizer
D. hot water and shampoo

___ 14. When relaxing virgin hair, the relaxer is always combed through the

A. scalp hair right away
B. entire length of the strand
C. ends of each strand right away
D. none of the above

___ 15. It is harmful to the hair to leave a chemical relaxer on it longer than

A. 10 minutes
B. 15 minutes
C. 20 minutes
D. 25 minutes

___ 16. Chemical relaxers should be used carefully because the hair may

A. become oily
B. become porous
C. stretch
D. dissolve

___ 17. The suggested implement to use for cutting hair that has been chemically relaxed is the

A. electric clipper
B. thinning shears
C. razor
D. scissors

___ 18. When giving a chemical relaxer, the cosmetologist must wear

A. a coverall apron
B. thick soled shoes
C. safety glasses
D. protective gloves

___ 19. When subsectioning the hair around the face for application of the relaxer, it is best to part the hair

A. diagonally
B. up and down
C. vertically
D. horizontally

___ 20. Just before applying the relaxer, the hair is subdivided into

A. eight sections
B. four sections
C. six sections
D. two sections

___ 21. If too much pressure is applied during the relaxing service, the hair will

A. revert to curl
B. stretch
C. dissolve
D. break

165

22. During neutralizing, the hair should be shampooed at least how many times?

   A. as many as needed
   B. 1 to 2
   C. 2 to 3
   D. 3 to 4

23. When applying a chemical relaxer be careful NOT to

   A. apply it to the scalp
   B. apply too much to the middle of the hair
   C. apply it with a brush
   D. apply it with a bottle

24. In which area of the head should a chemical relaxer application begin?

   A. front hairline
   B. nape hairline
   C. resistant crown
   D. normal top

25. What is the ideal amount of time for the application of a chemical relaxer in EACH section?

   A. 2 minutes
   B. 4 minutes
   C. 6 minutes
   D. 20 minutes

Poss.	Wrong	%	Right
25	0	100%	25
25	1	96%	24
25	2	92%	23
25	3	88%	22
25	4	84%	21
25	5	80%	20
25	6	76%	19
25	7	72%	18
25	8	68%	17
25	9	64%	16
25	10	60%	15

---

22 THERMAL PRESSING POST-TEST 1

23 Questions

1. After the hair is pressed, the thermal iron forms the curl by rotating the iron using

   A. a clicking action
   B. sliding actions
   C. an oval action
   D. a back and forth action

2. After a thermal wave, the hair is brushed and combed into a hairstyle

   A. after the lanolin has been applied
   B. while the hair is still hot
   C. when the hair has been cooled
   D. while the hair is lukewarm

3. When thermal waving the hair, fine, short hairs around the hairline are best curled with

   A. some pin curls
   B. a smaller iron
   C. a crimper
   D. some perm rods

4. The clicking referred to when thermal waving means how the iron is

   A. heated
   B. cleaned
   C. cooled
   D. opened and closed

5. Once the hair strand has been scorched (burned) during a thermal pressing service, how can it be repaired?

   A. reconditioning
   B. use of a filler
   C. cutting the hair
   D. applying more oil

6. Before thermal waving super-curly hair, the cosmetologist should

   A. color it
   B. press it
   C. shape it
   D. comb it

___ 7. What is the name for the service in which the hair is pressed twice on the top of the strand, and once on the underside?

    A. one press
    B. light press
    C. comb press
    D. soft press

___ 8. When pressing the hair, hair texture has to be considered, as well as the

    A. temperature of the comb
    B. chemicals to be used
    C. setting pattern
    D. cutting method

___ 9. Before pressing the hair, it should be

    A. combed and brushed
    B. shampooed and dried
    C. shampooed and marcelled
    D. dried and curled

___ 10. If the hair is pressed twice on each side of the strand before it is curled, this press is called a

    A. soft press
    B. hard press
    C. firm press
    D. double press

___ 11. Temporarily straightening the hair with the hot comb is called hair

    A. crimping
    B. straightening
    C. pressing
    D. molding

___ 12. To adequately straighten the hair, the pressing comb should be

    A. perfectly even
    B. hot enough
    C. curved enough
    D. heavy enough

___ 13. Hair that has been chemically relaxed cannot be silked, or

    A. set
    B. curled
    C. brushed
    D. pressed

___ 14. The temperature of the pressing comb is determined by its reaction to the

    A. touch
    B. tissue
    C. client
    D. litmus paper

___ 15. What would be the results of pressing lightened hair that was NOT thoroughly dried?

    A. it would be scorched
    B. it would be shiny
    C. it would be slightly curly
    D. it would be very curly

___ 16. Before thermal pressing the hair, what should be done first?

    A. shampoo and condition it
    B. shampoo and dry it thoroughly
    C. shampoo, condition, then dry it thoroughly
    D. nothing, just press it

___ 17. Should you accidently burn the client's scalp during a thermal pressing service, what should you apply to the burn?

    A. Neosporin ointment
    B. violet jelly
    C. butter coating
    D. alcohol solution

___ 18. When giving a pressing service, the cosmetologist should use

    A. moderate pressure and heat
    B. moderate pressure and intense heat
    C. firm pressure and intense heat
    D. B and C only

___ 19. As a safety consideration, before pressing the hair, the practitioner should check the scalp for

    A. flakes
    B. abrasions
    C. discoloration
    D. oiliness

20. How can gradual breakage of the hair happen as the result of thermal hair pressing?

   A. too much oil
   B. too much brushing
   C. having the hair pressed too often
   D. having the hair shampooed too often

21. What is used to remove carbon build-up from your thermal iron?

   A. sand paper
   B. steel wool
   C. an emery board
   D. all of the above

22. If the hair has been pressed, but the desired result was not achieved, what happened?

   A. not enough heat
   B. not enough pressure
   C. not enough curl
   D. A and B only

23. Which of the following hair textures will be difficult to press?

   A. fine, curly hair
   B. coarse, wiry hair
   C. medium hair
   D. fine, gray, curly hair

Poss.	Wrong	%	Right
23	0	100%	23
23	1	96%	22
23	2	91%	21
23	3	87%	20
23	4	83%	19
23	5	78%	18
23	6	74%	17
23	7	70%	16
23	8	65%	15
23	9	61%	14

22 THERMAL PRESSING POST-TEST 2

17 Questions

1. The temperature of the pressing comb is determined by its reaction to the

   A. touch
   B. tissue
   C. client
   D. litmus paper

2. Hair that has been chemically relaxed cannot be silked, or

   A. set
   B. curled
   C. brushed
   D. pressed

3. To adequately straighten the hair, the pressing comb should be

   A. perfectly even
   B. hot enough
   C. curved enough
   D. heavy enough

4. Thermal pressing usually begins in the

   A. nape section
   B. crown section
   C. side section
   D. top section

5. Temporarily straightening the hair with the hot comb is called hair

   A. crimping
   B. straightening
   C. pressing
   D. molding

6. If the hair is pressed twice on both sides of the strand before it is curled, this press is called a

   A. soft press
   B. hard press
   C. firm press
   D. double press

7. Before pressing the hair, it should be

   A. combed and brushed
   B. shampooed and dried
   C. shampooed and marcelled
   D. dried and curled

8. When pressing the hair, hair texture has to be considered, as well as the

   A. temperature of the comb
   B. chemicals to be used
   C. setting pattern
   D. cutting method

9. A single hair-pressing treatment with the hot comb is known as a

   A. one press
   B. light press
   C. comb press
   D. soft press

10. Before thermal waving super-curly hair, the cosmetologist should

    A. color it
    B. press it
    C. shape it
    D. comb it

11. The styling comb used in thermal waving should be made of

    A. aluminum
    B. steel
    C. hard rubber
    D. soft rubber

12. The clicking referred to when thermal waving means how the iron is

    A. heated
    B. cleaned
    C. cooled
    D. opened and closed

13. When thermal waving the hair, fine, short hairs around the hairline are best curled with

    A. some pin curls
    B. a smaller iron
    C. a crimper
    D. some perm rods

14. After a thermal wave, the hair is brushed and combed into a hairstyle

    A. after the lanolin has been applied
    B. while the hair is still hot
    C. when the hair has been cooled
    D. while the hair is lukewarm

15. When pressing the hair, what does the use of a pressing oil prevent?

    A. scorching
    B. breaking
    C. burning
    D. all of the above

16. After the hair has been thermal pressed, what will cause the hair to revert back to its natural curliness?

    A. heat
    B. moisture
    C. hairspray
    D. all of the above

17. Which of the following hair textures would most likely be given a hard press?

    A. fine hair
    B. medium hair
    C. coarse hair
    D. all of the above

Poss.	Wrong	%	Right
17	0	100%	17
17	1	94%	16
17	2	88%	15
17	3	82%	14
17	4	76%	13
17	5	71%	12
17	6	65%	11

18 Questions

___ 1. Before applying a curl reformation straightener, what should you do?

A. make a client record
B. apply the neutralizer to nape
C. apply a base to hairline
D. give a scalp treatment

___ 2. During a curl reformation, how much tension is used to wrap the hair on the rods?

A. no tension
B. moderate tension
C. slight tension
D. firm tension

___ 3. The client is receiving a curl reformation. The rearranger has been applied, capped, and put under the dryer. How often should the processing be checked for relaxation?

A. every 5 minutes
B. every 10 minutes
C. every 15 minutes
D. it doesn't need to be checked

___ 4. What is the name for the product that straightens the hair in the curl reformation service?

A. chemical relaxer
B. chemical rearranger
C. hair straightener
D. hair filler

___ 5. The double-application service in which super-curly hair is straightened, then curled on permanent wave rods, is called a(n)

A. recurl
B. structuring
C. Afro-pick
D. none of the above

___ 6. Before applying the neutralizer to the rods when doing a curl reformation, the hair should be

A. conditioned
B. rinsed with hot water
C. rinsed with tepid water
D. rinsed with cold water

___ 7. To be successful, what size rod subsections should the cosmetologist use when doing a curl reformation?

A. small subsections
B. medium subsections
C. large subsections
D. none of the above

___ 8. Which type of hair will curl the fastest?

A. coarse hair
B. hair with elasticity
C. porous hair
D. fine hair

___ 9. During a curl reformation, the hair dries out while you are wrapping it on the rods. What should you do?

A. apply more waving solution
B. apply water to dry strands
C. use spray-on conditioner
D. use two end wraps

___ 10. When giving a curl reformation, it is very important to wear

A. a hair net
B. an operator apron
C. protective shoes
D. none of the above

___ 11. When doing a curl reformation, how often should the rearranger be tested?

A. 1–2 minutes
B. 3–5 minutes
C. 6–8 minutes
D. 9–10 minutes

___ 12. What is the main chemical used in the neutralizer of most curl reformation products?

A. hydrogen peroxide
B. sodium bromate
C. ammonium thioglycolate
D. sodium chloride

___ 13. What is the one thing to watch out for when you are about to give a curl reformation?

A. too many test curls
B. client allergies
C. using too many rods
D. tangled hair

___ 14. If the client is scheduled for a curl reformation and tells you that he/she had a chemical hair relaxer last month, what should you do?

A. give the service
B. condition the hair, then give the service
C. give the service, then condition the hair
D. refuse to give the service

___ 15. When giving a curl reformation, how many turns is the rod unwound in order to test curl the strand?

A. 1-1/2 to 2 turns
B. 2-1/2 to 3 turns
C. 3-1/2 to 4 turns
D. 4-1/2 to 5 turns

___ 16. Which of the following is part of the curl reformation service?

A. place cap over hair during processing
B. test curl strand
C. apply curl booster
D. all of the above

___ 17. When applying the curl rearranger, you should wear

A. gloves
B. an operator apron
C. protective sleeves
D. all of the above

___ 18. In which of the following situations would you advise against the giving of a soft curl?

A. the hair has been previously pressed
B. the hair has been previously shampooed
C. the hair has been previously relaxed with thio
D. the hair has been conditioned

Poss.	Wrong	%	Right
18	0	100%	18
18	1	94%	17
18	2	89%	16
18	3	83%	15
18	4	78%	14
18	5	72%	13
18	6	67%	12

24 DESCRIBE THE SKIN POST-TEST 1

19 Questions

___ 1. If a suntan lotion has a rating of 15, how much exposure to the ultra-violet rays of the sun will you be exposed to?

A. none
B. 40%
C. 60%
D. 80%

___ 2. What will increase the strength of the sun's rays?

A. water
B. snow
C. swimming pool
D. all of the above

___ 3. The stratum corneum layer of the skin is also called the

A. clear layer
B. horny layer
C. basal layer
D. cutis layer

___ 4. The common name for subcutaneous tissue is

A. muscle tissue
B. nerve tissue
C. fatty tissue
D. blood tissue

____ 5. The scientific study of the structure, function, and diseases of the skin is known as

A. angiology
B. psychology
C. dermatology
D. osteology

____ 6. Any harmful or abnormal change in the skin is called a(n)

A. irritation
B. rash
C. lesion
D. patch

____ 7. The term used to describe the cause of a skin disease is

A. etiology
B. pathology
C. radiology
D. physiology

____ 8. The type of keratin that the skin is made of is

A. soft
B. hard
C. fragile
D. horny

____ 9. A simple word for the medical term hyperkeratosis would be

A. freckle
B. mole
C. callus
D. liver spot

____ 10. A person with albinism would have

A. pink skin
B. white hair
C. pink eyes
D. all of the above

____ 11. What skin condition does the word melanoderma describe?

A. hypopigmentation
B. hyperpigmentation
C. liver spots
D. areata

____ 12. What effects will over-exposure to sunlight have on the skin?

A. premature aging
B. wrinkling
C. thickening
D. all of the above

____ 13. What is the disorder called when the body does not perspire (sweat) at all?

A. hyperhidrosis
B. miliaria rubra
C. bromhidrosis
D. anhidrosis

____ 14. What is the name for the odor used to describe sweat that has been contaminated by bacteria?

A. sweat
B. bacteria
C. body odor
D. halitosis

____ 15. The general term used to describe both types of sweat glands is

A. superior
B. sebaceous
C. sudoriferous
D. carnivorous

____ 16. In a very warm climate, the flow of sebum tends to

A. increase
B. decrease
C. remain the same
D. B and C

____ 17. There are more and larger sebaceous glands located on the

A. palms and soles
B. arms and legs
C. scalp and face
D. chest and face

____ 18. The layer of the skin containing the keratin-forming and melanin-forming cells is the

A. prickle layer
B. granular layer
C. basal layer
D. horny layer

___ 19. The only two places on the body that the lucid layer of the skin will be found are the

A. forehead and nose
B. elbows and knees
C. ears and neck
D. palms and soles

Poss.	Wrong	%	Right
19	0	100%	19
19	1	95%	18
19	2	89%	17
19	3	84%	16
19	4	79%	15
19	5	74%	14
19	6	68%	13

---

25 FACIAL TREATMENTS POST-TEST 1

22 Questions

___ 1. Emollient cream is used in facial massage as a(n)

A. astringent
B. lubricant
C. cleanser
D. toner

___ 2. What type of lamp is used for dry skin when an emollient is used?

A. ultra-violet
B. infrared
C. quartz
D. actinic

___ 3. When the skin is exposed to ultra-violet rays, there is an increase in Vitamin

A. D
B. C
C. E
D. K

___ 4. An ultra-violet lamp should be placed

A. 36″ from the client
B. 72″ from the client
C. 84″ from the client
D. 96″ from the client

___ 5. Ultra-violet rays are also called

A. red
B. sunlight
C. white
D. actinic

___ 6. What percentage of the sunlight is represented by infrared rays?

A. 40%
B. 60%
C. 80%
D. 90%

___ 7. The word used to describe a kneading or rolling facial movement is

A. effleurage
B. petrissage
C. friction
D. tapotement

___ 8. The most common type of skin tumor is a

A. freckle
B. mole
C. stain
D. callus

___ 9. Lesions are also called

A. liver spots
B. boils
C. vesicles
D. freckles

___ 10. The pigment that colors the skin is called

A. melanin
B. tyrosinase
C. tyrosine
D. keratin

11. After a blackhead has been removed, the cosmetologist should apply a(n)

   A. hot towel
   B. antiseptic
   C. fumigant
   D. deodorant

12. A clay pack is recommended for skin that is

   A. dusty
   B. oily
   C. dry
   D. flakey

13. Of all the light from the sun, ultra-violet rays make up about

   A. 8% of it
   B. 12% of it
   C. 24% of it
   D. 36% of it

14. Ultra-violet rays are also called

   A. red rays
   B. gold rays
   C. actinic rays
   D. deep penetrating rays

15. Of all the light from the sun, infrared rays make up about

   A. 20% of it
   B. 40% of it
   C. 60% of it
   D. 80% of it

16. In the presence of severe acne, the cosmetologist should

   A. avoid facial massage
   B. use tapotement massage
   C. use kneading massage
   D. avoid use of emollient cream

17. The main purpose of a massage is to stimulate and strengthen

   A. nerve branches
   B. fatty tissue
   C. muscle tone
   D. cartilage

18. Of the choices below, select the preparation or product that should be used when giving a facial to normal, or oily skin.

   A. mask
   B. pack
   C. oil-based emollient cream
   D. cotton

19. What is the effect of sponging the skin during a facial treatment?

   A. removes impurities and excess oil
   B. obtains deeper penetration of the oil
   C. softens the skin
   D. allows the fingertips to slide more easily across the skin

20. What purpose does the application of witch hazel to the skin serve in the facial process?

   A. softens the skin
   B. moisturizes the skin
   C. soothes and cleanses the skin
   D. makes skin hard and leathery

21. How is a facial pack usually removed from the face?

   A. alcohol scrub
   B. witch hazel rub
   C. cutting from edges
   D. peeling from the edges

22. Before giving clients a pack or mask treatment, it is important to

   A. give an allergy test
   B. ask them why they want one
   C. heat the pack or mask on the stove
   D. all of the above

Poss.	Wrong	%	Right
22	0	100%	22
22	1	95%	21
22	2	91%	20
22	3	86%	19
22	4	82%	18
22	5	77%	17
22	6	73%	16
22	7	68%	15
22	8	64%	14
22	9	59%	13
22	10	55%	12

31 Questions

___ 1. Tapotement is a massage movement that uses a

A. kneading technique
B. pinching technique
C. stroking technique
D. tapping technique

___ 2. When the petrissage movement is used, it has a(n)

A. soothing effect
B. relaxing effect
C. invigorating effect
D. mellowing effect

___ 3. The massage movement that uses a kneading technique is called

A. petrissage
B. effleurage
C. friction
D. vibration

___ 4. The effleurage massage movement is done lightly and slowly, so it is

A. stimulating
B. soothing
C. exciting
D. irritating

___ 5. Cold cream is used on the face as a

A. foundation
B. base
C. emollient
D. cleanser

___ 6. To some extent, the skin is protected from ultra-violet sun rays by skin

A. melanin
B. keratin
C. cuticles
D. oil

___ 7. A vibration massage technique affects the skin by

A. soothing it
B. cooling it
C. relaxing it
D. stimulating it

___ 8. Massage that uses deep rubbing movements requires a

A. friction technique
B. tapping technique
C. stroking technique
D. vibrating technique

___ 9. Fast massage movements given with moderate pressure will cause body tissue to be

A. stimulated
B. relaxed
C. cooled
D. fatigued

___ 10. The high-frequency facial treatment is advised for skin that has

A. freckles
B. moles
C. acne
D. warts

___ 11. To prevent sagging facial muscles and wrinkling of the skin, what direction should all facial movements be given to the client?

A. downward toward the skin
B. across, from ear to ear
C. upward, toward the front hairline
D. all of the above

___ 12. If a client's eyes and skin are over-exposed to ultra-violet rays, the injury will appear as a

A. deep cut
B. large scab
C. severe burn
D. large abrasion

___ 13. Deep penetrating light rays used in light therapy are

A. blue
B. red
C. green
D. yellow

14. During a treatment using infrared or ultra-violet light, cotton pads saturated with water are used to cover the client's

A. hands
B. eyes
C. forehead
D. ear

15. What is the rubbing facial movement that is done with the flat of the hand or fingertips?

A. effleurage
B. petrissage
C. tapotement
D. friction

16. A facial mask should be used on which of the following skin types?

A. normal skin
B. oily skin
C. dry skin
D. moist skin

17. What effect does alcohol have on the skin?

A. moisturizing
B. drying
C. lusterizing
D. beautifying

18. When should you advise the client against having a facial treatment?

A. the face is bruised
B. the face has diseased skin
C. the face has broken, open sores
D. all of the above

19. What direction are facial movements most used to benefit the sagging and wrinkling of the client's skin?

A. downward movements
B. upward movements
C. circular movements to the side
D. strong stretching movements about the eyes

20. Where on the face is it important to be very careful when using pointed facial implements?

A. eye area
B. nose area
C. ear area
D. lower cheek area

21. Which of the following facial implements should be recapped immediately after use during a facial?

A. bottles
B. jars of facial creams
C. facial preparations
D. all of the above

22. Of the choices below, select the preparation or product that should be used when giving a facial to normal, or oily skin.

A. mask
B. pack
C. oil-based emollient cream
D. cotton

23. What is the effect of sponging the skin during a facial treatment?

A. removes impurities and excess oil
B. obtains deeper penetration of the oil
C. softens the skin
D. allows the fingertips to slide more easily across the skin

24. What purpose does the application of witch hazel to the skin serve in the facial process?

A. softens the skin
B. moisturizes the skin
C. soothes and cleanses the skin
D. makes skin hard and leathery

25. How is a facial pack usually removed from the face?

A. alcohol scrub
B. witch hazel rub
C. cutting from the edges
D. peeling from the edges

___ 26. Before giving clients a pack or mask treatment, it is important to

A. give an allergy test
B. ask them why they want one
C. heat the pack or mask on the stove
D. all of the above

___ 27. Why is the Wood's Light used mainly in the analysis of the skin?

A. to see it better magnified for fine details
B. to detect inflamed, or overactive oil glands
C. to pick up subtle skin tone not seen otherwise
D. to select the correct makeup

___ 28. For what skin condition is a mildly abrasive skin cleanser recommended?

A. normal skin
B. oily skin
C. dry skin
D. all of the above

___ 29. When using a clay mask, what areas of the face should you be careful to avoid?

A. mouth
B. nose
C. eyes
D. all of the above

___ 30. To prevent the spread of disease, what should be done as part of the facial procedure?

A. sponge the face with an antiseptic
B. wash the face with soap and water
C. vacuum the face with a facial machine
D. massage the face with alcohol

___ 31. With respect to makeup, what does it have a tendency to do to the pores of the skin?

A. clog them
B. cleanse them
C. close them
D. open them

Poss.	Wrong	%	Right
31	0	100%	31
31	1	97%	30
31	2	94%	29
31	3	90%	28
31	4	87%	27
31	5	84%	26
31	6	81%	25
31	7	77%	24
31	8	74%	23
31	9	71%	22
31	10	68%	21
31	11	65%	20

---

26 APPLYING MAKEUP POST-TEST 1

23 Questions

___ 1. To tweeze the eyebrows correctly, this should be done in the direction

A. toward the forehead
B. toward the chin
C. of their natural growth
D. opposite their natural growth

___ 2. To maintain sanitation, color applied to the lips should be done with a sanitized

A. pledget
B. brush
C. crayon
D. cotton ball

___ 3. If base makeup is applied correctly, the cosmetologist should be able to conceal

A. eye lids
B. blemishes
C. wrinkles
D. facial hair

___ 4. Knowledge of facial structure is important for the application of makeup to achieve the most attractive facial shape which is

A. round
B. square
C. diamond
D. oval

177

___ 5. Removal of unsightly matter on the facial area can be best achieved with a(n)

A. cleanser
B. astringent
C. freshener
D. emollient creme

___ 6. Foundation makeup is applied to the facial area to enhance the client's skin tone and

A. smooth it
B. dampen it
C. blend it
D. cleanse it

___ 7. Which of the following should be applied to remove cleansing creme from oily skin?

A. soap
B. astringent
C. toner
D. lotion

___ 8. Lash and brow tint is applied with, then against, the natural direction of the hair's

A. insertion
B. growth
C. follicle
D. strand

___ 9. When applying corrective or contour makeup, the rule is "lights in the valley, shadows on the hills." This means that indentations should be filled, and protrusions should be

A. shadowed
B. lightened
C. toned up
D. highlighted

___ 10. When tinting lashes and brows, petroleum jelly is used to protect the skin from

A. injury
B. abrasion
C. stain
D. scratches

___ 11. What should be applied down the center of the nose to create an illusion that will make the nose appear longer?

A. corrective stick
B. rouge line
C. shadow
D. highlighter

___ 12. When tweezing the eyebrows, this should be done in which direction?

A. against the growth direction
B. with the growth direction
C. in an upward direction
D. downward toward the nose

___ 13. The application of semipermanent lashes is also referred to as

A. temporary lashes
B. permanent lashes
C. strip lashes
D. eye tabbing

___ 14. If strip eyelashes are to fit correctly, what must be done before the lashes are put on the client?

A. measuring
B. weighing
C. cleansing
D. arching

___ 15. In terms of the client's natural eyelashes, where are the strip lashes placed?

A. below
B. above
C. even with
D. on

___ 16. When the foundation-base makeup protrudes from the surface of the skin, what should this tell you about the alkalinity of the skin?

A. high
B. low
C. neutral
D. zero

17. Small eyes can be made to appear larger. What type of makeup is applied to create this illusion?

    A. contour
    B. foundation
    C. lip
    D. white

18. To blend in facial scars and blemishes, what kind of makeup stick should be used?

    A. contour
    B. rouge
    C. corrective
    D. powder

19. Powder is applied over foundation makeup to

    A. black it out
    B. set it
    C. cover it
    D. blend it

20. What type of movement should be used when tweezing the eyebrows?

    A. slow, sliding movement
    B. quick movement
    C. circular movement
    D. zig-zag movement

21. After strip lashes are correctly positioned, the outside and inside ends are held in place for

    A. one minute
    B. two minutes
    C. three minutes
    D. four minutes

22. What effect does the freshener have on the pores?

    A. medicates
    B. cleanses
    C. opens
    D. sanitizes

23. When applying semipermanent lashes, dip the end of the lash in adhesive, stroke the client's lash, then

    A. remove it
    B. attach it
    C. slip it over
    D. slide it onto the lid

Poss.	Wrong	%	Right
23	0	100%	23
23	1	96%	22
23	2	91%	21
23	3	87%	20
23	4	83%	19
23	5	78%	18
23	6	74%	17
23	7	70%	16
23	8	65%	15
23	9	61%	14

27 NAIL ANATOMY, DISORDERS, AND DISEASES POST-TEST 1

17 Questions

1. Nail diseases are identified by

   A. the thickness of the nail
   B. the size of the nail plate
   C. oval shaped nails
   D. signs of infection

2. How many generally recognized nail forms are there?

   A. two
   B. three
   C. four
   D. six

3. Horizontal, uneven lines across the nail plate are caused by minor injury to the nail or

   A. weak eyes
   B. incorrect filing
   C. internal disease
   D. thickening of the nail plate

___ 4. Poor blood circulation may be indicated by fingernails that are

   A. pink
   B. red
   C. orange
   D. blue

___ 5. White spots on the nail plate is a disorder known as

   A. agnails
   B. leukonychia
   C. hangnails
   D. tinea

___ 6. The humerus is the large bone of the

   A. forearm
   B. wrist
   C. upper arm
   D. finger

___ 7. Tinea unguis (ringworm of the nails) is actually tinea of the

   A. hands
   B. scalp
   C. legs
   D. arms

___ 8. The humerus, ulna, and radius are bones found in the

   A. fingers
   B. palm
   C. wrist
   D. arm

___ 9. Hangnails may be caused by injury, or dryness of the

   A. cuticle
   B. free edge
   C. nail plate
   D. lunula

___ 10. The phalanges are the

   A. upper arm
   B. fingers
   C. forearm
   D. shoulder

___ 11. The light arc-shaped half moon form found at the base of the nail is known as the

   A. hyponychium
   B. nail bed
   C. lunula
   D. nail groove

___ 12. The radius is located in the

   A. forearm
   B. hand
   C. upper arm
   D. back

___ 13. The visible hard portion of the top side of the fingernail is the

   A. free edge
   B. nail plate
   C. nail root
   D. nail matrix

___ 14. The number of bones in the wrist would be

   A. 2
   B. 4
   C. 6
   D. 8

___ 15. The wrist is made up of eight bones called

   A. metacarpals
   B. carpals
   C. phalanges
   D. radius

___ 16. The technical term for nail biting is

   A. agnails
   B. leukonychia
   C. onychophagy
   D. eponychium

___ 17. The long bones that form the palm of the hand are

   A. metacarpals
   B. carpals
   C. humerus
   D. ulna

Poss.	Wrong	%	Right
17	0	100%	17
17	1	94%	16
17	2	88%	15
17	3	82%	14
17	4	76%	13
17	5	71%	12
17	6	65%	11

27 NAIL ANATOMY, DISORDERS, AND DISEASES POST-TEST 2

17 Questions

___ 1. The symptoms of athlete's foot are white patches between the toes, and

A. flat, oval patches
B. red, inflamed open sores
C. clear, water-filled blisters
D. round, white patches all over the foot

___ 2. The eponychium is the

A. skin that surrounds the entire nail
B. outside point where the skin overlaps the nail
C. inside point where the nail enters the skin
D. deep fold of skin where the nail root is imbedded

___ 3. Tinea (onychomycosis) is a disturbance of nail growth due to a vegetable fungi that is

A. very common
B. contagious
C. noncontagious
D. beneficial

___ 4. Nail growth can be decreased or slowed down because of

A. illness
B. old age
C. poor nutrition
D. all of the above

___ 5. The basic nail shapes are oval or pointed, and

A. square or round
B. round or ridged
C. all of the above

___ 6. The average daily growth rate of the nail is

A. .7 mm
B. .5 mm
C. .3 mm
D. .1 mm

___ 7. The inner part of the nail that affects the nail's shape, size, regeneration, and growth is

A. nail wall
B. matrix
C. lunula
D. nail root

___ 8. The nail root is located

A. at each side of the nail wall
B. beneath the skin at the base of the nail
C. beyond the end of the fingertip
D. near the skin directly beneath the nail's free edge

___ 9. That portion of the skin directly beneath the nail's free edge is the

A. mantle
B. eponychium
C. hyponychium
D. nail groove

___ 10. Onychogryposis is the technical name for

A. ingrown nails
B. ringworm
C. claw nails
D. felon

___ 11. Overgrowth or thickening of the nail is known as

A. hypertrophy
B. hypotrophy
C. tinea
D. agnails

___ 12. When the skin around the nail is very sore, inflamed, swollen, and infectious, this disease is known as

A. onycholysis
B. onychophagy
C. paronychia
D. bosphorus

181

13. The inner part of the nail that affects its shape, size, and growth is known as the

A. plate
B. matrix
C. lunula
D. cuticle

14. When the cuticle sticks to the base of the nail as it grows out, this condition is known as

A. agnails
B. tinea
C. blue nails
D. pterygium

15. Trimming or filing nails too deeply into corners can cause

A. hangnails
B. ingrown nails
C. nail thickening
D. brittle nails

16. If hangnails are neglected, they may become

A. brittle
B. fragile
C. infected
D. loose

17. Once a nail becomes infected, it should be treated by a

A. barber
B. cosmetologist
C. manicurist
D. physician

Poss.	Wrong	%	Right
17	0	100%	17
17	1	94%	16
17	2	88%	15
17	3	82%	14
17	4	76%	13
17	5	71%	12
17	6	65%	11

28 MANICURING AND PEDICURING POST-TEST 1

23 Questions

1. The product that softens the cuticle and the dead skin beneath the free edge is the

A. polish remover
B. nail base coat
C. nail peeler
D. cuticle remover

2. Filing nails and applying polish are alike because both should be done with

A. quick and smooth strokes
B. choppy and heavy strokes
C. jerky and light stokes
D. circular and oval strokes

3. The product that prevents the polish from chipping is the sealer, or

A. solvent coat
B. base coat
C. top coat
D. cuticle coat

4. The best time to apply nail enamel is

A. after the coat has dried
B. before the base coat is applied
C. before the cuticle cream is applied
D. right after the nails have been filed

5. A substitute for nail bleach would be

A. hydrogen peroxide
B. cleanser
C. styptic
D. alum

6. The product used to remove oil or stains from the nails is

A. stain remover
B. polish remover
C. nail bleach
D. cuticle remover

7. The fingerbowl used in manicuring usually contains liquid soap and

   A. alcohol
   B. hydrogen peroxide
   C. warm water
   D. sodium bromate

8. The art of caring for the toenails, feet, and legs is known as

   A. manicuring
   B. dermatology
   C. pedicuring
   D. nail wrapping

9. Manicure implements should be sanitized

   A. once a week
   B. twice a week
   C. twice a month
   D. after every use

10. If a minor cut should occur during a manicure, apply powdered styptic, or a(n)

    A. shampoo
    B. antiseptic
    C. creme rinse
    D. disinfectant

11. Should a small cut occur during the manicure, the cosmetologist should apply a(n)

    A. piece of cotton
    B. paper towel
    C. antiseptic
    D. bandage

12. Fingernail shaping with an emery board should be done from

    A. center to corner
    B. corner to corner
    C. corner to center
    D. curved across

13. One way to fix a torn fingernail would be to apply

    A. alum
    B. an artificial nail
    C. high-frequency current
    D. cuticle cream

14. The application of cuticle cream during the manicure prevents

    A. enamel from sticking
    B. free edge from splitting
    C. dry skin around nails
    D. chapping of hands

15. Implements to be used for manicuring should be

    A. rinsed in water
    B. wiped off with a towel
    C. cleaned and sanitized
    D. cleaned with a sponge

16. A glass container, that has cotton and alcohol at the bottom of it, is used to keep

    A. manicure implements sanitized
    B. cold waving combs sanitized
    C. hair color bottles sanitized
    D. styling combs sanitized

17. Brittle fingernails, or dry cuticles should be given a(n)

    A. oil manicure
    B. regular manicure
    C. pedicure
    D. foam manicure

18. An oil pedicure is recommended for the client with which of the following skin types?

    A. oily, fragile skin
    B. normal skin
    C. dry, callused skin
    D. thin skin

19. Before applying artificial nails, it is necessary to

    A. remove all polish
    B. remove all polish and thoroughly dry the nails
    C. buff all nails
    D. buff all nails and apply artificial nails to moist fingernails

20. The free edge of the nail is shaped using a(n)

    A. orangewood stick
    B. nail pusher
    C. nail sponge
    D. emery board

183

21. One way to prevent nails from splitting is to apply a strengthener, which is called a nail
    A. builder
    B. lever
    C. coat
    D. cover

22. When manicuring, the cuticle will be softened in the
    A. polishing step
    B. fingerbowl step
    C. polish removal step
    D. base coat step

23. What is the most important thing that a salon should have when artificial nails are offered as a service?
    A. comfortable chairs
    B. good ventilation
    C. an adequate supply of cold water
    D. proper supervision

Poss.	Wrong	%	Right
23	0	100%	23
23	1	96%	22
23	2	91%	21
23	3	87%	20
23	4	83%	19
23	5	78%	18
23	6	74%	17
23	7	70%	16
23	8	65%	15
23	9	61%	14

29 WIGS AND HAIRPIECES POST-TEST 1

10 Questions

1. To prevent a canvas block from molding and giving an odor, it is advisable to cover it with
   A. a nylon cap
   B. synthetic fiber
   C. a plastic bag
   D. a rubber sheet

2. Small, circular-based hairpieces usually made from angora and yak hair are termed
   A. postiches
   B. switches
   C. falls
   D. chignons

3. If a wig is made of human hair, it should be cleaned with a
   A. liquid shampoo
   B. mild detergent
   C. dry cleaning fluid
   D. wet cleaning fluid

4. When selecting a hairpiece for a client, you will be able to match the color more easily by using a
   A. pH color chart
   B. color triangle
   C. JL color ring
   D. color comparison chart

5. The most expensive type of human hair is classified as
   A. Oriental
   B. Asiatic
   C. European
   D. West Indian

6. The size of the canvas block should correspond with the
   A. length of the hair the wig contains
   B. client's head size
   C. texture of hair the wig contains
   D. amount of hair the wig contains

7. To secure a wig on a canvas block, use
   A. bobby pins
   B. hair pins
   C. common pins
   D. T-pins

___ 8. A hairpiece that covers 80 to 100 percent of a client's head is called a

    A. wiglet
    B. cascade
    C. wig
    D. toupee

___ 9. Hand-tied hairpieces are quite expensive because the hair in them is

    A. synthetic
    B. constructed in an area where labor costs are high
    C. in great demand
    D. individually attached to the netting by hand

___ 10. The most expensive type of hair from which hairgoods are made is

    A. synthetic hair
    B. yak hair
    C. angora hair
    D. human hair

Poss.	Wrong	%	Right
10	0	100%	10
10	1	90%	9
10	2	80%	8
10	3	70%	7
10	4	60%	6

---

30 SHAVING POST-TEST 1

10 Questions

___ 1. What is the name for the stone used to sharpen a straight razor?

    A. hone
    B. whetstone
    C. strop
    D. crop

___ 2. When shaving, what purpose does the application of lather serve?

    A. softens the skin
    B. smoothes the beard
    C. softens the beard
    D. feels soothing

___ 3. If you should accidently draw blood when giving the client a shave, what should you do first?

    A. apply pressure to stop the bleeding
    B. put on rubber gloves
    C. apply antiseptic
    D. put styptic on wound

___ 4. Which of the following should be used to put a finishing edge on your straight razor?

    A. towel
    B. strop
    C. hone
    D. comb

___ 5. What should be used to sanitize a straight razor?

    A. wet sanitizer
    B. soap and water
    C. 70% alcohol
    D. towel

___ 6. What type of motion should be used when applying lather to the face before shaving?

    A. circular
    B. back and forth
    C. zig zag
    D. up and down

___ 7. How should an ingrown hair be removed from the skin?

    A. dig it out with a needle
    B. scrap it to the surface
    C. apply a drying lotion
    D. use a tweezers

___ 8. In which area of the neck should you be extra careful?

    A. Adam's apple
    B. base of the chin
    C. jaw line
    D. base of the neck

9. If the client's skin is mildly inflamed, which step of the shaving procedure should you skip?

    A. lathering the beard
    B. shaving
    C. feathering the razor's edge
    D. the steamer towel

10. If you use a straight razor, how do you protect yourself and your client from accidental cuts during the shaving service?

    A. use of a guard
    B. protective spray
    C. use an upward motion
    D. being very careful

Poss.	Wrong	%	Right
10	0	100%	10
10	1	90%	9
10	2	80%	8
10	3	70%	7
10	4	60%	6

31 PLANNING A SALON POST-TEST 1

23 Questions

1. When retailing in the salon, it is important to keep the merchandise

    A. clean and neat
    B. priced with a sticker
    C. attractively labeled and displayed
    D. all of the above

2. What is the name for the person that answers the phone and schedules appointments in the salon?

    A. clerk
    B. receptionist
    C. sales person
    D. appointment clerk

3. In the absence of a written agreement, each person in a partnership has

    A. limited liability
    B. specific assets
    C. limited assets
    D. unlimited liability

4. Restrictions on size, shape, and location of a beauty salon's sign is controlled by local

    A. statutes
    B. rules
    C. ordinances
    D. notices

5. The type of business ownership that limits, or protects, a person from individual losses is called a

    A. partnership
    B. corporation
    C. proprietorship
    D. sole ownership

6. The lessor should state in writing that the beauty salon will be kept at

    A. 68–72 degrees
    B. 73–76 degrees
    C. 77–80 degrees
    D. 81–84 degrees

7. If a planned beauty salon intends to employ several operators, it must be zoned

    A. commercial
    B. residential
    C. industrial
    D. accessible

8. When purchasing an existing salon, the buyer should receive information and advice from an

    A. accountant
    B. advisor
    C. attorney
    D. all of the above

____ 9. If all other sale terms are acceptable, the buyer of an existing salon should have how many years remaining on the lease?

A. 1 to 2
B. 3 to 4
C. 4 to 6
D. 7 or more

____ 10. For a beauty salon, the lessor should provide a space that has good plumbing, lighting, and

A. neighbors
B. hair dryers
C. parking
D. styling chairs

____ 11. If the lessor verbally agrees to make certain building changes, these changes should be in the

A. agreement
B. lease
C. contract
D. arrangement

____ 12. For most written legal agreements, there is need for a(n)

A. lawyer
B. doctor
C. banker
D. accountant

____ 13. The highest fixed cost percentage associated with planning a beauty salon is the cost for

A. supplies
B. advertising
C. laundry
D. rent

____ 14. If the planning stage for installation of a beauty salon indicates a low population density for the area, it means that

A. no one lives in the area
B. only a few people live in the area
C. the area has many other salons
D. a lot of people live in the area

____ 15. The salon operator is protected from dollar losses resulting from service lawsuits by

A. mortgage insurance
B. liability insurance
C. malpractice insurance
D. major-medical insurance

____ 16. Before purchasing an existing beauty salon, one should consider the

A. cost of supplies
B. available parking
C. attitude of the landlord
D. all of the above

____ 17. The written legal agreement between the owner of a building and a tenant is called a

A. lease
B. lessee
C. lessor
D. mortgage

____ 18. When selecting a name for a beauty salon, avoid the name of the

A. lessor
B. owner
C. landlord
D. assignor

____ 19. If a client slips and falls to the floor and files a lawsuit for the injury, the salon owner is protected from dollar loss by

A. income insurance
B. liability insurance
C. malpractice insurance
D. major-medical insurance

____ 20. A partnership operates best when there is a written partnership

A. lease
B. agreement
C. declaration
D. contract

____ 21. Before signing a lease, advice should be obtained from a licensed

A. physician
B. chiropractor
C. attorney
D. cosmetologist

___ 22. When one person owns a business, this legal form of ownership is called a

A. corporation
B. partnership
C. sole proprietorship
D. company

___ 23. The person who grants someone the use of a building is called the

A. assignee
B. assignor
C. lessee
D. lessor

Poss.	Wrong	%	Right
23	0	100%	23
23	1	96%	22
23	2	91%	21
23	3	87%	20
23	4	83%	19
23	5	78%	18
23	6	74%	17
23	7	70%	16
23	8	65%	15
23	9	61%	14

32 SALON OPERATIONS POST-TEST 1

16 Questions

___ 1. The basic accounting equation is Assets equals

A. Liabilities + Proprietorship
B. Expense - Costs
C. Proprietorship + Liabilities
D. Liabilities - Expenses

___ 2. Tax laws mandate that each business keep proper and accurate

A. advertising
B. records
C. supply bills
D. telephone bills

___ 3. The usual effect on the salon that accepts credit cards is

A. decrease in sales
B. theft by employees
C. losses from stolen credit cards
D. increase in overall sales

___ 4. The best way to control supply and demand is to increase the price until the demand is

A. greater than supply
B. less than supply
C. equal to supply
D. all of the above

___ 5. After all expenses have been deducted, the remaining money from the business is called

A. lien
B. liability
C. asset
D. profit

___ 6. If a salon can afford to pay 8 percent of their gross income for supplies, and the supply bill last year was $3,200, their gross income is

A. $20,000
B. $25,000
C. $35,000
D. $40,000

___ 7. What is the communications link between the salon and the manufacturer of supplies used in the salon?

A. salesperson
B. magazines
C. newsletters
D. telephone calls

___ 8. The largest single expense in operating a beauty salon is

A. advertising/telephone
B. salaries/commissions
C. supplies/depreciation
D. dues/travel

188

9. Who pays for Workman's Compensation Insurance?

   A. the employer
   B. the employee
   C. both employer and employee
   D. all of the above

10. When salon equipment such as dryers and chairs have been purchased on time payments, what would happen if you made a monthly payment late?

   A. the equipment would be repossessed
   B. you would be sued
   C. there would be a service charge
   D. the business would be bankrupt

11. The general concept of how many people would be willing to pay for the salon services offered in a particular area is known as

   A. supply
   B. density
   C. demand
   D. socio-economic

12. Who pays for FUTA?

   A. the employer
   B. the employee
   C. both the employer and employee
   D. all of the above

13. Depending on which services are given in the salon, time will determine the difference between

   A. services accepted
   B. employees fired
   C. supplies used
   D. profit or loss

14. A written set of items that specifies what an employer expects from an employee is called the salon's

   A. want list
   B. requirement list
   C. operating policies
   D. reading policy

15. In addition to other taxes, salon owners are responsible for payment of employee

   A. social security taxes
   B. stamp taxes
   C. coupon taxes
   D. ticket taxes

16. Besides rent and salaries, the next largest expense is

   A. advertising
   B. supplies
   C. towels
   D. education

Poss.	Wrong	%	Right
16	0	100%	16
16	1	94%	15
16	2	88%	14
16	3	81%	13
16	4	75%	12
16	5	69%	11

32 SALON OPERATIONS POST-TEST 2

17 Questions

1. Who pays for FICA?

   A. the employer
   B. the employee
   C. both the employer and employee
   D. none of the above

2. What is one of the disadvantages for the salon that accepts credit cards for services?

   A. time for writing a sales slip
   B. the fee charged by the card company
   C. collecting uncollectible accounts
   D. employee errors in making a sale

189

___ 3. Your supply costs can be larger than they need to be if you are not careful in terms of

A. using one application of product for two clients
B. product duplication
C. ordering enough supplies for three months
D. ordering from 2 or 3 suppliers

___ 4. If everything that affects demand is kept constant except the price, then the price will determine

A. demand for a service
B. supply of a service
C. consumption of a service
D. elimination of a service

___ 5. Fixed-costs tend to

A. increase
B. decrease
C. remain constant
D. become variable

___ 6. Which of the items below will determine the demand for a service?

A. price of a service
B. family income
C. price of substitute service
D. all of the above

___ 7. The main disadvantage of ordering supplies C.O.D. is

A. handling
B. time
C. bookkeeping
D. cost

___ 8. An asset means something a business

A. owes
B. owns
C. delivers
D. supplies

___ 9. After making an application for a job interview, the applicant should

A. be on time
B. wear neat and clean clothes
C. have his/her hair styled
D. all of the above

___ 10. The best place to borrow money is from a

A. credit fund
B. neighbor
C. union fund
D. commercial bank

___ 11. FUTA is an abbreviation for

A. Federal Unitary Travel Area
B. Forced Unit Tax Act
C. Future Tax Act
D. Federal Unemployment Tax Act

___ 12. The cost of purchasing new equipment will increase depending on the

A. color of the equipment
B. fabric of the equipment
C. styles of the equipment
D. all of the above

___ 13. In terms of the dollars taken into a beauty salon, usable supplies should represent

A. 2%
B. 4%
C. 6%
D. 8%

___ 14. For tax purposes, you must report all tips received and pay income tax if those tips exceed

A. $10.00 per month
B. $20.00 per month
C. $30.00 per month
D. $40.00 per month

___ 15. If cash is paid for equipment, the purchaser can usually expect

A. better equipment
B. a friendly dealer
C. a discount
D. a rebate

___ 16. The beauty salon owner should decide the amount to be paid the supply house from

A. statements
B. packing slips
C. bills of lading
D. invoices

17. An employer is likely to ask a prospective employee	Poss.	Wrong	%	Right
	17	0	100%	17
A. the cosmetology school that he/she graduated from	17	1	94%	16
	17	2	88%	15
B. names of others who have employed the student or operator	17	3	82%	14
	17	4	76%	13
C. his/her place of residence	17	5	71%	12
D. all of the above	17	6	65%	11

___ 17. An employer is likely to ask a prospective employee

A. the cosmetology school that he/she graduated from
B. names of others who have employed the student or operator
C. his/her place of residence
D. all of the above

33 PHYCHOLOGY OF INTERPERSONAL SKILLS & RETAILING POST-TEST 1

20 Questions

___ 1. What is at least one factor that society uses to determine the success or failure of a person's career?

A. how tall they are
B. how much money they make
C. what kind of car they drive
D. how they dress

___ 2. What is the common goal set between you and your clients before you have done anything to their hair, nails, or face?

A. improve their appearance
B. to make money
C. to buy a new car
D. make their hair shinier

___ 3. How does the cosmetologist obtain personal satisfaction and financial gain from working in the salon?

A. scheduling a lot of appointments
B. answering the phone frequently
C. helping others
D. taking risks

___ 4. When the stylist and the client have developed a common set of thoughts, what is the term used to describe this relationship?

A. rapport
B. charisma
C. charm
D. poise

___ 5. Given two students with identical training, what factors determine why one student will graduate from school and earn a lot more money than the other?

A. the greater money earner gives many free services
B. the one making more money treats their clients better
C. the student earning less money can't technically do the desired work
D. the student earning less money didn't attend school regularly

___ 6. What can be done to make the client want to come into the salon?

A. make them feel good about their salon experience
B. sell them products they don't need
C. always call them by their first names
D. all of the above

___ 7. Today, salon stylists should think of themselves as

A. salespersons
B. helpers
C. educators
D. all of the above

___ 8. What is the greatest fear faced by people in sales-related jobs?

A. which clothes to wear
B. what to do with the client's hair
C. what to do with the client's face
D. how to overcome rejection

9. What is the first step in becoming a
   successful cosmetologist?

   A. styling the hair well
   B. answering the phone well
   C. realizing you are a sales person
   D. knowing that you can help all clients

10. What is the name for the establishment of a
    positive emotional relationship between you
    and your client?

    A. caring
    B. bonding
    C. rapport
    D. support

11. When you are asking clients questions about
    their needs, what strategy are you using to
    provide services or products to them?

    A. grilling
    B. discovery
    C. anticipation
    D. all of the above

12. Talking with your client about the possible
    solutions to some of their appearance
    problems is known as a

    A. meeting
    B. consultation
    C. conversation
    D. revelation

13. When a cosmetologist has so many
    appointments that it is difficult to fit in new
    clients, what is this called?

    A. booked solid
    B. full book
    C. booked-up
    D. booked to the hilt

14. If a client is booked for a permanent wave,
    which of the following would be classified
    as an extra service?

    A. haircut
    B. frosting
    C. protein conditioner
    D. all of the above

15. How is a stylist usually paid for the sale of
    retail products in the salon to their clients?

    A. $2.00 per item
    B. $3.00 per item
    C. $5.00 per item
    D. a commission

16. What is the term used to describe a new
    client visiting you for a service as the result
    of another client sending them to you?

    A. word of mouth
    B. a referral
    C. lucky to have good friends
    D. a random chance

17. How does a stylist provide additional money
    for themselves in addition to the money
    earned for providing services?

    A. retail sales
    B. rebook client before they leave the salon
    C. stealing clients from co-workers
    D. hogging phoned-in appointments

18. If you are at a social event, such as a party,
    what would be an effective way to let fellow
    party goers know what kind of work you do,
    and where you can be contacted for
    cosmetology services?

    A. write your phone number on a napkin
    B. ask them to look you up in the book
    C. pass out business cards
    D. ask your friends to write your number
       down on a scrap of paper and pass it
       along to others

19. What percentage of your business should
    come from friends recommending your
    services to friends?

    A. 1–2%
    B. 2–3%
    C. 4–6%
    D. all of the above

20. What is the term used for describing the
    relationship between you and your client that
    keeps them coming back into the salon

    A. client retention
    B. bonding
    C. referral
    D. client rapport

Poss.	Wrong	%	Right
20	0	100%	20
20	1	95%	19
20	2	90%	18

20	3	85%	17
20	4	80%	16
20	5	75%	15
20	6	70%	14

34 PRINCIPLES OF ELECTRICITY POST-TEST 1

15 Questions

___ 1. What is the electrical device that reduces 120 volts of electricity down so that it can be used for facial treatments?

A. wall plate
B. resistor
C. transformer
D. reformer

___ 2. When a current and heat are used together to remove unwanted hair, this method is known as

A. the blend
B. waxing
C. epilating
D. zipping

___ 3. What is the name for the electrical process that forces chemicals through the unbroken skin?

A. osmosis
B. phoresis
C. photosynthesis
D. static

___ 4. Faradic electro-therapy is used on the skin to

A. maintain muscle tone
B. reduce circulation
C. reduce production of sebum
D. maintain skin color

___ 5. Which current is used in a high-frequency treatment?

A. faradic
B. galvanic
C. tesla
D. sinusoidal

___ 6. If a high-frequency treatment is given indirectly, the metal electrode is held by the

A. cosmetologist
B. receptionist
C. client
D. operator

___ 7. High-frequency scalp treatments are only used on hair that is

A. dry
B. wet
C. damp
D. towel dry

___ 8. The device that stops the flow of electricity when wires are overloaded is called a fuse or

A. live wire
B. circuit breaker
C. electric breaker
D. electric stopper

___ 9. A continuous flow of electricity that only flows in one direction is known as

A. mm
B. c c
C. d c
D. a c

___ 10. An ohm is a measure of electrical

A. potential
B. strength
C. resistance
D. pressure

___ 11. A measure of electrical potential or pressure is called a(n)

A. ampere
B. volt
C. current
D. ohm

_____ 12. The device that regulates the flow of electricity is called a(n)

A. regulator
B. conductor
C. insulator
D. rheostat

_____ 13. Something that easily allows electricity to travel along it is called a(n)

A. electron
B. conductor
C. insulator
D. inductor

_____ 14. Traveling units of electricity are called

A. protons
B. electrons
C. electrolytes
D. leukocytes

_____ 15. Which of the following is not a benefit of using a high-frequency unit on the scalp?

A. normalizing
B. stimulating
C. germicidal
D. relaxing

Poss.	Wrong	%	Right
15	0	100%	15
15	1	93%	14
15	2	87%	13
15	3	80%	12
15	4	73%	11
15	5	67%	10

35 CHEMISTRY OF COSMETOLOGY POST-TEST 1

32 Questions

_____ 1. On the pH scale, if a solution is neutral, what is the pH of that solution?

A. 4
B. 5
C. 6
D. 7

_____ 2. What is the smallest structural unit of a substance?

A. atom
B. molecule
C. micron
D. element

_____ 3. The pH range of a cold-waving solution would be

A. 3.5 to 4.5
B. 5.0 to 6.0
C. 6.0 to 7.5
D. 8.5 to 9.5

_____ 4. Compounds are a combination of two or more

A. elements
B. atoms
C. molecules
D. substances

_____ 5. A solution that has more hydrogen ions is said to be

A. acid
B. alkali
C. a base
D. neutral

_____ 6. Suspensions generally have an appearance that is

A. clear
B. cloudy
C. translucent
D. opaque

_____ 7. The pH value of distilled water would be

A. 3
B. 5
C. 7
D. 9

___ 8. Organic chemistry is mainly interested in things that used to be

    A. dead
    B. materials
    C. alive
    D. chemicals

___ 9. The basic unit for a substance is a(n)

    A. element
    B. compound
    C. carbon
    D. reduction

___ 10. Mixtures differ from compounds in that they are not mixed

    A. in a liquid form
    B. physically
    C. chemically
    D. in a gaseous form

___ 11. A solution containing an equal number of hydrogen and hydroxyl ions is said to be

    A. acid
    B. alkaline
    C. neutral
    D. none of the above

___ 12. The expression acid-balanced refers to a product that has a pH in the range of

    A. 2.5 to 3.5
    B. 3.5 to 4.5
    C. 4.5 to 5.5
    D. 5.5 to 6.5

___ 13. Hydrogen ions are electrically charged particles of

    A. hydrogen
    B. oxygen
    C. sulfur
    D. hydroxis

___ 14. Particles dissolved by a solvent are called

    A. acids
    B. solutes
    C. bases
    D. compounds

___ 15. Chemical energy is released during which of the following services?

    A. temporary color
    B. lightening
    C. air waving
    D. shaping

___ 16. When a new product is made by joining two or more substances, this would be called a

    A. compound
    B. base
    C. atom
    D. element

___ 17. When a solid is mixed with a liquid, the new substance is called a(n)

    A. alkaline
    B. acid
    C. base
    D. suspension

___ 18. The smallest unit of a substance that still has all the properties of that substance is a(n)

    A. millimeter
    B. atom
    C. compound
    D. carbon

___ 19. Anything that occupies space and has weight is called

    A. a molecule
    B. an atom
    C. matter
    D. velocity

___ 20. An atom is the smallest part of a(n)

    A. element
    B. neutron
    C. mixture
    D. eon

___ 21. The chemical properties of a substance are changed during

    A. air waving
    B. permanent coloring
    C. bleaching
    D. B and C

22. Inorganic chemistry deals mainly with things made from

A. salt
B. minerals
C. compounds
D. carbon

23. An example of a gas used in a beauty salon is

A. ammonium
B. ultra-violet
C. high-frequency
D. formaldehyde

24. The science that deals with the makeup of matter and its changes is called

A. etiology
B. chemistry
C. bacteriology
D. cosmetology

25. Hydrogen peroxide would have a pH value in the range of

A. 3.5 to 4
B. 4.5 to 5.5
C. 6.5 to 7.5
D. 8 to 8.5

26. When something has a definite form, such as wood, glass, or ice, they are examples of a

A. liquid
B. solid
C. gas
D. gel

27. A solution containing more hydroxyl than hydrogen ions is a

A. sugar
B. salt
C. base
D. crystal

28. Chemical relaxers would have a pH value in the range

A. 4.5 to 5.5
B. 6 to 7.5
C. 8 to 8.5
D. 11.5 to 14

29. Kitchen salt is an example of a

A. base
B. compound
C. gas
D. liquid

30. Elements joined together but which keep their individual identities are called

A. atoms
B. solutes
C. mixtures
D. solvents

31. A liquid used to dissolve one substance into another one is called a(n)

A. solvent
B. organic
C. substitute
D. suspension

32. The main function of an emulsifying agent is to

A. suspend one liquid in another
B. break up and dispense color
C. break up water into separate droplets
D. suspend a mixture in water

Poss.	Wrong	%	Right
32	0	100%	32
32	1	97%	31
32	2	94%	30
32	3	91%	29
32	4	88%	28
32	5	84%	27
32	6	81%	26
32	7	78%	25
32	8	75%	24
32	9	72%	23
32	10	69%	22
32	11	66%	21

30 Questions

___ 1. The term physiology relates to the function of the

    A. skin
    B. body
    C. glands
    D. scalp

___ 2. The technical name given to what encases the cell is called a

    A. wall
    B. curtain
    C. membrane
    D. case

___ 3. The process that builds up a cell is called

    A. anabolism
    B. catabolism
    C. metabolism
    D. cytoplasm

___ 4. Epithelial tissue serves to

    A. protect the inside of the heart
    B. cover the liver
    C. line all surfaces of the body
    D. move blood throughout the body

___ 5. The ability of one part of the body to communicate with another part is provided by which system?

    A. endocrine
    B. vascular
    C. muscular
    D. nervous

___ 6. Tissue that binds, supports, protects, and nourishes the body is called

    A. connective
    B. nervous
    C. endocrine
    D. none of the above

___ 7. Bones, ligaments, and cartilage are examples of what kind of tissue?

    A. connective
    B. adipose
    C. corrective
    D. epithelial

___ 8. Osteology relates to which system of the body?

    A. vascular
    B. skeletal
    C. endocrine
    D. muscular

___ 9. Cancellous tissue is usually found on the inside of

    A. round bones
    B. long bones
    C. oval bones
    D. square bones

___ 10. What is the yellow fluid substance that serves as a cushion, and lubricates the long bones?

    A. periosteum
    B. sheath
    C. synovial
    D. corium

___ 11. Blood nourishes the inner layers of the bone by flowing through vessels found in the

    A. cancellous tissue
    B. compact tissue
    C. periosteum
    D. marrow

___ 12. Bands of connective tissue that support and hold bones in place are the

    A. cartilage
    B. ligaments
    C. compacts
    D. attachments

___ 13. To prevent friction during movement, bones are lubricated by

    A. oil
    B. inorganic fluid
    C. synovial fluid
    D. cranial fluid

___ 14. The single name given to all the bones that form the head is the

A. epicranius
B. cranium
C. occipital
D. skull

___ 15. The cranium is formed by the meeting of two bones that form the top and sides of the head. They are the

A. temporal bones
B. lacrimal bones
C. zygomatic bones
D. parietal bones

___ 16. The butterfly-shaped bone located at almost the exact center of the head is the

A. concha
B. nasal
C. ethmoid
D. sphenoid

___ 17. The bone that forms the upper part of the jaw is the

A. zygomatic
B. frontal
C. mandible
D. maxillae

___ 18. The U-shaped hyoid bone is located in the

A. pharynx
B. larynx
C. metatarsal
D. carpals

___ 19. The breastbone is also called the

A. corium
B. zygomatic
C. sternum
D. trunk

___ 20. Clavicles are commonly called the

A. ribs
B. metatarsals
C. collarbones
D. shinbones

___ 21. The large bone of the upper arm is the

A. humerus
B. radius
C. occipitalis
D. temporalis

___ 22. Phalanges or digits are found in the

A. toes
B. fingers
C. ears
D. eyes

___ 23. The bone on the thumb side of the forearm is the

A. ulna
B. radius
C. humerus
D. clavicle

___ 24. Myology is the study of the

A. bones
B. nerves
C. muscles
D. blood

___ 25. The term muscle is described as

A. a bundle of tough elastic fibers
B. a body of peripheral tissue
C. tendons that connect bones
D. a union of movements

___ 26. The type of muscles that we voluntarily control are called

A. smooth
B. striated
C. non-striated
D. cardiac

___ 27. Cardiac muscle tissue is found only in the

A. scalp
B. palms
C. lungs
D. heart

___ 28. The muscle attachment that moves the most
when the muscle is flexed is called the

    A. axial
    B. origin
    C. insertion
    D. cardiac

___ 29. The frontalis and occipitalis muscle form the

    A. skull
    B. head
    C. epicranium
    D. masseter

___ 30. The orbicularis oculi muscle

    A. closes the eyelids
    B. clenches the hand
    C. closes the lips
    D. bends the elbow

Poss.	Wrong	%	Right
30	0	100%	30
30	1	97%	29
30	2	93%	28
30	3	90%	27
30	4	87%	26
30	5	83%	25
30	6	80%	24
30	7	77%	23
30	8	73%	22
30	9	70%	21
30	10	67%	20
30	11	63%	19

37 ANATOMY – VASCULAR & ENDOCRINE POST-TEST 1

31 Questions

___ 1. What gland is related to weight loss or
weight gain?

    A. pituitary
    B. thyroid
    C. hypothalamus
    D. pancreas

___ 2. The gland that has the special job of
regulating the water balance in the body is
called the

    A. pituitary
    B. thyroid
    C. hypothalamus
    D. adrenal

___ 3. The endocrine system controls

    A. reproduction
    B. general health
    C. growth
    D. all of the above

___ 4. The endocrine system releases special
chemicals in the blood called

    A. serums
    B. steroids
    C. hormones
    D. platelets

___ 5. The brachial artery divides in the arm to
become the radial and

    A. fumer arteries
    B. ulnar arteries
    C. humerus arteries
    D. tibi arteries

___ 6. The facial artery that supplies blood to the
lower part of the face, mouth, and nose is the

    A. external maxillary
    B. superficial temporal
    C. transverse facial
    D. ophthalmic

___ 7. The largest artery in the body is the

    A. aorta
    B. internal carotid
    C. external carotid
    D. pulmonary

___ 8. If the pancreas is not functioning the way it
should, what condition develops?

    A. hair loss
    B. diabetes
    C. hyperthyroidism
    D. hardening of the arteries

9. A special set of vessels that carry chyle in the lymph system is called

A. lacteals
B. platelets
C. lymphocytes
D. lymph nodes

10. The vascular system is divided into two systems, the circulatory system and the

A. endocrine system
B. lymphatic system
C. nervous system
D. respiratory system

11. The colorless cells that cause blood to clot are

A. erythrocytes
B. leukocytes
C. thrombocytes
D. melanocytes

12. Leukocytes are also called

A. red blood cells
B. white blood cells
C. blue blood cells
D. none of the above

13. The yellow, watery fluid part of the blood is

A. red blood cells
B. thrombocytes
C. plasma
D. erythrocytes

14. The thyroid gland is located in the

A. stomach
B. head
C. neck
D. chest

15. The gland found at the base of the brain is the

A. pituitary
B. renal
C. hypothalamus
D. adrenal

16. The body's ability to withstand stress is determined by the chemical known as

A. iron
B. potassium
C. thiamine
D. adrenaline

17. The endocrine system contains only

A. ducted glands
B. ductless glands
C. compact bones
D. cancellous bones

18. The posterior auricular artery supplies blood to the scalp behind and above the

A. neck
B. occipital
C. forehead
D. ear

19. The main artery branch of the aorta that supplies blood to the head, face, and neck is the

A. posterior auricular
B. anterior auricular
C. common carotid
D. common fumer

20. The large lymphatic vessels empty into the

A. chest
B. stomach
C. heart
D. pancreas

21. A colorless liquid that comes from plasma is

A. lacteals
B. lymph
C. platelets
D. vena cava

22. Blood cells that fight infection in the body are called

A. white
B. red
C. erythrocytes
D. thrombocytes

_____ 23. Blood platelets cause the blood to

    A. oxygenate
    B. clot
    C. flow
    D. hydrogenate

_____ 24. Which blood cells are the main infection fighters of the body?

    A. leukocytes
    B. erythrocytes
    C. hemoglobin
    D. red blood cells

_____ 25. Vessels that carry blood from the heart to the body tissue are called

    A. veins
    B. arteries
    C. capillaries
    D. lymphatics

_____ 26. The substance that gives blood its characteristic red color is

    A. thrombocytes
    B. leukocytes
    C. hemoglobin
    D. plasma

_____ 27. Generally, the temperature of the body and blood is

    A. 97.6 degrees
    B. 96.6 degrees
    C. 98.6 degrees
    D. 99.6 degrees

_____ 28. Which item below rids the body of carbon dioxide?

    A. kidneys
    B. heart
    C. lungs
    D. liver

_____ 29. Very small blood vessels that are composed of only one layer of tissue are

    A. veins
    B. arteries
    C. ventricles
    D. capillaries

_____ 30. Angiology is related to the study of

    A. bones
    B. muscles
    C. blood
    D. nerves

_____ 31. The circulatory system functions to bring food materials and what else to the cells or the body?

    A. oxygen
    B. melanin
    C. hydrogen
    D. calcium

Poss.	Wrong	%	Right
31	0	100%	31
31	1	97%	30
31	2	94%	29
31	3	90%	28
31	4	87%	27
31	5	84%	26
31	6	81%	25
31	7	77%	24
31	8	74%	23
31	9	71%	22
31	10	68%	21
31	11	65%	20

PRACTICAL TEST 1

Use the drawing(s) on each page to answer the questions on each page of this section.

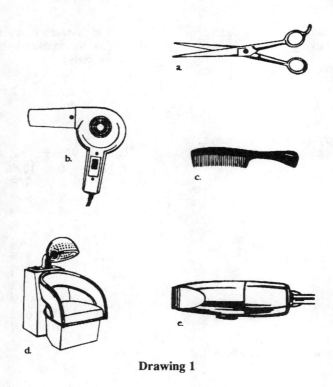

Drawing 1

___ 1. Which of the items above should be completely immersed in a wet sanitizer?
A.–a, B.–b, C.–c, D.–d, E.–e, F.–a and b only

___ 2. Select the item that should be sanitized with 70% alcohol.
A.–a, B.–b, C.–c, D.–d, E.–e, F.–b and c only

___ 3. Which is the item most likely to be used to apply a chemical hair relaxer?
A.–a, B.–b, C.–c, D.–d, E.–e, F.–a and d only

___ 4. Can you identify the implement used to shorten the hair?
A.–a, B.–b, C.–c, D.–d, E.–e, F.–a and e only

___ 5. Pick out the item that requires you to be the most careful when using.
A.–a, B.–b, C.–c, D.–d, E.–e, F.–a and e only, G.–a, b, and e only

___ 6. Which of the implements pictured requires the most caution when styling long hair?
A.–a, B.–b, C.–c, D.–d, E.–e

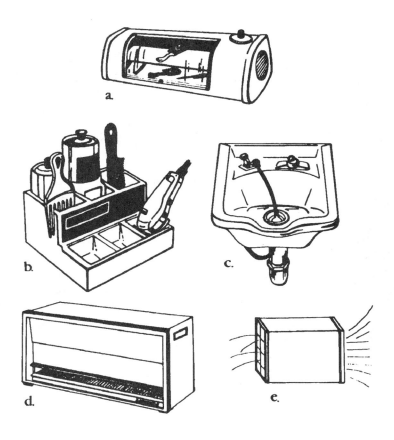

Drawing 2

___ 7. From the equipment pictured above, can you choose the one that purifies air in the salon?
     A.–a, B.–b, C.–c, D.–d, E.–e

___ 8. Which piece of equipment should be sanitized after each use?
     A.–a, B.–b, C.–c, D.–d, E.–e

___ 9. Can you identify the equipment that uses ultraviolet light?
     A.–a, B.–b, C.–c, D.–d, E.–e, F.–b and c only, G.–a and d only

___ 10. Can you select the piece of equipment that uses a vacuum breaker?
     A.–a, B.–b, C.–c, D.–d, E.–e, F.–a and b only

___ 11. Which piece of equipment is used as a dry sanitizer?
     A.–a, B.–b, C.–c, D.–d, E.–e, F.–a and d only

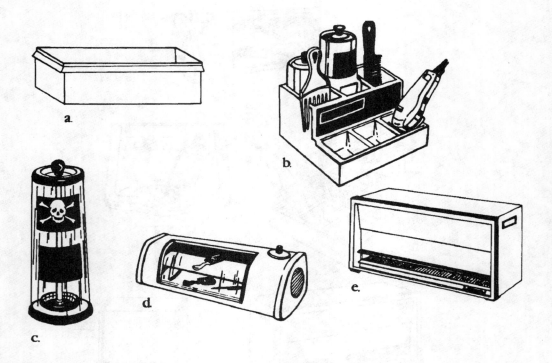

Drawing 3

___ 12. Select the wet sanitizer in the drawing above.
A.–a, B.–b, C.–c, D.–d, E.–e, F.–d and c only, G.–a, b and d only

___ 13. Which of the above would be used to store dry , clean combs and brushes?
A.–a, B.–b, C.–c, D.–d, E.–e, F.–a and c, G.–b, c, d and e

___ 14. In which piece of equipment would you use quats?
A.–a, B.–b, C.–c, D.–d, E.–e, F.–a and c, F.–none of the above

___ 15. Inside of which piece of equipment would you use a fumigant?
A.–a, B.–b, C.–c, D.–d, E.–e, F.–a, b and c, G.–none of the above

___ 16. Which of the above is a wet sanitizer used for the storage of combs?
A.–a, B.–b, C.–c, D.–d, E.–e, F.–a, b and c, F.–none of the above

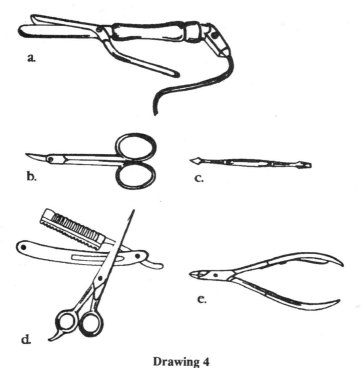

Drawing 4

_____ 17. Which of the above implements should be placed in a disinfectant solution during the service?
       A.–a, B.–b, C.–c, D.–d, E.–e, F.–a and b, G.–b, c and e

_____ 18. Can you select the implement that would be cleaned using steel wool?
       A.–a, B.–b, C.–c, D.–d, E.–e

_____ 19. A safety guard should be used with which of the implements?
       A.–a, B.–b, C.–c, D.–d, E.–e

_____ 20. Which of the above pictured implements should be sanitized with alcohol?
       A.–a, B.–b, C.–c, D.–d, E.–e, F.–a and b, G.–b, c, d and e

_____ 21. Can you identify the implement that should NOT be submerged in a wet sanitizer?
       A.–a, B.–b, C.–c, D.–d, E.–e, F.–b and e

_____ 22. Which of the implements would be used during the manicuring service?
       A.–a, B.–b, C.–c, D.–d, E.–e, F.–a and b, G.–b, c and e

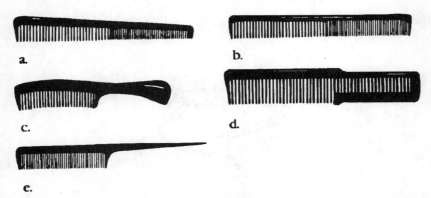

Drawing 5

___ 23. Can you identify the comb normally used to finger wave the hair?
  A.–a, B.–b, C.–c, D.–d, E.–e

___ 24. Which comb would normally be used to taper the sideburns when doing a haircut on a male client?
  A.–a, B.–b, C.–c, D.–d, E.–e

___ 25. Can you select the comb most often used for parting and wrapping a permanent wave?
  A.–a, B.–b, C.–c, D.–d, E.–e, F.–b and e

___ 26. Which of the combs above are used for hair cutting?
  A.–a, B.–b, C.–c, D.–d, E.–e, F.–a, b and d , G.–a, b, d and e

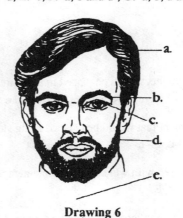

Drawing 6

___ 27. Which letter correctly labels capilli hair?
  A.–a, B.–b, C.–c, D.–d, E.–e

___ 28. Which letter correctly labels cilia hair?
  A.–a, B.–b, C.–c, D.–d, E.–e
___ 29. Which letter of Drawing 6 correctly labels barba hair?
  A.–a, B.–b, C.–c, D.–d, E.–e

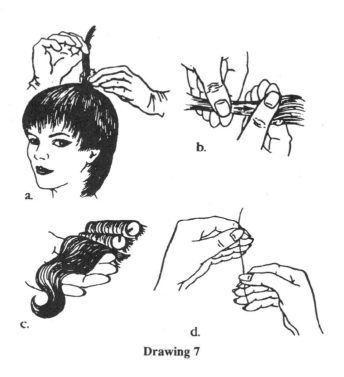

Drawing 7

___ 30. Which letter in Drawing 7 correctly labels a test for hair elasticity?
A.–a, B.–b, C.–c, D.–d, E.–e

___ 31. Can you select the drawing that demonstrates a permanent wave test curl?
A.–a, B.–b, C.–c, D.–d, E.–none shown

___ 32. Choose the drawing that correctly labels a test for hair porosity.
A.–a, B.–b, C.–c, D.–d, E.–none shown

___ 33. Which of the drawings demonstrates a permanent color strand test?
A.–a, B.–b, C.–c, D.–d, E.–none shown

___ 34. Which drawing gives an example of how a patch test should be given?
A.–a, B.–b, C.–c, D.–d, E.–none shown

PRACTICAL TEST 2

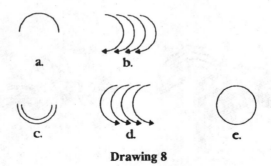

Drawing 8

_____ 1. Which drawing indicates a clockwise direction?
   A.–a, B.–b, C.–c, D.–d, E.–e

_____ 2. Select the letter that shows a counterclockwise direction.
   A.–a, B.–b, C.–c, D.–d, E.–e, F.–none shown

_____ 3. Which two illustrations when placed together would form a wave pattern?
   A.–a and b, B.–b and d, C.–c and d, D.–a and d, E.–b and d.

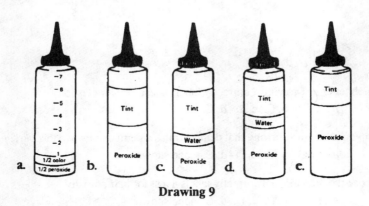

Drawing 9

_____ 4. Referring to Drawing 9, which drawing illustrates a mixuture of "double peroxide" for use in a permanent hair coloring formula?
   A.–a, B.–b, C.–c, D.–d, E.–e

_____ 5. Which would be an illustration of an "equal peroxide" color formula?
   A.–a, B.–b, C.–c, D.–d, E.–e, F.–a and b, G.–c and d

_____ 6. Can you select the bottle from the drawing that illustrates a a formula that has been diluted?
   A.–a, B.–b, C.–c, D.–d, E.–e, F.–a and b, G.–c and d

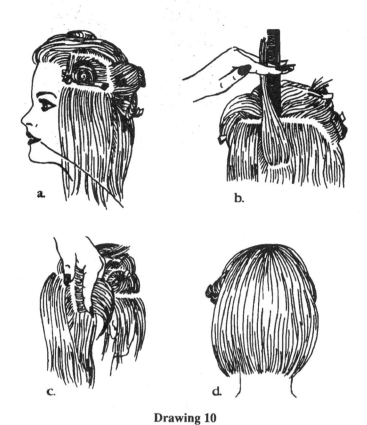

Drawing 10

___ 7. Which letter correctly identifies a procedure that will use a guideline for cutting the hair?
      A.–a, B.–b, C.–c, D.–d

___ 8. Can you select the drawing that shows the use of vertical hair sections?
      A.–a, B.–b, C.–c, D.–d, E.–none shown

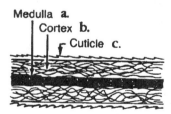

Drawing 11

___ 9. Referring to Drawing 11, determine in which layer of the hair the melanin is concentrated?
      A.–a, B.–b, C.–c

___ 10. Which layer of the hair is sometimes not present?
      A.–a, B.–b, C.–c

a.

b.

c.

d.

Drawing 12

___ 11. Which letter correctly labels the basic sectioning procedure for applying a tint?
   A.–a, B.–b, C.–c, D.–d

___ 12. Can you select the drawing that defines the top area of the head?
   A.–a, B.–b, C.–c, D.–d

___ 13. Select the drawing that defines the division between the top and side section of the head.
   A.–a, B.–b, C.–c, D.–d

___ 14. Which drawing illustrates the basic sectioning technique for a cutting guideline for a haircut?
   A.–a, B.–b, C.–c, D.–d, E–none shown

___ 15. What angle is formed where the combs meet in "c" of Drawing 12?
   A.–20 degrees, B.–25 degrees, C.–40 degrees, D.–90 degrees

a.

b.

c.

d.

Drawing 13

___ 16. Can you choose the illustration that identifies the pattern that will result in a horizontal wave formation?

      A.–a, B.–b, C.–c, D.–d

___ 17. Select the setting pattern that will result in a skip wave.

      A.–a, B.–b, C.–c, D.–d

___ 18. Which setting pattern shows alternating rows of shapings and sculpture curls?

      A.–a, B.–b, C.–c, D.–d, E.–a, b and c

___ 19. Which pattern will result in a diagonal wave formation?

      A.–a, B.–b, C.–c, D.–d, E.–b, c and d

a.   b.

c.   d.

Drawing 14

___ 20. Which of the above drawings correctly labels the client receiving a frosting?
A.–a, B.–b, C.–c, D.–d, E –none shown

___ 21. Can you identify the client receiving a foiling service?
A.–a, B.–b, C.–c, D.–d

___ 22. Identify the client receiving a painting service.
A.–a, B.–b, C.–c, D.–d

___ 23. To achieve maximum lightening for the services in the above drawing, what type of bleach would you use?
A.–cream, B.–oil, C.–powder, D.–peroxide only

___ 24. For the service shown above, which of the following would you add to the bleaching product?
A.–water, B.–sodium, C.–neutralizer, D.–peroxide

Drawing 15

___ 25. Which of the head samples above is an example of giving the client a strand test?
  A.–a, B.–b, C.–c, D.–d

___ 26. From the examples in Drawing 15, what would be an example of streaking the hair?
  A.–a, B.–b, C.–c, D.–d

___ 27. Can you identify the example of the sectioning of the top section of the head?
  A.–a, B.–b, C.–c, D.–d

___ 28. Which of the examples would illustrate the sections for a ponytail permanent wave wrap in which only a very little amount of curl is the desired effect?
  A.–a, B.–b, C.–c, D.–d

PRACTICAL TEST 3

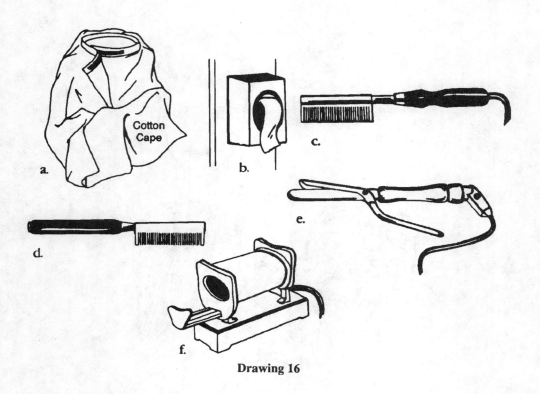

Cotton
Cape

a.

b.

c.

d.

e.

f.

Drawing 16

___ 1. Referring to Drawing 16, which is an example of a thermal stove?
   A.–a, B.–b, C.–c, D.–d, E.–e

___ 2. Can you identify what should be used around the client's neck before securing the cape?
   A.–a, B.–b, C.–c, D.–d, E.–e

___ 3. Which item would be placed in the stove?
   A.–a, B.–b, C.–c, D.–d, E.–e

___ 4. Identify the implement that has a "barrel".
   A.–a, B.–b, C.–c, D.–d, E.–e

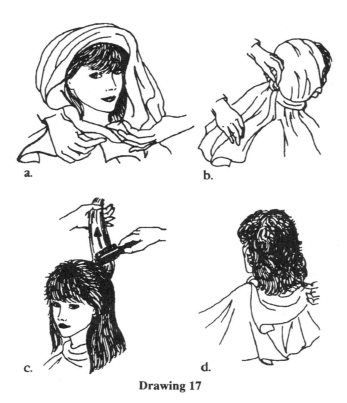

a.

b.

c.

d.

Drawing 17

___ 5. Referencing Drawing 17, which one would NOT be a preparation procedure before the application of a chemical hair relaxer service?

A.–a, B.–b, C.–c, D.–d

___ 6. Which is the best drawing to identify what should be done during the processing of a relaxer?

A.–a, B.–b, C.–c, D.–d

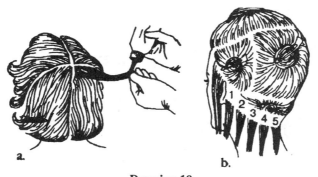

a.

b.

Drawing 18

___ 7. Checking Drawing 18, which is an example of a permanent hair color strand test?

A.–a, B.–b

215

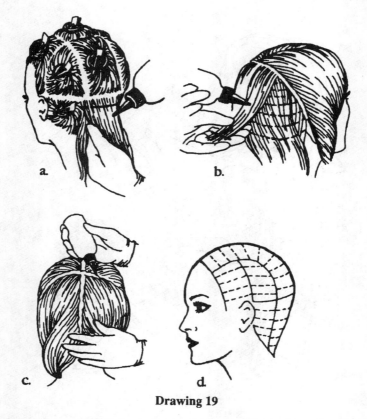

Drawing 19

___ 8. In Drawing 19, which picture shows how the hair would be sub-divided for permanent waving?
A.–a, B.–b, C.–c, D.–d

___ 9. From the choices above, select the one that demonstrates the procedure for a tint retouch.
A.–a, B.–b, C.–c, D.–d

___ 10. Can you choose the drawing that illustrates the application of a filler?
A.–a, B.–b, C.–c, D.–d, E–none shown

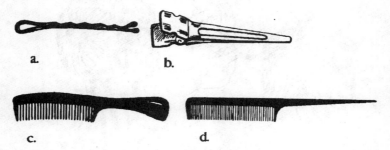

Drawing 20

___ 11. Referring to Drawing 20, which item would be used during the tinting service?
A.–a, B.–b, C.–c, D.–d, E–not shown

216

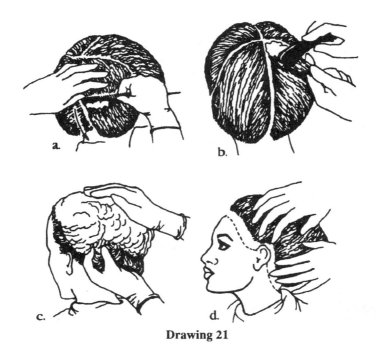

Drawing 21

___ 12. Which drawing shows the application of the chemical relaxer cream?

       A.–a, B.–b, C.–c, D.–d

___ 13. Select the drawing that best shows the activation of the relaxer cream.

       A.–a, B.–b, C.–c, D.–d

___ 14. What is present in the above drawings that makes it clear to you that the cosmetologist is concerned about their own safety, too?

       A.–combs, B.–foam, C.–towel, D.–gloves

___ 15. Which section of the head is usually the most resistant to a chemical relaxer?

       A.–nape, B.–crown, C.–front hairline, D.–nape, E.–none shown

___ 16. Which picture above shows the neutralizing of the chemical relaxer?

       A.–a, B.–b, C.–c, D.–d, E.–none shown

___ 17. Select the drawing above that illustrates the neutralizing shampoo.

       A.–a, B.–b, C.–c, D.–d, E.–none shown

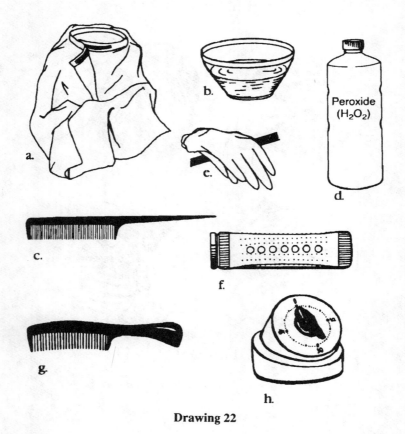

b.

Peroxide
(H₂O₂)

a.

e.

d.

c.

f.

g.

h.

Drawing 22

____ 18. Can you select the item above that will help you determine how long to process a chemical hair relaxer?

A.–a, B.–b, C.–c, D.–d, E.–e, F.–f, G.–g, H.–h, I.–a and c

____ 19. From the drawing above, select the item that acts as the catalyst for a permanent hair color.

A.–a, B.–b, C.–c, D.–d, E.–e, F.–f, G.–g, H.–h

____ 20. Which item is used to apply the chemical relaxer cream?

A.–a, B.–b, C.–c, D.–d, E.–e, F.–f, G.–g, H.–h, I.–c and g

____ 21. Select the item above that is used to protect the client.

A.–a, B.–b, C.–c, D.–d, E.–e, F.–f, G.–g, H.–h, I.–g and h

____ 22. Can you choose the item that is used to protect the cosmetologist?

A.–a, B.–b, C.–c, D.–d, E.–e, F.–f, G.–g, H.–h

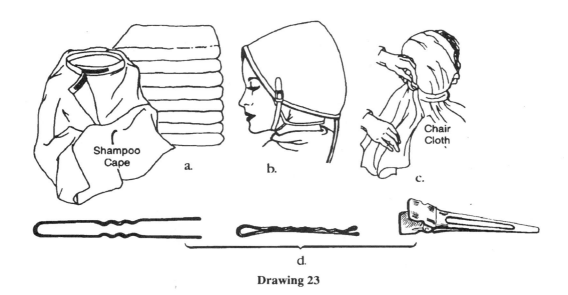

Shampoo Cape a.

b.

Chair Cloth c.

d.

Drawing 23

_____ 23. Can you select the item that would be used to secure a sculpture curl into its shaping?
A.–a, B.–b, C.–c, D.–d

_____ 24. Considering safety, which item should be used in the thermal pressing service?
A.–a, B.–b, C.–c, D.–d

_____ 25. Which of the above would NOT be used before the application of a chemical relaxer?
A.–a, B.–b, C.–c, D.–d

_____ 26. Which of the above would you recommend for use on the client that will be having a permanent wave service?
A.–a, B.–b, C.–c, D.–d, E.–none shown

_____ 27. Can you select the item that would be used to thermal press the hair?
A.–a, B.–b, C.–c, D.–d, E.–none shown

_____ 28. Select the item that you would use on the head to frost the hair?
A.–a, B.–b, C.–c, D.–d, E.–none shown

PRACTICAL TEST 4

Drawing 24

___ 1.   Which of the above items is used to weave the client's hair?
         A.–a, B.–b, C.–c, D.–d

___ 2.   Select the drawing that shows how a permanent wave could be wrapped.
         A.–a, B.–b, C.–c, D.–d

___ 3.   Identify the drawing that illustrates the streaking service.
         A.–a, B.–b, C.–c, D.–d

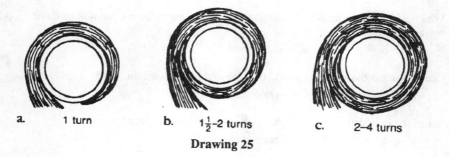

Drawing 25

___ 4.   Which of the curls in Drawing 25 would give the maximum amount of curl to the client's hair?
         A.–a, B.–b, C.–c

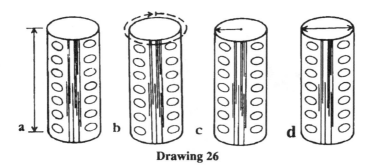

Drawing 26

___ 5. Which letter correctly labels the length of the roller?
A.–a, B.–b, C.–c, D.–d

___ 6. Can you select the drawing that shows the radius of the roller?
A.–a, B.–b, C.–c, D.–d

___ 7. Select the roller that shows the circumference of a roller.
A.–a, B.–b, C.–c, D.–d

___ 8. Which roller shows the diameter of the roller?
A.–a, B.–b, C.–c, D.–d

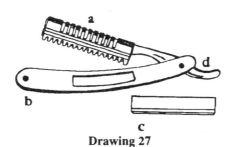

Drawing 27

___ 9. Referring to Drawing 27, which letter correctly labels the tang of the razor?
A.–a, B.–b, C.–c, D.–d

___ 10. Which item in the drawing illustrates the razor guard?
A.–a, B.–b, C.–c, D.–d

___ 11. Can you identify the letter that identifies the handle of the razor?
A.–a, B.–b, C.–c, D.–d

___ 12. Indicate which letter correctly labels the blade of the razor.
A.–a, B.–b, C.–c, D.–d

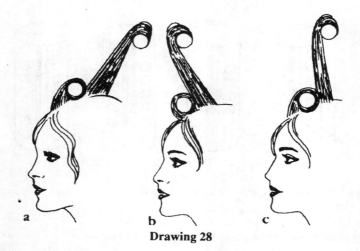

Drawing 28

___ 13. Can you determine which roller position will give the client's hairstyle maximum height and fullness?

       A.–a, B.–b, C.–c

___ 14. Which position will give the hairstyle medium height and fullness?

       A.–a, B.–b, C.–c

___ 15. And which position will give the hairstyle only a minumum degree of height and fullness?

       A.–a, B.–b, C.–c

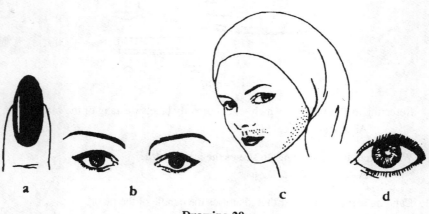

Drawing 29

___ 16. After checking Drawing 29, identify which of the items should NOT have an aniline tint applied to it.

       A.–a, B.–b, C.–c, D.–d, E.–all items shown

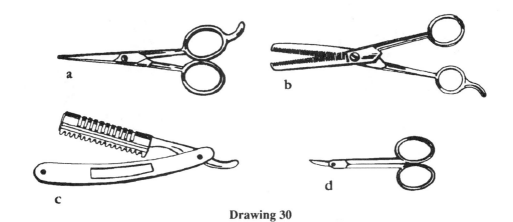

Drawing 30

____ 17. Which of the above implements would be used to remove bulk from the hair?
      A.–a, B.–b, C.–c, D.–d, E.–a, b and c

____ 18. Identify the implement normally used to remove bulk and shorten wet hair.
      A.–a, B.–b, C.–c, D.–d

____ 19. What cutting implement should be used to trim the nail cuticle?
      A.–a, B.–b, C.–c, D.–d

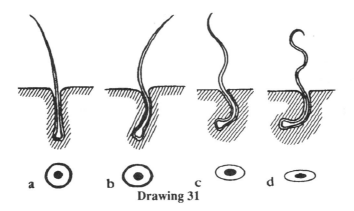

Drawing 31

____ 20. Correctly select the letter that labels the follicle that results in wavy hair.
      A.–a, B.–b, C.–c, D.–d

____ 21. Which follicle shape will result in nearly straight hair?
      A.–a, B.–b, C.–c, D.–d

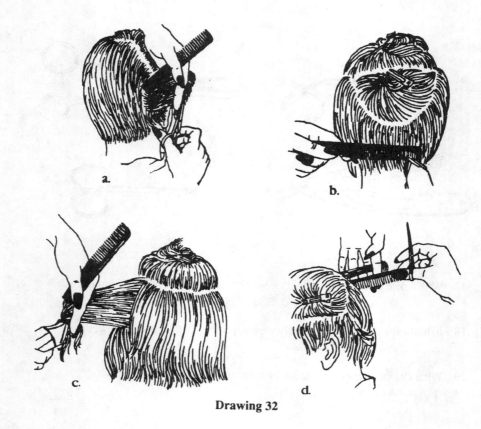

Drawing 32

___ 22. Which drawing demonstrates the use of establishing a cutting guideline?
A.–a, B.–b, C.–c, D.–d, E.–b and d

___ 23. Can you select the drawing that labels the establishment of a guideline in the crown?
A.–a, B.–b, C.–c, D.–d

___ 24. Referring to Drawing 33 below, which correctly labels the growing cycle of a normal hair?
A.–a, B.–b, C.–c

A.   catagen, anagen, telogen

B.   anagen, catagen, telogen

C.   telogen, catagen, anagen

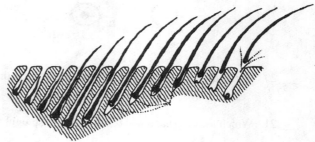

Drawing 33

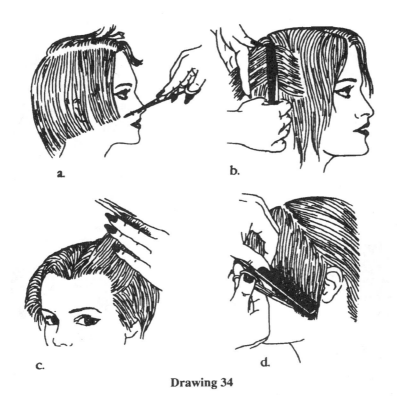

Drawing 34

___ 25. Select the drawing that demonstrates the cutting procedure used for checking the cutting pattern for corners.

A.–a, B.–b, C.–c, D.–d

___ 26. In which of the drawings above should you be the most careful when working on the client's head?

A.–a, B.–b, C.–c, D.–d

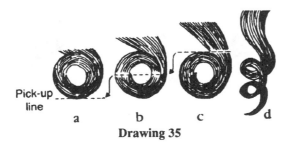

Pick-up line

Drawing 35

___ 27. Which letter identifies the sculpture curl pick-up line that will result in a no-stem curl formation?

A.–a, B.–b, C.–c, D.–d

___ 28. Can you select the curl formation that will result in a long (full) stem curl?

A.–a, B.–b, C.–c, D.–d

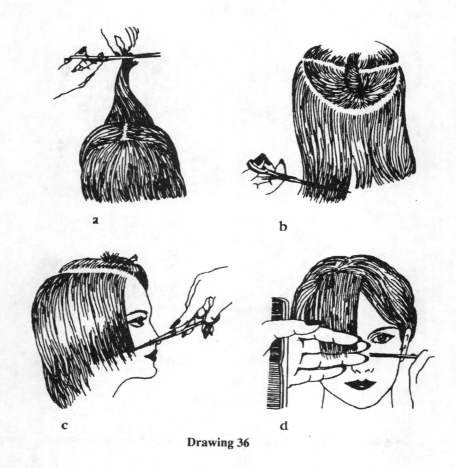

a

b

c

d

Drawing 36

____ 29. Correctly label the drawing that demonstrates the most concern for the safety of the client.
A.–a, B.–b, C.–c, D.–d, E.–all of the above, F.–a and d, E.–b and c

____ 30. Which of the drawings illustrates the blunt hair cutting method?
A.–a, B.–b, C.–c, D.–d, E.–all of the above

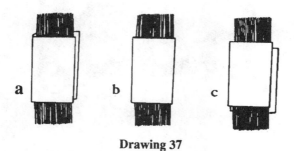

a   b   c

Drawing 37

____ 31. In the drawing above, select the drawing that is the best illustration of the book-end fold
wrapping method sometimes used for wrapping a permanent wave.
A.–a, B.–b, C.–c

226

PRACTICAL TEST 5

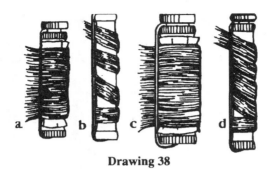

Drawing 38

___ 1. Referring to Drawing 38, which rod is the best example of a correctly wound spiral permanent wave wrap?

A.–a, B.–b, C.–c, D.–d

___ 2. If all the hair strands were the same length, which of the above rods would result in the least amount of curl?

A.–a, B.–b, C.–c, D.–d

Drawing 39

___ 3. When having a permanent wave, in which area of the head would a client be the most likely to get a chemical burn?

A.–a, B.–b, C.–c, D.–d

___ 4. Which area of the head are the smaller rods normally used?

A.–a, B.–b, C.–c, D.–d

___ 5. In which area of the head are larger rods used?

A.–a, B.–b, C.–c, D.–d

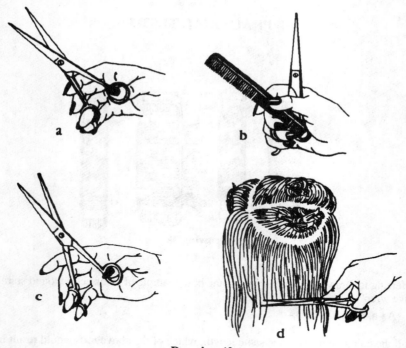

Drawing 40

___ 6. Which of the drawings best demonstrates the safest position of your scissors when sectioning the hair?

A.–a, B.–b, C.–c, D.–d

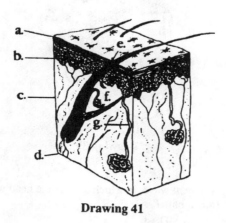

Drawing 41

___ 7. Select the letter that correctly labels the duct to the sebaceous gland.

A.–a, B.–b, C.–c, D.–d, E.–e

___ 8. Select the letter that correctly labels the papilla of the hair.

A.–a, B.–b, C.–c, D.–d, E.–e

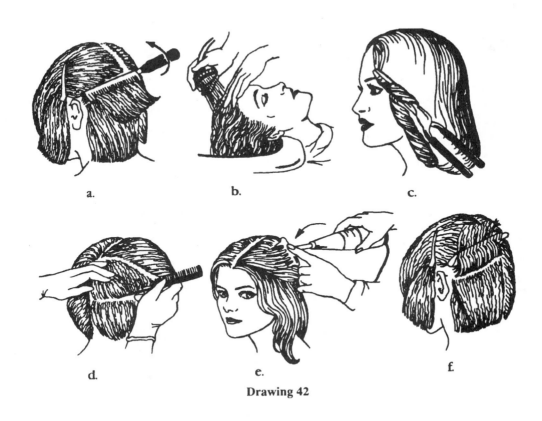

a.   b.   c.

d.   e.   f.

Drawing 42

___ 9. Can you choose the drawing that demonstrates hair pressing?
        A.–a, B.–b, C.–c, D.–d, E.–e, F.–f

___ 10. Select the drawing that shows the correct way to place the high frequency electrode on the scalp.
        A.–a, B.–b, C.–c, D.–d, E.–e

___ 11. Which of the drawings demonstrates how to protect the client's face during the neutralization of a permanent wave?
        A.–a, B.–b, C.–c, D.–d, E.–e, F.–f, G.–none shown

___ 12. From the drawings above, choose the one that demonstrates thermal curling.
        A.–a, B.–b, C.–c, D.–d, E.–e, F.–f, G.–none shown

___ 13. Identify the drawing that illustrates the wrapping of permanent wave rods.
        A.–a, B.–b, C.–c, D.–d, E.–e, F.–f, G.–none shown

Drawing 43

___ 14. Which of the drawings shows the application of a temporary rinse?
   A.–a, B.–b, C.–c, D.–d

___ 15. Can you identify the drawing that illustrates the application of a semipermanent hair color?
   A.–a, B.–b, C.–c, D.–d, E.–all of the above

___ 16. Select the drawing that would require an allergy patch test before actually giving the color.
   A.–a, B.–b, C.–c, D.–d

___ 17. During which of the above procedures could a strand test be given?
   A.–a, B.–b, C.–c, D.–d, E.–all of the above

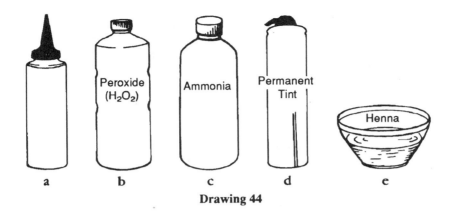

Drawing 44

___ 18. Which two products should be mixed together for a test for metallic salts?

A.–a, B.–b, C.–c, D.–d, E.–e

___ 19. Can you select the two items in the drawing that would be mixed together for the application of a virgin tint?

A.–a and b, B.–a and d, C.–b and c, D.–b and d

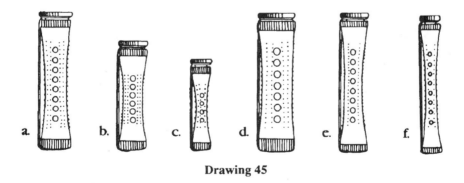

Drawing 45

___ 20. For permanent waving of long hair, which rod size would result in the largest wave pattern?

A.–a, B.–b, C.–c, D.–d, E.–e, F.–f

___ 21. Can you select the rod that would most likely be used in the nape section of short hair?

A.–a, B.–b, C.–c, D.–d, E.–e, F.–f

___ 22. From the rods shown, select the rod most likely to be used in the crown section of medium-length hair.

A.–a and d, B.–a, d, e and f, C.–c, D.–d, E.–e

231

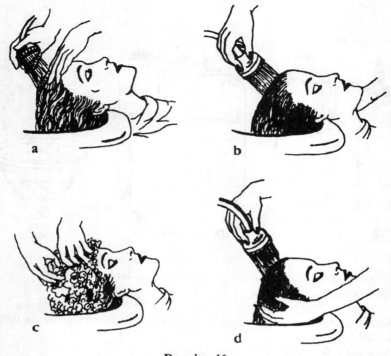

Drawing 46

____ 23. Which of the drawings demonstrates the best protection for the client's face?
        A.–a, B.–b, C.–c, D.–d

____ 24. Select the drawing that shows the monitoring of the water temperature.
        A.–a, B.–b, C.–c, D.–d

____ 25. Can you choose the drawing that illustrates the neutralizing of a chemical relaxer?
        A.–a, B.–b, C.–c, D.–d

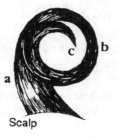

Scalp

Drawing 47

____ 26. Where along this hair strand should the application of a virgin tint to lighten the hair begin?
        A.–scalp to a, B.–scalp to b, C.–scalp to c, D.–a to b, E.–b to c

232

Drawing 48

___ 27. Can you choose the best illustration of a tapered neckline hair shaping?
A.–a, B.–b, C.–c, D.–d

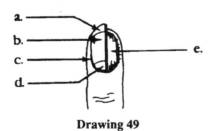

Drawing 49

___ 28. On the drawing above, correctly label the point that shows the nail bed.
A.–a, B.–b, C.–c, D.–d, E.–e

___ 29. Choose the letter that labels the lunula of the nail.
A.–a, B.–b, C.–c, D.–d, E.–e

___ 30. Can you select the letter that shows the nail wall?
A.–a, B.–b, C.–c, D.–d, E.–e

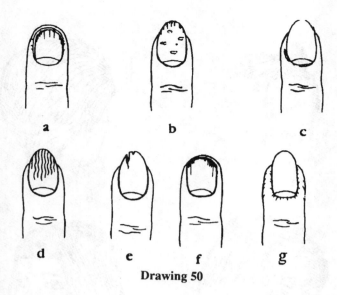

Drawing 50

_____ 31. In the drawing above, which is an example of leukonychia?
A.–a, B.–b, C.–c, D.–d, E.–e, F.–f, G.–g

_____ 32. Referring to the same drawing, which is an example of onychorrhexis?
A.–a, B.–b, C.–c, D.–d, E.–e

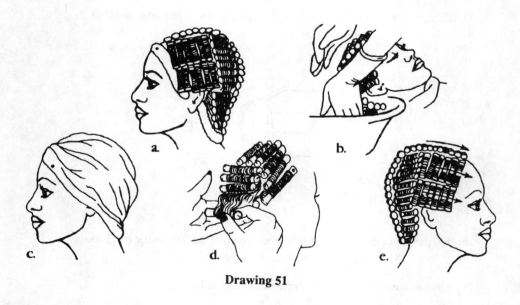

Drawing 51

_____ 33. Study Drawing 51 of the recurl service, then choose the correct steps in the order in which they should be done.
A.–a, b, c, d, and e; B.–c, d, e, a, and b; C.–e, a, c, d, and b; D.–d, e, a, b, and c; E.–a, c, d, e, and b

234

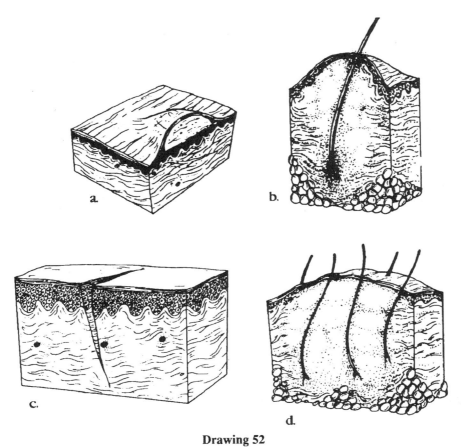

a.

b.

c.

d.

Drawing 52

___ 34. Any abnormal change in the skin is known as a

       A.–lesion, B.–abrasion, C.–scrape, D.–macule

___ 35. From the drawing above, can you select the one that is the most common to the fingertips of the hand, and the heels of the feet?

       A.–a, B.–b, C.–c, D.–d

Answer Key

State Board Review Questions